NICKELODEONS AND BLACK VAUDEVILLE

NICKELODEONS
and
BLACK VAUDEVILLE

The Forgotten
Story of Amanda Thorp

KATHI CLARK WONG

The University of Tennessee Press
Knoxville

LIBRARY OF CONGRESS CATALOGING-IN-PUBLICATION DATA

Names: Wong, Kathi Clark, 1955– author.

Title: Nickelodeons and Black vaudeville : the forgotten story of Amanda Thorp /
Kathi Clark Wong.

Description: First edition. | Knoxville : The University of Tennessee Press, [2023]. |
Includes bibliographical references and index. | Summary: "Amanda Thorp was a theater
entrepreneur influential in bringing Black vaudeville and early movie theaters to Richmond, Virginia,
and more widely to the southeastern US. Thorp, a White woman, opened theaters and nickelodeons
exclusively for Black patrons during a period of entrenched segregation and outright opposition
to Black patronage in the South. And though Thorp's mission was not expressly philanthropic,
she nonetheless expanded access to early movies when demand for the silver screen had just begun
to rival the theater business. Wong sheds light on Thorp's early life in Ohio, her travel to a culturally
nascent Richmond, and her remarkable contributions to theater culture in the South"
—Provided by publisher.

Identifiers: LCCN 2023006217 (print) | LCCN 2023006218 (ebook) |
ISBN 9781621908029 (hardcover) | ISBN 9781621908036 (pdf)

Subjects: LCSH: Thorp, Amanda, 1863–1927. | Motion picture theater owners—
United States—Biography. | Businesswomen—United State—Biography. |
Motion picture industry—United States—History. | Vaudeville—United States—History. |
African American theater—United States—History. |
BISAC: Biography & Autobiography | Women | Performing Arts | Film | General

Classification: LCC PN1998.3.T486 W66 2023 (print) | LCC PN1998.3.T486 (ebook) |
DDC 384/.8092 [B]—dc23/eng/20230411
LC record available at https://lccn.loc.gov/2023006217
LC ebook record available at https://lccn.loc.gov/2023006218

CONTENTS

ILLUSTRATIONS

PREFACE

A social-media post showed up in my feed in the midst of the COVID-19 pandemic one day in January 2021. Jennifer Raines had recently purchased a building at 18 West Broad Street in Richmond, at the intersection of Brook Road, and wanted to know more about the building's history. She knew, she wrote, that it once had housed the Dixie Theater, a nickelodeon, but wondered what else there was to know about it.

As an avocation, I enjoy researching the history of buildings, and so I responded to her that I'd be glad to take a look and see what I could find. Soon after, I forwarded an article to her that I had found after quickly searching a newspaper archives website. Headlined, "Charles A. Somma, Sr., Dies Here after Short Illness," it noted that Somma, after getting his start in business in his father's Richmond ice cream shop, "soon became interested in the amusement field and opened the Dixie Theater at Brook Avenue and Broad Street in 1912." That was easy, I thought.

The only trouble was, it was wrong.

What followed was a year-long unraveling of what the Dixie Theater was and, as the information revealed itself, a sense of diminution and sometimes outright erasure of the accomplishments of the woman, Amanda Thorp, who actually started the theater, the first in Richmond dedicated to showing (silent) movies. The full story of the theater is really the story of Thorp herself, and it includes themes of perseverance in the face of many challenges, unusual relationships, and a remarkable story about the presence of early Black vaudeville in Richmond. Since Thorp started out her career as a movie exhibitor in Bucyrus, Ohio, the folks there will also find something of interest within these pages.

The author owes thanks to several people. Ms. Raines, of course, put me on to the story, but she also offered encouragement, gave me tours of

Fig. 1a. The building (2022 photograph) which housed the former Dixie at 18 West Broad, Richmond. The distinctive angle on the west side reflects its relationship to the triangular intersection of Brook and Broad. Photo by the author.

the building at 18 West Broad, and even gifted me with adorable items from her store that is now there. John Kurtz of the Bucyrus, Ohio, Historical Society answered many emails from me and helped me hunt down images. Thorp spent her early adult years in Newark, Ohio, and Donna Gregory at the Licking County Historical Society there sent me a multitude of scans of

Fig. 1b. The back of the building (2022 photograph) which once housed the Dixie. Photo by the author.

historical photographs from that area. Nearly daily I consulted *Celebrate Richmond Theater*, the definitive book on Richmond theater written by Kathyrn Fuller-Seeley. Formerly with Virginia Commonwealth University (VCU) here in Richmond, Fuller-Seeley is currently a professor at the University of Texas at Austin. She was also kind enough to answer my early emails as well as later give me useful guidance as I became immersed in the project. Another important resource was Gibson Worsham's outstanding blog, *Urban Scale Richmond*, about historical aspects of Richmond buildings including the city's many significant theaters. Via email, Worsham, an architectural historian, pointed out features of the building at 18 West Broad that I otherwise would not have understood. Ben Anderson, who works at the Maggie L. Walker National Historic Site in Richmond's Jackson Ward and has also written on Thorp, helped me refine some of my early ideas about her. Robbie Rhodes, editor of the Mechanical Music Digest (online as mmdigest.com) in Etiwanda, California, answered many of my email questions about Hope-Jones orchestras (later known as Wurlitzer organs). The folks at the Byrd Theater generously invited me to the theater to talk to Bob Gulledge who plays its Wurlitzer organ—the original instrument still in operation today—and from him and the other passionate folks who work there, I gained insight which I needed at that point. I thank the good people of Richmond's wonderful museums and libraries who went above and beyond, despite the ongoing COVID-19 pandemic, to provide me with resources or information. These include the Boatwright Library of the University of Richmond, VCU's James Branch Cabell Library, the Valentine Museum of Richmond (a museum of Richmond history), the Library of Virginia, and the Virginia Museum of History and Culture. More good people at the University of Tennessee Press were ever-patient and kind to this author who was putting together her first work of this magnitude. The work of mostly anonymous journalists in the early twentieth century who reported darned near everything in their communities, sometimes in almost excruciating detail, must also be acknowledged (may we never be without newspapers). My friend Nancy Holdren Stockdale looked over the final draft and caught typos that continued to elude me. But, finally, and most of all, I thank my husband, who put up with my disappearing for many hours at a time on many, many days, to put all this material together; this, in the midst of the pandemic, when other company was unavailable to him as we self-isolated. He also read many drafts, providing feedback that improved the final product considerably, and he accompanied me on several photography expeditions, including a notable one on a very cold rainy day when we hunted down Thorp's grave in a very large cemetery with little information to guide us.

This book corrects many errors in the story of Amanda Thorp and it gives her credit for her many accomplishments, though it is inevitable that there are new, hopefully minor, errors. These, of course, are entirely my responsibility.

Editorial Notes

Though the Thorp family sometimes used the spelling "Thorpe," throughout this narrative "Thorp" is used instead, since the family appears to have settled on that spelling later in life. In addition, the spelling of the word "theater" used to be "theatre" in the early 1900s when it referred to the building as opposed to the activity. Except when it appears in quotes, however, the spelling "theater" is used in this narrative with the exception of when it refers to the "Byrd Theatre," since that theater uses the old spelling.

Punctuation, spelling, and grammar conventions of items from old newspapers and trade magazines generally have been edited to reflect 2023 norms. A notable exception involves references when they involve racialized African Americans: words originally used, including the terms "colored" and "negro," are retained because the terminology puts the references squarely into the overtly racist times and prevailing segregationist thought. The word "Black" is capitalized to reflect current ideas that when it is so-written it refers to people of the African diaspora rather than to a color.[1] Since "Black" is capitalized, the word "White" is as well when it is used to refer to people who are racialized as White in the United States, including those who identify with ethnicities and nationalities that can be traced back to Europe.

INTRODUCTION

It was not Amanda Thorp's intention to open a theater in Richmond when she booked an excursion from her home in Bucyrus, Ohio, to the 1907 Jamestown Exposition in Norfolk, Virginia. But always one to seek out a new adventure, she had stopped in Richmond to check the city out. It was late April or early May, when the weather was beautiful, and temperatures were comfortable. In her long Edwardian skirts, she would have walked along Broad Street and marveled at how broad it actually was. She would have picked her way carefully through the busy traffic, among the many pedestrians, horse-drawn buggies, and electric street cars. The shopping district would have been thriving, with customers pushing in and out the doors of big department stores with names like Thalhimer's and Miller and Rhoad's. But what really would have grabbed her attention were the theaters centered around Eighth and Broad, and even more than that: what was not there. She herself was in the theater business, but of a different sort than these theaters in Richmond. Back home in Bucyrus, she ran a moving picture theater, the Wonderland, catering to people without a lot of money to spend. She charged only a nickel for admission, and she made a lot of nickels. It was only a matter of time before someone figured out that someone could do the same here, and it would cross her mind that maybe that someone should be her. On her walk, she met Jack Jacobson showing films outdoors in a tent on an empty lot next door to the Colonial Theater at 714 East Broad. Within days, she bought the rights to his show for $250, rented a room inside the Colonial, and opened on May 4 what she called the Dixie Theater, the first in Richmond showing moving pictures as its major draw. Like Jacobson had been doing, and like she had done at her Wonderland, she charged five cents admission. The newspapers called the theater a nickelodeon.[1]

Fig. 2. Thorp in a photo likely
taken ca. 1907, possibly while still
in Bucyrus. In 1907 she would
have been 44, and she does appear
to be around that age in this
photo. *RTD*, Jan. 10, 1926.

Mrs A. E. THORP

Perhaps in this day and age, when the movie theater industry seems to be facing its biggest challenges yet,[2] this story about a woman in the early days of the theater exhibition business might seem of interest only as an idle curiosity. But Thorp in the early 1900s had gotten in on the ground floor of a popular cultural phenomenon which would grow over time to become enormously influential. From the industry's first flickering beginnings, she believed in the potential of movies to entertain the masses even though many people were saying they were just a fad. History proved she was right: in the early years of the century, the industry hardly existed, but by 1910, one-third of Americans would attend a movie each week, and by 1920, it would be fifty percent.[3] Now, a hundred years later, more than 1 billion people world-wide subscribe to online video streaming services.[4]

Thorp was an entrepreneur at a time when women entrepreneurs were not at all common. Those that did exist generally built their companies around products and ideas that were considered to be of feminine interest—fashion, cooking, makeup—and even then, most women who were able to succeed in business were able to do so because their startups received financial assistance from family members. The movie theater business, on the other hand, was without question a man's world. Women film exhibitors were an infinitesimal minority and even when they existed, they were likely to be in partnership with a spouse, dividing labor responsibilities along traditional gender roles.[5] Thorp did the "man's work" in owning and operating her theaters, and she did it as a self-made single woman, all the more noteworthy because she was already in her forties when she opened her first theater in Bucyrus.

After Thorp moved to Richmond and expanded her chain of nickelodeons in that and other nearby cities, she tested other theater ventures. Among them were segregated venues specifically developed for African American patrons. She had seen for herself that African Americans, like their White counterparts though relatively speaking, were beginning to have more time and more money to spend on leisure activities. However, racist norms or even outright Jim Crow laws prevented African American access to most theaters except for rare all-Black venues or the occasional segregated seating made available to them in galleries of White theaters. Thorp was not the only one in Richmond who came to see that providing entertainment to Black audiences in Richmond was a money-making proposition, but she was by far the most successful at the time.

Nearly all early moving-picture theaters of the early 1900s also offered the occasional vaudeville act to supplement their film offerings, and Thorp's theaters were no exception. In Richmond, Thorp's earliest permanent theater was located at the intersection of Brook Road and Broad Street, near what is today the historic Black community of Jackson Ward. She converted it to all-Black patronage in late 1908 and began bringing in early Black vaudeville acts on a regular basis, de-emphasizing the showing of films. This strategy was so successful that in 1913 she built the much larger Hippodrome Theater a few blocks away in the heart of Jackson Ward's business district. Built expressly to showcase early Black vaudeville, the Hippodrome brought in bigger acts than was possible at the Dixie. The Hippodrome is well known for its contributions to Black vaudeville in Richmond and the Southeast, and although a few articles and books rightly attribute to her its founding, many more give other people (men) the credit. What does not appear to be published anywhere, however, is the fact that Black vaudeville acts were performing at a significant level at her Dixie Theater even before she built the Hippodrome: more than fifty Black vaudeville acts appeared at the Dixie before the Hippodrome ever opened. In interviews she gave later in life, Thorp herself never spoke of the early Black vaudeville she brought to her Dixie and Hippodrome theaters, suggesting that she herself failed to see its importance and likely was a reflection of racist views of the time that would have judged cultural activities of African Americans as less important than those of Whites.

In addition to her pioneering theater exhibition work, acknowledged during her lifetime not only in Bucyrus and Richmond but regionally and even nationally, Thorp mentored men who worked for her or who she otherwise saw as having promise. She was their boss and teacher amid an industry dominated by them. In particular, without Amanda Thorp, there would have been no Walter Coulter in the movie theater business, and without Walter Coulter, there would have been no Byrd Theatre, the historic Richmond landmark he built and which still shows pictures today.

By the time Thorp came to Richmond from Ohio, she knew from experience how to create a moving picture theater from the ground up and how to bring in the kinds of entertainments, whether film or vaudeville, that people would pay to see. She spent two decades in Richmond developing amusement houses that were enjoyed—albeit in segregated circumstances by a great many of her customers—by pretty nearly everyone. Her bigger houses that she began to build about mid-career could seat well more than a thousand people a night in multiple showings, and those patrons would come week after week as the programs changed.

The development of "talking pictures" in the 1920s was the beginning of a new era for the motion picture industry. Independent exhibitors like Thorp found it more and more difficult to compete with the large corporate interests which could afford to build ever more spectacular facilities to show these new films that brought in even more people. Thorp died of cancer just about that time. And then she was largely forgotten.

1

IT'S OKAY FOR A GIRL TO BE SMART

On January 28, 1928, the Capitol Theater ran a one-third-page display ad in the *Richmond Times-Dispatch* announcing the pre-release showing of *The Jazz Singer*.[1] Filmed with Vitaphone technology, it was the first feature-length picture with both a synchronized recorded musical score and lip-synchronous singing and speech. Later, people would call these kinds of movies "talkies," but that term was so new it wasn't even mentioned the next day in the gushing newspaper reviews of the amazing spectacle that Richmonders had flocked to see. *The Jazz Singer* was the first of its kind to be shown in Richmond and, in fact, Virginia, and it signaled the beginning of the end of the silent movie era there as it did across the country. Six months earlier, another event also marked the passing of the silent film era in Richmond: the death of Amanda E. Thorp, the woman who in 1907 had opened the city's first "picture house,"[2] as she sometimes referred to it, to show silent movies.

Formative Years

Amanda Thorp was born Amanda E. Baughman on April 13, 1863, in Granville, Licking County, Ohio.[3] By the 1870 census, her mother Catherine was 41 and married to Amanda's much older father Isaac, who was 71. Isaac, originally from Ohio, was a shingle maker in an area of Ohio populated mostly by farmers; Catherine, an Ohio native, was a housekeeper, and may or may not have worked outside the home. Amanda, at seven years old, attended school in the village of about 850 people; her two younger brothers, Isaac S. Baughman, 5, and John E. Baughman, 2, stayed home.[4] Education was a cultural mainstay of the village, particularly for young girls, with

Fig. 3. Pataskala, Ohio, late 1800s. Collection of Licking County, Ohio, Historical Society, Newark, Ohio.

the Granville Female Seminary (equivalent to a high school today) having been established in 1832.[5] While it is not known how long Amanda went to school or even if she went to the girls' school in Granville, she spent at least some time in this small town where the mindset was that it was okay for a girl to be smart.

Things likely got tougher as Amanda grew older; by 1880, her mother was widowed and working as a housekeeper. Amanda, 17, still lived at home but also worked as a housekeeper. Amanda's younger brother Isaac, 14, was a cigar maker; her other, younger brother John disappears from the record and may have died. Where they then lived in Licking County, Ohio, was Pataskala, a village of 634 people, even smaller than their former community of Granville which lay about 10 miles east. Pataskala consisted of several small households in the densely populated little area, though extended Baughman family members close by who might have lent support do not appear to exist. Several of their neighbors worked for the railroad that ran through the village, and several others also had surprisingly diverse skilled or professional occupations: there was a carpenter, sewing machine salesman, piano salesman, cooper, weaver, schoolteacher, dry goods store owner, wagonwright, and a bridge carpenter, among others.[6] It seems likely that Amanda and what was left of her family did not live far from poverty, so perhaps it is not surprising that at age 18, on May 30, 1881, she married Franklin (Frank) T. Thorp, a man older than she by 21 years.[7] A pregnancy which produced a son, Walter (Waldo) Franklin, born November 4, 1881, just over five months later, might have been another reason for their marriage.[8]

Fighting for the Union—But Only the Union

Amanda's husband was born January 2, 1843, in New York state.[9] His mother was Sarah Anderson, and his father's first name is unknown.[10] Frank first appears in 1850 census records in Jersey Township, Licking County, Ohio, in an odd entry where at eight years old he is shown as the single inhabitant of a household.[11] Perhaps he was home alone at the time and the census taker found it fruitless to try to interview a child so young.

On July 18, 1861, when he was eighteen, Frank was conscripted as a Union soldier in the Ohio 27th Infantry Regiment and assigned as a private to Company C.[12] The 27th was organized during summer 1861 at Camp Chase in Columbus, Ohio, to serve a term of three years. Initially engaging in occasional skirmishes with Confederate troops as it traveled on a steamboat down the Mississippi River, the regiment ultimately joined the Union advance on Corinth, Mississippi, in April 1862. In the midst of the Union siege on that town, in July, Frank was injured. Listed as having an eye "imperfection," he was discharged from service on a surgeon's certificate of disability almost exactly a year to the day after he had enlisted.[13] In May 1863, he filed for and received approval for a modest invalid pension based on the injury.[14]

What Frank did between his discharge from service and his marriage to Amanda in 1881 is unknown, with one exception: in October 1865, six months after the close of the Civil War, he was in Newark, Ohio, signing a petition that he was one of the "boys in blue" who had fought for the union not because they "believed in negro equality," but rather because they believed in a united America. They declared that they supported "a White man's country and a White man's government for which President Johnson has so decidedly declared himself."[15]

In 1882, Frank was working as a chainman for the railroad in Newark,

Fig. 4. Architectural map of Newark, Ohio, ca. 1870, drawn just a few years before Amanda and her family moved there. Collection of Licking Co., Ohio, Historical Society, Newark, Ohio.

Ohio, undoubtedly making a home there with Amanda and Waldo about eight miles east of Amanda's childhood home in Granville. With a population at the time of about 10,000, Newark was much larger than Granville, much less Pataskala, and it was growing. Even by the 1840s, when its population was only 2,000 people, it boasted three newspapers, ten grocery stores, two gristmills, an iron foundry, a wool factory, a bookstore, two hardware stores, the railroad, and several other businesses.[16] The Ohio and Erie Canal, which ran just south of Newark, peaked in its importance to the region in the 1830s and 1840s, but it had contributed to the prosperity of the little town.

Frank's job as a chainman, one he may have had for several years, involved helping to survey for new railway construction.[17] Perhaps it was through this work, traveling the rails of the area, that he had met Amanda in nearby Pataskala. The first mention of her living in Newark was in 1887, when she was already Frank's wife, and a newspaper brief noted that she had visited Hartford, Ohio, about twenty miles to the northwest, to judge a baby contest.[18]

Fig. 5. Turn-of-the-century police officers in Newark, Ohio. Frank is not likely to be among those photographed, but these were likely his colleagues. Collection of Licking Co., Ohio, Historical Society, Newark, Ohio.

Frank held a number of odd jobs over the years, though none of them would have provided a generous income to support his small family: he worked in low-level law enforcement off and on when he could, he was a baker for a while, he apparently was in a small cornet band, he was a mail carrier, and may well have had other short-term positions. Once, while working as a police officer in 1886, charges were dropped against alleged perpetrators he had arrested and instead he was himself charged with drunkenness.[19] During all this time, Frank also would have been receiving his Civil War invalid pension which in 1883 amounted to $6 per month, about the cost of a couple weeks' groceries.[20]

Occupation: Loafing

When Amanda and Frank stopped living together is not clear, though it occurred after 1889 when the local paper reported she had organized a birthday party for him[21] and before 1894 when Waldo was thirteen and an application was made to admit him as an orphan to the Ohio Soldiers' and Sailors' Orphans' Home.[22] The Home, located in a remote area near

XENIA : OHIO SOLDIERS' AND SAILORS' ORPHANS'
HOME.

Fig. 6. The Ohio Soldiers' and Sailors' Orphans' Home as it appeared in
1891. Moses Forster Sweetser, *King's Hand-book of the United States*, 1891,
planned and edited by M. King. Osgood, McIlvaine & Co., 670.

Dayton, was about 100 miles southwest of Newark. Created after the war
to care for children whose fathers had perished in the conflict, it eventually
was opened to children whose veteran parent or spouse might need to leave
their children there due to serious financial difficulties. Waldo's eligibility
was based on Frank's service with the Union Army, and the application
was made despite the fact that both parents were still living, though, the
application states, separated. Amanda filled out the form, indicating Waldo
was in her custody and listing Frank's occupation at the time as "loafing."
She listed her address as 28 Park House, a rooming house in Newark. She

reported Frank's Civil War pension as $17 a month at a time when a pair of shoes cost $3.[23] The pension was not enough to support one man alone much less one man and his wife and son, especially with the man loafing and having no other stated income. At the time of Amanda's application, so many parents were seeking assistance from the home that it could not accept all the children.[24] The fact of the application fairly reeks of desperation, but it does not appear that Waldo was accepted.

Three years later, in 1897, at age fifty-four, Frank left Newark and took up residence at the Soldiers' and Sailors' Home in Sandusky, Ohio, about 100 miles north of Newark.[25] Like the Soldiers' and Sailors' Orphans' Home, it had been created after the Civil War to provide for Ohio's indigent, honorably discharged veterans. His move to the Home was likely a kind of retirement, though he returned once or twice a year to Newark through at least 1903 to visit friends.[26]

Some of Them from Excellent Families

Shortly after Frank's self-removal to the Soldiers' and Sailors' Home, Amanda and Waldo show up in the record at the same time in Newark on November 5, 1898: Waldo, then 17, was arrested on a complaint initiated by Amanda for going through her pocketbook.[27] Given the problems with the law that Waldo was to have in the following years, it is highly likely that Amanda's accusation wasn't just a mother's momentary pique with her son but rather the result of some years' history of pre-existing exasperation with him. It might also help further explain Amanda's decision to try to place him in the orphans' home, as well as Frank's decision to leave his son (and wife) to move to Sandusky when Waldo was 16.

The outcome of Amanda's charges is not known, but Waldo's legal problems quickly escalated. An 1899 arrest for disorderly conduct[28] was followed by another in January 1900 when Waldo, then nineteen, was among twenty-three young men of the Hercules Athletic Club, a Newark boxing venue, who were arrested *en masse* for burglarizing men's clothing, notions, and a small amount of cash from a dry goods store, also in Newark. A highly sensational and scandalous affair in the small town, the crime and its aftermath were reported in excruciating detail in the local paper, attracting even wider attention with the wire services carrying the story to neighboring cities and towns. The Licking County courtroom was crowded with spectators for the resultant court cases—after all, some twenty-three families or so were painfully interested in the outcome—and "hundreds" of

Fig. 7. Photograph (2016) of the Licking County Jail. The jail closed in 1987 and is currently a historical property said to be haunted by prisoners and staff who perished there. Paranormal tours are open to the public. Library of Congress, Washington, D.C.

people were turned away. All twenty-three of the young men spent several days in jail being held on suspicion of the charges. Eventually they turned on each other, though confessions exonerated seventeen of them—"some (of those) from excellent families."[29] Among the small number of club members actually indicted on charges of burglary and larceny was Waldo, who was alleged to have crafted the homemade rope ladder the perpetrators used for lowering themselves into the store through a hatch in the roof.[30] The 1900 census, taken on June 11, shows Waldo as being incarcerated in the Licking County Jail.[31]

Either the publicity or the fact of the likely escalation of Waldo's challenges must have been difficult for Amanda: a note in the newspaper's personals column in February 1900 noted she had been confined to bed for four weeks but was improving, though it did not give a specific reason.[32]

Amanda by this time was likely the manager or owner of an unknown boarding or hotel establishment as she had pressed charges on a man for failing to pay his hotel bill.[33] Waldo may actually have been working for her at that same establishment at the time of the robbery: the 1900 jailhouse census, in addition to de facto noting he was incarcerated, somewhat oddly indicated his occupation as bellboy.[34] On June 27, 1900, a brief in the Newark Advocate noted that Amanda had moved her mother from Columbus, Ohio, to West Main Street in Newark to live with her.[35]

Waldo's jail stay does not appear to have been long; on Valentine's Day 1901, the twenty-year-old Waldo married Della E. Baker, the nineteen-year-old daughter of George and Anna Griffin Baker of Licking County.[36] The Advocate noted that "the announcement of the marriage will be a surprise to the many friends of the young people" and added, perhaps in a snide nod to Waldo's dry goods heist notoriety, that the groom was a "well known" employee of the Citizen's Electric Light plant in Newark. The address of the bride was noted as being 210 West Main Street, which would have been almost directly across the street from that of the groom's mother (Amanda) given as 249 West Main Street, the latter of which, the Advocate said, was where the young married couple would "commence housekeeping."[37] Six months later, a child, Thelma Pauline Thorp, was born to Waldo and Della.

There is no building at 249 West Main today, only an empty lot next to Raccoon Creek. Despite the house number implying it is closer to town, it is about a five-block walk to Newark's main square (and for Amanda, convenient to the jailhouse for visiting purposes). Surviving nearby homes of the period are large, boxy clapboard affairs, many with vestiges of midwestern Victorian ornamentation. Given her later career trajectory, it is not unlikely that Amanda would have had lodgers or even run a small boarding house, a "hotel," at 249 West Main—perhaps the same one from which the previously-mentioned errant lodger tried to leave without paying his bill. In later years, she would say her work in the hotel business preceded her entry into the moving picture business, and this may have been her start.[38] It is not known how Amanda would have obtained the money to start a boarding house or hotel; maybe she had been hiding away pin money over the years. Or perhaps some funds had come from sort of settlement from Frank when he left for the Soldiers' and Sailors' Home in Sandusky. Or possibly Amanda's mother had been able to contribute to the investment when she came to live in Newark with her daughter.

Whenever or however Amanda was able to get her start in the lodging business, by May 1901, she was running the Commercial House, also a boarding establishment. Located on Newark's South Fifth Street, the quirky street numbering system puts it only a couple of blocks away from the town center, better-situated than the West Main home.[39] By fall, she had done well enough that she took a month off for a vacation to Buffalo, Cleveland, and Chicago.[40] She was firmly established at Commercial House by the time of the 1902 Newark City Directory which noted that she was indeed its proprietor, a word that was used in the day to indicate the owner. Waldo, who by this time and perhaps not surprisingly was divorced from Della, was also listed in the city directory as living at Commercial House.[41]

It might be noted here that Amanda was already showing propensities that would serve her well over the coming decades as she grew as a businesswoman: she enjoyed travel and she kept and cultivated relationships with friends and acquaintances, even over some distance. A spattering of articles in the Newark paper attested to this—starting with the ones earlier mentioned in which she judged the baby contest in Hartford, Ohio, as well as her more extensive, month-long, vacation trip—but there were also several other, social sojourns reported in the personals column of the local paper. Additionally, she also hosted friends from other towns who visited her.[42]

How long Amanda ran Commercial House is unclear. Two newspaper articles in early to mid-1902 show her pressing charges against patrons for problems which presumably arose there: one had tried to leave without paying, and another, she claimed, had engaged in an illicit sex act.[43] An advertisement which appeared in the paper in February 1903 gives an idea of her business model: she charged board at $4 per week and offered twenty-one meal tickets in a package deal for a cost of $3.[44] She may have sold and left that business by May, however, because by then she was advertising meals available at her nearby Crescent Café at 47 North Fourth Street where she raised her prices: she charged $3.25 for a ticket for twenty-one meals. The 1904 Newark City Directory shows her as living as a boarder at 47 North Fourth. Waldo was living nearby at 41½ North Fourth. He was employed as a fireman, likely for the railroad, meaning he shoveled coal into the furnace and tended the boilers on the steam locomotives of the day. Surprisingly, Amanda's husband, Frank, also shows up in the directory as a clerk at Newark's Hotel Seiler located at 62 South Second Street, having at least apparently temporarily left the Soldiers' and Sailors' Home. Perhaps he did so in what might be charitably described as an effort to try and help deal with the problems with Waldo. Though Frank was back in town, Amanda left no doubt about how she viewed their relationship: the same 1904 Newark City Directory identified her as Frank's widow—a ruse about her marital status she would continue to use throughout the rest of her life, all the more intriguing because she began it in a town where a great number of people would have known the truth. The city directory did not provide relationship status of men.

Troubles, and Leaving Newark Behind

Waldo's problems with the law continued to mount. In mid-May 1902, he had been arrested on a charge of obtaining $2 on false pretenses when he apparently tried to sell stolen goods to a second-hand dealer.[45] Ten days later he was arrested for assault and battery on his wife, Della, likely precipitating their divorce.[46] A month later he was arrested for being drunk and driving a buggy too fast, hitting a five-year-old boy (who survived) in the process.[47] In February 1903, while in court on a charge of leaving the Bretzius Boarding House without paying for his lodging and also for taking with him several

Fig. 8. Early 1900s photograph of Newark's Steam Laundry. Waldo's room would have been one of those upstairs. Collection of Licking Co., Ohio, Historical Society, Newark, Ohio.

articles of clothing he had stolen from a lodger there, he was arrested (inside the courtroom) for actually wearing clothing he was alleged to have stolen from a patron at (Amanda's) Commercial House in July 1902.[48] The charges for the theft at the Commercial House were amended in May 1903 to show that among the items Waldo allegedly stole included two watches and a revolver.[49] In the Bretzius case, where Waldo was answering to a charge of grand larceny for property theft and despite stating he worked for the B&O Railroad, he was appointed counsel because he said he had no money to hire one.[50] He was eventually convicted of the Bretzius charge and sentenced to three years at the state penitentiary in Columbus, Ohio, the most serious official punishment he had yet received. Amanda, who was in the courtroom when the verdict was announced, collapsed and had to be carried home.[51] While serving his sentence, Waldo, along with two of his buddies in prison, then managed to make their problems worse by trying to escape. Waldo, apparently no more than a passive participant, received no further punishment and was released a short time later upon payment of $500 bond. It can safely be assumed that Amanda paid it, though it was likely the customary ten percent promissory note.[52]

In September 1904 Waldo was in the news again. The local paper described his narrow escape from serious injury in a room he was renting above the Newark Steam Laundry: Waldo had poured gasoline on his bed to disinfect it (the squalor he was living in at the time can only be imagined), and afterward sat down on the side of the bed and struck a match to light a cigarette. The resulting fire was quickly put out and no one was injured, but he was lucky to escape with his life.[53] After this bit of misfortune, he did receive the good news in November that the February 3, 1903, felony judgment for grand larceny was to be lowered to a misdemeanor, and even that was dropped because the witness for the prosecution was unable to testify (in fact, he was a co-conspirator who had turned state's evidence before fleeing to Canada).[54] The outcome of the July 1902 theft charges from the Commercial House is not known, but since Amanda was the owner of the establishment and the victim one of her patrons, it can be assumed that Amanda was able to negotiate with the client to get Waldo off the hook.

The 1905 Newark City Directory catches up with all three members of the Thorp family once again: Amanda, whose name appears as "Mrs. A. E. Thorpe" in bold-faced type, a perk she would have had to pay extra for, was shown as proprietor of and living at the Hotel Franklin, formerly the Ford Hotel, located at the rear of 21 South Third behind Peoples National Bank in Newark.[55] Waldo, listed as an electrician, was also living at the

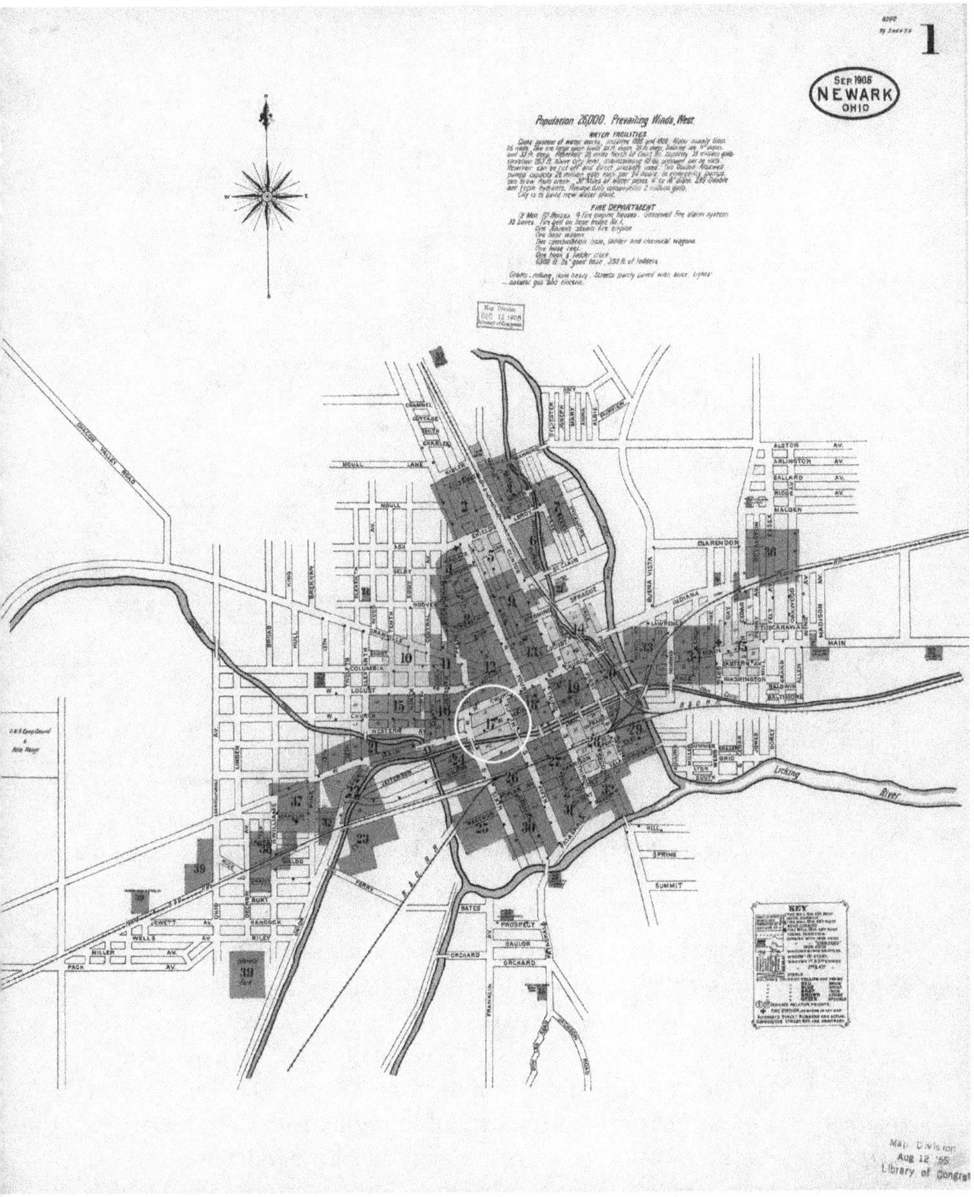

Fig. 9a. 1905 Sanborn Fire Insurance map of Newark, Ohio. The Franklin Hotel (figure 9b.) was in area 17 (circled), a prime spot in regard to the center of town which was area 18. Library of Congress, Washington, D.C.

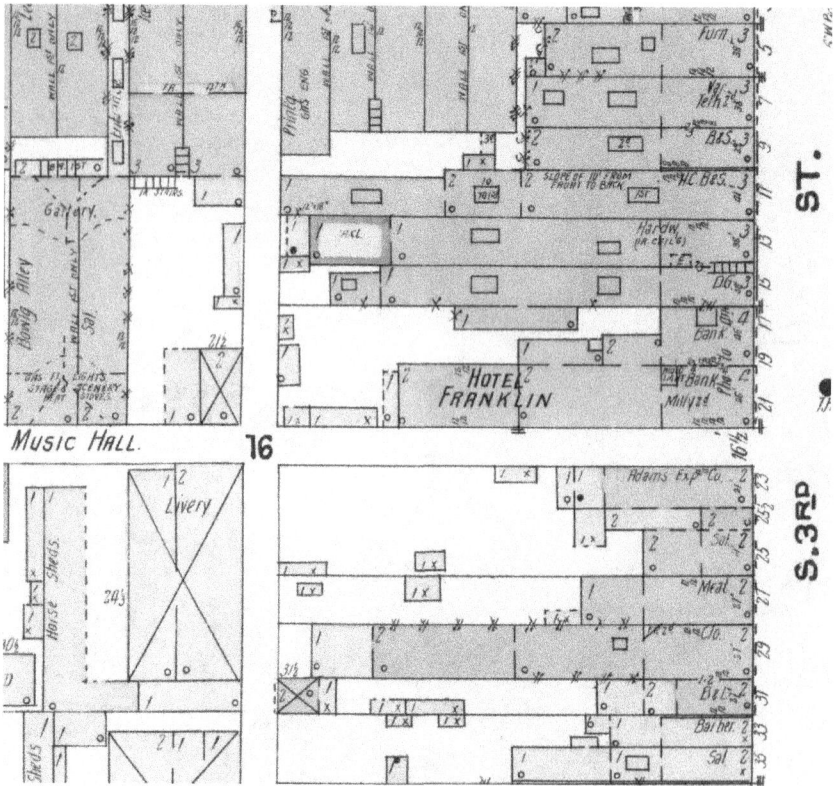

Fig. 9b. Detail of 1905 Newark, Ohio, Sanborn Fire Insurance map showing Franklin Hotel. Library of Congress, Washington, D.C.

hotel. Frank, apparently still in town, was living at 11½ West Main and working as a baker.[56]

Amanda may have taken ownership of the hotel as early as April 5, 1904, when the Newark paper reported she had installed a telephone there, although at the time it was still called the Ford Hotel.[57] The choice to rename the hotel in October 1904 to Franklin Hotel is an interesting one, given that Franklin was the name of her erstwhile husband, but it was also Waldo's middle name.[58]

Once again, Waldo managed to find trouble: in August 1905, the *Cincinnati Enquirer* reported that he was arrested along with another man from Newark for lowering themselves with a rope at 2 a.m. from a window in a Springfield, Ohio, hotel in an effort to avoid paying for their room. The paper noted that with the arrest, it had come to light that Waldo had just gotten married in nearby Covington, Ohio, to the underage Ethelda Mae Schmutzler of Newark. She had turned sixteen just three months earlier; he was twenty-four.[59] Some of the details in the paper may have been an effort by the families to cover up something they possibly considered even more sordid: a Licking County marriage certificate shows Waldo and Ethelda were not married until August 28 in Newark,[60] indicating they were not yet married at the time of the Springfield caper. Even without that illustrative point, the whole thing was highly scandalous. Waldo's first wife Della helpfully provided the Newark paper with colorful commentary that the initial press had missed, including new and soapy particulars about Waldo's other escapades over the years.[61] Waldo's arrest for trying to avoid paying a hotel bill must have been particularly galling to Amanda who had been known to press charges against guests who had failed to pay her.[62]

It wouldn't have been especially surprising if Amanda, now forty-three, was growing weary of Newark and the repetitive perceived blows to her reputation as Waldo's mother. Though the disposition of most of the latest cases against Waldo is not known, he seems to have once again escaped the worst of what could have happened to him, and Amanda may have thought that a change in venue for Waldo might also change the trajectory of his life. When her mother, at age 72 and living with her, was involuntarily committed to a mental hospital in Columbus, Amanda may have felt she no longer had a compelling reason to remain in Newark.[63] She already considered herself a widow and, anyway, by this time Frank appears to have retreated once again back to the Soldiers' and Sailors' Home.[64]

One intriguing court case involving Amanda, mentioned in Newark's newspaper several months before Amanda left town, may help explain how she had gotten the idea of what she would do wherever she might settle next. While still in Newark, she apparently had sold a "moving picture outfit" on credit to a man named Joseph Nies who had failed to make payments, and she wanted the device back.[65] The resolution to the court case cannot be found, but it suggests that Amanda was starting to toy with the idea of the film industry. It is possible she had begun showing some films, referred to in the day as "amusements," to guests in the Hotel Franklin. In fact, that could be why she had left the café and bought the old Ford Hotel: only a block from the Newark's city center and likely much larger than the cafe, it definitely would have been in a good location for making a little extra cash by engaging in the "amusements" business.

By leaving Newark, Amanda Thorp once again was establishing a pattern that she would follow the rest of her life. She had moved frequently within the town of Newark in the twenty-four years she had lived there. She had often tested her skills there as an entrepreneur, defining herself not as one who developed a business over time, but one who bought a business, established it, sold it, and then moved onward and upward. She probably hadn't made a great deal of money, but she had made a living and most likely earned enough extra income to bail Waldo out of his legal troubles multiple times. For whatever the reason—whether it was because of fallout from Waldo's shenanigans or a desire to engage in a new business—in July 1906, at age forty-three, she decided to leave Newark. She leased part of a building at 201 South Sandusky Avenue in Bucyrus, Ohio, a space likely originally intended as a retail shop, and began renovating it for the installation of an "automatic moving picture show."[66]

Fig. 10. Photograph (2021) of 201 South Sandusky Avenue, Bucyrus, Ohio, which housed Thorp's Wonderland Theater, 1906–1907. Photo by John K. Kurtz, MD, Bucyrus, Ohio.

2

MEET ME AT THE WONDERLAND

The Wonderland Theater in Bucyrus, Ohio

The rapid growth of commercialized entertainment is one of the most strik-
ing differences between the nineteenth and twentieth centuries in the United
States. In the early- to mid-1800s, puritanical criticisms of recreational
activities equated theaters, dance halls, circuses, and even organized sports
with immoral behavior. As incomes rose and leisure time expanded after the
turn of the nineteenth century, however, and affordable commercial "amusements" democratized free time across socioeconomic classes, entertainment
became a major industry in and of itself. Playhouses, which before this shift
had in the main presented performances put on by traveling theater troupes,
expanded their offerings to include vaudeville acts—such as ventriloquists,
magicians, hypnotists, tight rope walkers, and jugglers—as well as poets,
comedians, choirs, and orchestras. The new "moving pictures"—short in
length, often without plot, and always without integrated sound—would
occasionally be added to the mix. Itinerant exhibitors arose, traveling from
one town to another and showing these new moving pictures to audiences
under rented tents or in churches and other venues as part of fund-raising
or so-called educational events. Nickelodeon theaters were next to emerge,
exhibiting movies as their main offerings and enabling entertainment for
the public that cost only five cents a throw, an incredibly low price for an
evening's entertainment especially compared to the price of the cheapest
tickets of a show at the traditional playhouses that were often just down
the street.

What made (and makes) film such a popular form of entertainment?
Film historian Roger Manvell writes, "There is something mildly hypnotic
about the illusion of movement that captures and holds the attention. The

motion picture gives viewers a strong sense of presence; the film image is
in the present tense. There is also the concrete nature of film: it appears to
show actual people and things. The setting for viewing a motion picture is
no less important: spectators are no longer in their everyday environment,
but rather they are comfortably seated in the dark, in relative isolation from
others. They live in the world the motion picture unfolds before them."[1]

It can only be imagined what it must have been like in those days of
early film to have the experience of viewing a moving picture for the very
first time. Both filmed and presented with then-revolutionary technology,
the new medium influenced the way people viewed themselves as well as the
world around them in ways theretofore unknown. Films offered escapism
and largely were equally accessible to both rich and poor—though much
less so to people of color, though this was also true for other entertainments
of the era.

Why Thorp chose Bucyrus, about seventy miles north of Newark, for
her theater venture is unknown, but it may have been simply because there
wasn't one there yet. Ohio as a whole was saturated with nickelodeons
in 1906 (*Billboard* magazine showed seventy-three nickelodeons in Ohio,
the most of any state), and there was even one already in Newark.[2] With a
population of about 7,000, Bucyrus had a diminutive pool of potential patrons compared to Newark's population of about 20,000 but, like Newark,
it was a typical, bustling midwestern county seat surrounded by farmland
populated with folks who went into town to do their weekly shopping.[3]
Thorp would have hoped that while there, they would take a break from
purchasing their necessaries and indulge in an inexpensive amusement.

In about two weeks, Thorp had the place ready to show films; in truth,
in those days it wasn't very complicated. A prospective exhibitor would
typically rent out a space otherwise intended to function as a retail shop.
"Often the windows were not even taken out, but merely darkened with
paint, blinds, or shades," she told the *Richmond Times-Dispatch* in 1926.
"The [projector] was put in place in the easiest and most convenient spot,
a makeshift screen erected, and a gramophone . . . placed outside the theater to play its tunes and attract the crowd."[4] She would have added rows
of mismatched kitchen chairs or perhaps wooden benches. When she had
done all this, she opened the Wonderland Theater for business in Bucyrus
on Saturday, August 11, 1906.[5] It may have deliberately been a soft opening,
or Thorp may have just believed that if she opened the doors, they would
come, but a local friend of hers remembered it this way years later after
he had also entered the business: "While the building was being remod-
eled [into the Wonderland theater], discussion was rife as to her sanity. On

opening night, her only patron was the village drunkard." Things improved somewhat, he said: "The next day, several of the more venturesome saw the performance, but it was some days before any of the ladies ventured into the house."[6]

The titles of the very first films shown at Wonderland are lost to history; Thorp did not advertise them. But what patrons could expect was described in the local paper: "It [will be] a place of popular amusement with changes of program each Monday and Thursday and is to be a continuous performance of live moving pictures from 1–5 and 7–10 pm each weekday. The admission is five cents and that includes the entire entertainment of which the management says will be a 25-cent show for a nickel." Weekdays in the parlance at the time would have included Saturday; no businesses operated on Sunday, the day legally reserved for church-going. The picture show, the paper continued, would consist of about 800 feet of moving picture film interspersed with "illustrated songs,"[7] a kind of sing-along activity.

Merritt Russell writes in an academic piece about nickelodeons that "the show customarily began with a song, usually one of the popular ballads of the day—'Sunbonnet Sue,' 'Bicycle Built for Two,' 'The Way of the Cross,' or perhaps 'Down in Jungle Town'—or else a patriotic anthem. Hand-colored slides illustrated scenes from the song and a final slide projecting the lyrics encouraged the audience to join in the chorus. The manager might then present his first film, or bring on a live comedian, a dog act, or perhaps a ventriloquist."[8]

The early films Thorp exhibited at Wonderland would have been so-called trick pictures involving some kind of optical illusion, films of faraway places or scientific innovations, or accounts of disasters, scandals, or other events deemed newsworthy. If a film happened to have a plot, it would have fast-moving action which would develop linearly from one climax to another until it resolved itself in an explosion or a person being beaten.[9] Thorp recalled later that exhibitors such as herself did not know anything about the content or length of the early movies in advance of showing them in their theaters; however, it did not matter if there was no plot or even no rhyme or reason to the film, as long as the figures actually appeared to move.[10] Like all early theater managers, Thorp rented her films from a film distributor, called an exchange, located in a major city; the first one she recalled using was based in Cincinnati[11] and may have been a branch of a larger one headquartered in Chicago. The exchanges sent films to theater exhibitors who showed them and then paid to return them; all shipping was done by train.[12] Herbert Miles, who ran an exchange in San Francisco, recalled a price of $15 per reel for up to one week for the first reel his company rented out,[13] but the price varied according to the length of the film—not, it is noted, to its quality as a production.

With the price of admission five cents, ten shows a day, and a seating capacity of 150 people, Thorp could conceivably make $75 a day, less expenses, every day that she showed pictures.[14] Clearly, the more seats she could fill, the more money she would make. A week or so after opening, she began placing editorial announcements in the local paper to let potential patrons know what was showing. These announcements, which evolved into ads, were placed three to four times a week over the next year, and when taken together (Appendix 1—Films and Other Entertainments at the Wonderland), they provide a useful catalog for what early filmgoers typically saw when they went to see moving pictures in the United States during 1906–1907. The first films Thorp announced for the Wonderland were for showings on Wednesday, August 22: *Love vs. Title* or *An Up-to-Date Elopement* and *Angler's Dream*.[15] Thorp appears to have presented only films at Wonderland and not to have supplemented with vaudeville or other novelty acts, although on occasion she may have hired a local musician or two to help fill out a bill; a local speaker or one passing through also may have made some remarks now and again.

"Tobacco and Feet and Sweat"

A business such as the Wonderland would have taken at least two, maybe three, people to run it: one or two might be responsible for opening the theater, selling tickets at the door, ushering people into the theater, running the projector, overseeing the patrons' departure, and then closing the theater at the end of the day. Another person would have a more administrative role: ordering and returning films (a complex endeavor in and of itself), marketing the business, paying bills, and doing myriad other managerial tasks all the while filling in for other employees as needed. It is easy to imagine Amanda Thorp in the second role and Waldo in the first, a position where she could keep him close, keep him busy, and keep him out of trouble. In Newark, Waldo had worked at least briefly as an electrician, so he would have acquired at least a modicum of a useful skill that could have helped him deal with the inevitable equipment breakdowns that would occur in a business so heavily dependent on new technology. Projector operators, in fact, were in those days often called "electricians," and early nickelodeon theaters were sometimes called "electric theaters" to distinguish them from "live" or "legitimate" playhouses.

Fig. 11. Early photograph of the exterior of the Bucyrus Wonderland Theater, late 1906 or early 1907. Collection of Doug Godwin, Bucyrus, Ohio.

Two images survive of Thorp's early 1900s Bucyrus, Ohio, Wonderland, and elements pictured in them fit her 1926 *Richmond Times-Dispatch* description of early nickelodeons. The first image, which may originally have been what is known as a "real photo postcard," shows the entrance to Thorp's theater and appears to have been taken shortly after she opened it in August 1906. The two large front windows, typical for a building space originally intended as a retail store selling women's hats or questionable pharmaceuticals, retreat toward the interior and appear to have been painted black. The words "Always Good, The Wonderland, Bucyrus," are painted in primitive lettering on both windows. There is room under the theater name to post information about films that were currently appearing; both windows also have the word "Tonight" painted on them. The price of admission, "5 cents," is painted in large, prominent lettering on the two narrower windows which directly face the street, easily visible to persons passing by in farm wagons. Shadows detected inside the door may reveal a small area that might have functioned as the ticket selling area.[16]

The second image accompanies the 1926 *Richmond Times-Dispatch* interview and was likely taken on Independence Day, 1907. By the time of this photograph, a ticket booth has been constructed to jut out in front of

Fig. 12. Photograph of the exterior of the Bucyrus Wonderland Theater thought to have been taken around Independence Day 1907. Cox, "Woman," *RTD*, Jan. 10, 1926.

the entrance. A roundish item on the left is the horn of the gramophone, set up on a shelf outdoors in order to broadcast music to attract patrons, which was a tactic, she said years later, that worked "finely."[17] It sits at eye-level to make it convenient for an employee, perhaps the ticket seller, to wind it up frequently, but it also probably protected the machine from patrons jostling in line. A large and professionally lettered sign projects over the sidewalk and proclaims "WONDERLAND" in all caps. There is copious patriotic bunting swagged along the top and sides of the theater as well as around the ticket booth. Adding to the themed holiday effect are at least three pairs of crossed American flags; even the gramophone appears to have a ribbon tied to it. There is a single door as a patron entrance; a door toward the back of the building that opened on East Rensselaer Street would likely have functioned as the patron exit. The long, narrow architectural shape of the building would have been advantageous for exhibiting movies, since film, more so than live theater, is best seen from a position directly perpendicular to the plane of the screen. As previously noted, Thorp at some point enlarged the inside of the theater,[18] and it may have been done by this date, as the front of the theater is noticeably larger compared to that shown in the earlier postcard photo.

Thorp's Wonderland Theater was typical of nickelodeons of the day as she herself described it in the 1926 interview. Craig Morrison writes in his article on design of the early nickelodeons, "These early theaters were in no way great works of architecture, but their bravura evoked wide public admiration."[19]

In the early days, film reels ran from not more than a couple of minutes up to a maximum of about seven minutes. Films could also be supplemented with in-house live or recorded music, vaudeville-like acts, or even other films to make a lengthier show and to justify the ticket price. Film plots generally were not of huge concern: it was the movement on the screen that was the novelty that drew audiences to film showings. As plot elements were added, intertitles, or title cards, were used to help describe action which might not otherwise be clear. The early films are today called "silent" because they had no audible sound (other than the noisy whir of the projector or the accelerating clack-clack-clack when the end of each reel signaled its completion), but they were often accompanied by music either provided live by a local musician on piano or other instrument, or else the projectionist might play a scratchy wax cylinder record on a phonograph kept at arm's length nearby. If music was indeed part of the program, the choice of titles was at the discretion of the exhibitor; the earliest film producers seldom suggested what music went with their movies. Theater managers sometimes also attempted to provide synchronized sound effects produced by a local hire who improvised with whatever materials were at hand.

The theater owner, then, had no particular concern with acoustical demands for the film itself when considering the design of the theater's interior space. There would have been, however, in many of these early theaters, the Wonderland included, an area carved out near the screen—to one side so as not to block the patrons' view—which would provide a niche for an upright piano (perhaps a player piano) or a small group of live musicians. Though writing much later, James Agee, the well-known film critic from Knoxville, Tennessee, captured the filmgoer's experience in early picture palaces: "The barefaced honky-tonk and the waltzes by Waldteufel slammed out on a mechanical piano; the searing redolence of peanuts and demirep perfumery, tobacco and feet and sweat; the laughter of unrespectable people having a hell of a good time, laughter as silent and steady and deafening as standing under a waterfall."[20]

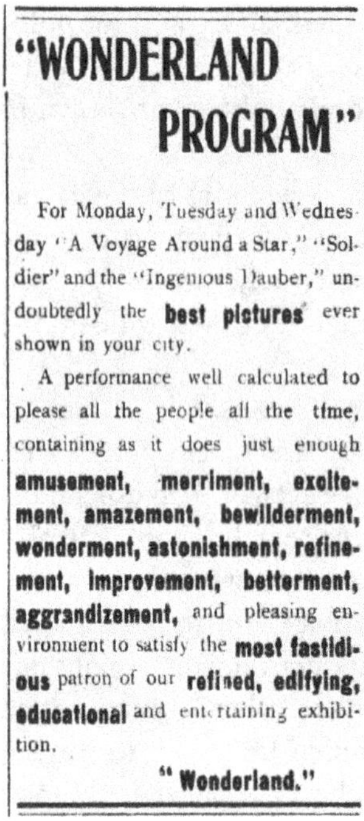

"WONDERLAND PROGRAM"

For Monday, Tuesday and Wednesday "A Voyage Around a Star," "Soldier" and the "Ingenious Dauber," undoubtedly the **best pictures** ever shown in your city.

A performance well calculated to please all the people all the time, containing as it does just enough **amusement, merriment, excitement, amazement, bewilderment, wonderment, astonishment, refinement, improvement, betterment, aggrandizement,** and pleasing environment to satisfy the **most fastidious** patron of our **refined, edifying, educational** and entertaining exhibition.

" **Wonderland.** "

"WONDERLAND."

Our moving pictures are as far ahead of those usually exhibited by 5c theatres as the electric light is the superior of the candle.

Pictures for Friday and Saturday Afternoon and Night are

"The Old Masher" & "False Coiners"

COME IN AND SEE FOR YOURSELF.

"WONDERLAND"

WHY WONDER? BE CONVINCED!

Many people wonder at the great success of Wonderland—It is due to advertising by word of mouth more than by printed advertising. An endless chain and the very best kind of advertising. As a lady visitor to this beautiful and prosperous little city recently said, "I cannot speak too strongly in praise of your Electric Theatre, the Wonderland." But Bucyrus proof should be good enough for Bucyrus people. We give you home evidence. Your townspeople furnish it. You must be convinced. We furnish proof of our claim. If you think that any other entertainment in Ohio can successfully aspire to the excellence of "Wonderland" you are mistaken. Any one in this city who is discouraged and sick at heart will only visit us it will do them good. This statement can not be denied. Watch for our next attraction which is billed for tonight, entitled "A Venetian Tragedy," "The Cab" and "Burglars at Work" which WONDERLAND you are politely requested to enjoy at

WONDERLAND

We have secured for Thursday, Friday and Saturday the highly-colored film,

"MEPHISTO'S SON"

Don't fail to see it at

WONDERLAND

Wonderland

"Passion Play." This film is hand-colored and is entirely different from anything in pictures ever shown in Bucyrus. No man, woman or child should miss seeing this wonderful depicting of the life of Christ. Tonight many of Jesus' miracles are exemplified in pictures, such as the ' Wedding Feast," where He changes water to wine; Mary Magdalene at the feet of Jesus, and His gracious forgiveness, followed by Jesus and the woman of Samaria. The restoring of the dying daughter of Jarius is very realistic, and is followed by another miracle—Jesus walking on the surface of the troubled waters of the sea; the draught of fishes, where Christ comes to the aid of the fishermaid and they catch plenty, and the raising of Lazarus are illustrated at

Wonderland

Fig. 13. Ads from the Bucyrus *Evening Telegraph* for the Wonderland Theater. Thorp placed ads in the newspaper nearly every week during the year she operated the theater in Bucyrus and they often revealed intriguing details about her business philosophy and marketing strategies. *BET*, Jan. 21, Feb. 16, Mar. 23, May 9, and June 17, 1907.

The number of films being shown on any given day at the Wonderland would be determined by the length of each individual film. A multi-tasking projector operator could show three to four titles for one audience set including the time expended for efficient reel changes as well as attending to the phonograph if required. That would have left just enough time to move patrons into and out of the theater as another group arrived. If it's possible to feel pity for Waldo, it might be in this: showing the same three to four very short films fifteen times a day for three or so days in a row and then repeating that with another set of films, again and again, week after week.

Widely held prejudice for early moving picture theaters ran toward the side of considering them to be disreputable (as Agee alluded), and Thorp knew that portraying the theater as a place of decency would be necessary to increase her patron pool and maximize her profits. She approached the challenge head-on in her advertising which not only noted films that would be playing but also directly addressed any potential personal conflicts with morality that might arise. Even though seeing a film at the Wonderland would provide "amusement, merriment, excitement, amazement, bewilderment, wonderment, astonishment, refinement, improvement, betterment, [and] aggrandizement" in a "pleasing environment," it would still "satisfy the most fastidious patron."[21] And anyway, her theater, she said, only attracted the best kinds of people: "[we] notice the increasing numbers of refined ladies who have cast aside their prejudices and have become a part of the always respectable audience at Wonderland. We doubt very much if any electric theater in Ohio can truthfully boast of such refined audiences as those that assemble at this cozy and moral entertainment. Nothing coarse or objectionable at this peerless theater."[22] Two weeks later, she praised her "select audiences" of "intelligent people," as proof that her theater was above reproach.[23] In mid-October, she started offering special Saturday afternoon matinee showings specifically for women and children to further draw in that audience demographic.

In another example of her innate marketing savvy, when other events that were happening in town had the potential to dampen her patronage, she would change her hours to accommodate them: "We are still here," she proclaimed in an October 9, 1906 ad, "Everybody will have plenty of time to go the opera house as our theater will open at 6:30."[24] But also there would be an occasional warning to head off scofflaws: "Remember, tickets good only the night purchased,"[25] and she wasn't above interjecting a bit of humor, "If the party with the bald head who could not remove his hat in the Wonderland last night will go to Kern's drug store, Mr. Kern will recommend a guaranteed hair restorer."[26]

By early December, she likely had already ordered at a cost of $200 the "fine new moving picture machine," an Edison which would be installed at the end of the year.[27]

Things appeared to be going well for Amanda. Even Waldo seemed to be staying out of trouble. But then a horrific event shattered the run of good luck. The Bucyrus newspaper reported on Monday, November 26, that "William Morey of Newark, part owner of the Wonderland Theatre, was blown to atoms near Straitsville (Ohio) Saturday morning by an explosion of nitroglycerine. Morey was a well shooter, and it is supposed that a can of fluid exploded while he was handling it."[28]

Getting Through the Month of August Safely

Natural gas was discovered in northwest Ohio in 1836 while a farmer was in the process of drilling a 10-foot-deep water well. Originally considered a nuisance, gas did not become a valuable commodity until the 1880s when people realized its usefulness. Today, most people think of other U.S. states as major exporters of oil and gas, but from 1895–1902, Ohio was the leading producer of oil and natural gas in the country. When wells would inevitably begin to slow in production, and paraffin wax or rocks were suspected to be restricting the flow, well-shooters like Morey would be hired to use explosives to try to increase output. Simplified, a well-shooter would lower an explosive-filled "torpedo" into a well and then detonate it to try to loosen any obstructions. Dynamite was used in earlier years, but nitroglycerin, though more dangerous to use because of its inherent instability, worked better.

William Morey, about sixty years old, had been shooting wells for more than twenty-five years for the Marietta, Ohio, Torpedo Company. If nothing else, because of his longevity in the business he was well known in the gas industry and among landowners who had gas wells on their property. Occasional news articles in newspapers across Ohio which regularly published gas industry news would sometimes mention him and whether or not his actions had been able to successfully increase gas production in a particular well—the technique was not guaranteed to succeed. Morey was fully mindful of the dangers of his job. He had tendered his resignation with the company on several occasions over the past two years before the accident, but each time was induced to remain.[29] On August 21, 1906, just three months before the fatal accident, the *Newark Advocate* carried a short news story in which Morey had announced that "if he (got) through the month of August safely," he intended to quit. The *Advocate* added, "He expects to engage in the moving picture business."[30] The story appeared ten days after Thorp had opened the Wonderland Theater in Bucyrus.

Immediately after hearing of Morey's accident, Thorp went to Corning, Ohio, located near the explosion site, but no follow-up to her trip there is documented.[31] Morey's estate, estimated to be worth about $5,000 (about $165,000 in 2023), was adjudicated,[32] but any effect his death had on his investment in Wonderland, if the story in the Bucyrus newspaper that he was part owner is accurate, is not known.

There are several curious side notes to this event in Thorp's story, not the least of which is the mention of William Morey as "part owner" of Wonderland. Morey considered his home to be Newark, and in fact he was planning to return there after completing the job in Corning.[33] His wife, May Wilson, originally of Utica, Ohio, had died of liver "trouble" in March 1904 at their Newark home;[34] Thorp had to have known William and May in Newark. The couple was childless, and therefore there were no direct descendants that stood to inherit Morey's estate assets. Morey had visited Bucyrus several times shortly before his death.[35] Was he just looking after his supposed investment? Morey was about the same age as Amanda's husband Frank, which is to say, nearly twenty years older than Amanda. It might be inevitable to wonder if there was a romantic involvement, but the age difference makes the question more speculative, even taking into account that Thorp previously had been married to a man that much older than she (a marriage which she regarded as having ended). The question also arises whether Thorp benefited financially from Morey's estate if he were indeed "part owner" of Wonderland. Was the probate court aware of the connection, and if not, could that have been the basis of a bit of wealth that allowed her to take on her later projects in Virginia? If the supposed investment was included in the estate, did Thorp have to buy out the asset and was it a hardship? And finally, of course, was Morey even really a past owner? In the 1926 Richmond interview, Thorp maintained she never had a business partner until she was in Virginia, though perhaps this was an instance of her bending the truth.[36]

William Morey's death clearly would have been an emotional setback to Thorp, whether or not a romantic connection between them existed. But the show must go on, and Thorp had to cope with the myriad technical and managerial problems and tasks associated with running Wonderland: electrical outages and equipment breakdowns, films arriving in poor condition or not when expected, keeping pace with technological advancements in a rapidly-changing industry, coordinating live or recorded music, upgrading or cleaning and otherwise maintaining the physical theater space, hiring employees, making bank deposits, paying bills and, of course, constantly ordering, receiving, and returning films while also keeping them secure and safe when they were in her possession—among other things.[37] This was not a business for the faint of heart. And competition was fierce, not only from

Fig. 14a. Modern-day
street view of 126 South
Sandusky Avenue, Bucyrus,
Ohio, the location of the
Hart Brothers store in
1906. Photo by John K.
Kurtz, MD, Bucyrus, Ohio.

existing, traditional theaters which would also show the occasional film,
but from threats by others who saw how many nickels were pouring into
Thorp's hands and were thinking about setting up their own moving picture
start-ups. In the face of all these challenges, Thorp ran the Wonderland with
creativity and with a remarkably savvy business sense.

When William Morey visited Bucyrus, he had stayed with Thomas
Hart.[38] Thomas was in business as a timberman in northern Ohio, supple-
menting his comfortable living by also renting out his land for farming.[39] He
and his wife, the former Barbara Rebeccah Bechtel, had three sons: Earl P.,
Harvey H., and Lloyd F., all born two years apart starting in 1884, with Earl
the oldest and Lloyd the youngest.[40] The sons did not follow their father

Fig. 14b. The Hart Brothers moved their store to several locations up and down Sandusky Avenue in Bucyrus. It can be seen here, second store from right. Postcard photo, ca. 1915. Collection of the author.

into the timber business, but somewhere in their youth discovered an affinity, and apparently a talent, for music. By around 1901, when the family moved about twenty miles east to Bucyrus, the Hart brothers, by then in their mid- to late teenage years, were starting to make a name for themselves as musicians, playing individually or together at churches, club meetings, community picnics, and school events. They played multiple instruments: Earl played violin, cornet, and piano, Harvey the trombone, and Lloyd cornet and piano. By 1903, they had become part of an eighteen-member community band and an eight-piece orchestra, were teaching music to a number of Bucyrus residents, and still performed individually as well as together in a small group they billed The Hart Brothers. They often traveled to nearby towns for their concert venues. At the end of 1904, they rented space in downtown Bucyrus and sold pianos along with other musical instruments while continuing to perform as well as teach. Their business did well; they continued to grow, moving several times to ever-larger spaces in Bucyrus, continually increasing their inventory and expanding into selling Edison records. In 1906, they moved into space at 126 South Sandusky Avenue in Bucyrus, across the street from the Wonderland Theater.[41]

Fig. 15. An ad for the Edison phonograph of the sort Thorp would have had in her early theaters. Note the cylindrically shaped molded records. *The Century Illustrated Monthly* (April 1904): 74.

It is not known how Thorp first met the Hart brothers. William Morey could have been her connection to them even before she left Newark, but certainly when she arrived in Bucyrus she would have gotten to know them as fellow colleagues in the entertainment business as well as neighboring business associates. At least occasionally, the brothers provided live music at the Wonderland accompanying the silent pictures and the illustrated songs—a mutually beneficial arrangement, since the illustrated songs were seen as a valuable promotional tool for marketing sheet music which the Hart Brothers sold in their store.[42] The brothers also likely facilitated Thorp's hiring of their students who would sometimes play at the theater. They also would have sold or lent Thorp their Edison records to play on her prized phonograph. When Thorp placed a piano in Wonderland, it goes without saying that she bought it from the Hart Brothers.[43]

A Refined Entertainment of Ever-changing Wonders

At the turn of the new year, Thorp published a thank-you note of sorts to the people of Bucyrus while in the course of promoting her theater in the local paper:

The electric theatre of Bucyrus is, as its name implies, a refined entertainment of ever-changing wonders—electrical possibilities managed and manipulated skillfully and with a full appreciation of the desires of a refined people who by their continued liberal patronage have demonstrated that they have no fear of seeing or hearing anything that would offend the most fastidious lady or gentleman of this city. A theatre with the price of admission within the reach of the most humble and respectable citizen and at the same time offering an amusement worth the endorsement of all mothers seeking recreation for themselves and children. The managers of Wonderland feel very grateful toward the good people of Bucyrus for the encouragement given them in their efforts toward conducting a good, moral, and clean place to spend an enjoyable evening, and it will be ever their highest aim to amuse and please their patrons to the full extent of their ability and to treat every person politely.[44]

By the time she placed that ad, she may have already heard rumors that significant competition was coming: the Theatorium, another nickelodeon, would open in the next month about a half-block down the street from the Wonderland.

Thorp modified her marketing strategy in response to the new threat. It began with a bean contest: whomever came closest to guessing the number of beans in a jar on display in the Hart brothers' music store window would win the prize of a cut-glass punch bowl complete with stand and tumblers.[45] The contest created a lot of buzz in Bucyrus, prompting the *Evening Telegraph* to write a feature about a feckless fellow named Al Blosier who was so obsessed with the beans that "he sees them in his sleep, he sees them in the air, and when the snowflakes gently fall, Al thinks it is raining beans."[46] Alas, Blosier did not win. Miss Lulu Mars of 316 Jump Street won with a guess of 2,565, missing the bean count by only one (there were 2,566).[47]

Next, Thorp ran a series of larger ads in the *Evening Telegraph*, some of which, in addition to listing upcoming films, had text which contained what may have been intended as not-so-subtle jabs at the Theatorium. A February 11, 1907, ad claimed: "Meritorious recognition has been accorded Wonderland, the electric theater of Bucyrus, by an ever-increasing attendance, stamping the approval of the generous people of an enterprising city upon the ability displayed and the indefatigable energy manifested in security for the amusement of the public and entertainment of extraordinary merit, each pleasing feature succeeded by one more entertaining." It ended with the clear invitation, "Meet me at the Wonderland."[48] Later the same month: "Remember our show is continuous. The latest moving pictures and beautifully illustrated songs. No long waits. Nothing stale. Nothing vulgar. Everything new and up to date. Strictly moral. Special attention to ladies." She then listed the films showing at the time—ironically not all of which might be said to uphold the adjectives she had just applied to them: *Officials, Smugglers, Bad Mother*, and *Birthday Cake*.[49] The next day: "[The Wonderland] is the finest of anything in the West. . . . Other five cent theatres are more or less actuated by consideration of economy. Not so at the peerless Wonderland."[50] Going to her theater, Thorp advertised, would even make her patrons better people: "Hello, girls! Our remarkable recipe, 'How to be Healthy, Beautiful, and Happy' and possess that bloom of countenance so much admired is labeled healthful recreation. No matter how or where you are employed you will obtain it by visiting Wonderland."[51] She often just touted the qualities of her theater over others: "You can see nothing better in moving pictures, no matter where you go or how much you pay. We exhibit the same pictures that are shown in the best theatres of New York, Paris, and London. Our machine is of the very latest model, and the films are all new and up-to-date and the best procurable in the world. The subjects selected are adapted for intelligent audiences and never fail to please the most exacting, critical, and fastidious audience."[52]

The Theatorium did the same sort of thing, but without Thorp's exuberant language, exemplified, for instance, on March 5, 1907: "The people say our pictures are the best they have seen," and March 7: "Ladies are especially welcome," then on March 18: "Theatorium Pictures. See them and be happy, miss them and be sad. The many expressions of delight by hundreds of patrons last week proves we give a show the people like," and another on April 4: "We present each evening a refined show which you will enjoy."[53]

In 1907, the two theaters consistently showed different films, attesting to the huge number of products being circulated by film exchanges at the time. Even on the two occasions when they overlapped themes, they were not showing the same films. Thorp would have found both these occasions particularly vexing, however, because they were otherwise significant showings.

The first time had to do with shows about the affair known as the Thaw-White tragedy, the sensational June 1906 New York City rooftop murder, witnessed by hundreds, of renowned architect Stanford White by Harry Kendall Thaw, heir to a multimillion-dollar coal and railroad fortune. Newspaper coverage of the murder and the accompanying back-story of alcohol, drugs, rape, a chorus girl, jealousy, insanity, and very wealthy people, had been widespread in the United States. In mid-April, in the same week, both moving picture houses in Bucyrus happened to be showing different media versions of the incident. The Wonderland was screening sixty-two slides divided into five sets involving different aspects of the backstory, trial, and subsequent commitment of Thaw to an insane asylum.[54] But the Theatorium had beaten them to the punch: a few days earlier, they had shown *The Unwritten Law*, an actual moving picture based on the killings—and they also had the advantage of screening it on Saturday.[55]

In the second instance, Thorp would have scooped the Theatorium when she scheduled the late-April showing of the *Passion Play*,[56] just three weeks after Easter. The films did not arrive on time, however, and in a very unusual occurrence, the Wonderland went dark on the Monday evening the films were supposed to open. The next day, on Tuesday, Thorp ran an ad saying they had arrived and would be showing that day. On Wednesday, she ran an ad saying the Tuesday showing had been canceled, because the films were "not of the high quality which Wonderland insists on giving its patrons." Wonderland resumed its next cycle of movies on Thursday with three other unrelated films.[57] New films did not come in until two months later, putting Thorp once again into direct competition with the Theatorium which was planning to show Passion Play films the same week.[58]

Expansion

At the same time as she was dealing with the competition the Theatorium presented, Thorp opened another theater in another little Ohio town, Washington Court House, often abbreviated by Ohio residents as Washington C.H. to distinguish it from Washington, D.C.[59] Located in Fayette County between Cincinnati and Columbus, Washington Court House is another mystifying location for Thorp to have chosen for a theater, although it may have been another case of finding one of the few places in Ohio that didn't already have one.[60] When Thorp established this new theater there, the downtown area of Washington C.H. consisted of the courthouse, some centralized utility offices, and a very small number of retail stores; the closest the town came to having any major industry was a grain elevator and milling company.[61] At about 6,000, the population size was similar to Bucyrus; however, though like Bucyrus it was also a county seat in rural Ohio, it wasn't the bustling borough that Bucyrus had become.[62] Perhaps someone coming through Bucyrus on their way to the popular recreational areas in northern Ohio had visited Thorp's theater and remarked that their own city could sure use a moving picture house. For whatever reason, the decision was made, and by April 2, 1907, Thorp had started making regular business trips to Washington Court House.[63]

Bucyrus and Washington C.H. were a hundred miles apart, nearly half a day's journey by rail, so the location of the new theater alone would create management difficulties.[64] Thorp resolved the issue by hiring eighteen-year-old Walter Coulter of Bucyrus to run the theater in Washington C.H.[65] It is not known how Thorp knew the Coulter family, though the Coulters had lived in Bucyrus since at least 1900. Walter's father Matthew worked at a farm implement company in town.[66] Thorp would have hired Walter to work at Wonderland for a time before sending him to Washington Court House to manage the theater there alone. She must have seen something impressive and trustworthy about the young man, but she still occasionally traveled there to check on him.[67] Walter's fourteen-year-old younger brother, Robert, worked at Wonderland in Bucyrus while Walter was in Washington C.H.; he sat behind the screen playing gramophone records and making sound effects by shooting off cap pistols.[68] As youngsters, the two brothers would have often walked past Wonderland while venturing out from their home four blocks away on Spring Street—it is easy to imagine them seeing a "Help Wanted" sign among the theater posters hanging outside and then applying within.[69]

3

THE BEST PLACE SHE COULD FIND

On the Way to Richmond, Virginia

For months, newspapers across the country had been running stories about the Jamestown Exposition, an event celebrating the 300th anniversary of the founding of the Virginia colony and the telling of many other aspects of American history. The Exposition would have been the talk of lunchrooms, barber shops, and waiting lines outside movie theaters in Bucyrus and across the country. Ads ran in the Bucyrus papers, touting special rates for excursions by rail to the Exposition in Norfolk on the Virginia coast. The *Telegraph-Forum* on April 19 noted that there were fifty-two different plans for traveling to the Exposition from Bucyrus, with rates ranging from $12 to $30.70, depending on time spent and route traveled.[1] En route stopover privileges were available.[2]

Thorp had never been to Virginia, or anywhere else in the South, but it had been an especially hectic month with the competition with the Theatorium and the fiasco of the Passion Play pictures. The theater in Washington C.H. was up and running, and she was confident in the abilities of Walter Coulter to run it. Waldo was staying out of trouble, or at least was staying out of the news for being in trouble, and the Hart Brothers were such good friends that she could likely count on them to help with any sudden emergencies (with Waldo, for example) that might come up, should she take a few days off.[3] She had a bit of breathing space, and it must have seemed a good time to take a small vacation.

The Exposition opened on April 26, 1907. It is not known whether Thorp planned to arrive for the opening ceremonies or for a day or two later. It appears she traveled alone, though if she took an excursion she would probably have become friendly with others on the same trip. How long she may have stayed at the Exposition is also unknown, although it could only have been two or three days. Even so, there was a lot to see and experience, especially for someone in the amusements business.

A series of moving pictures relating the history of Jamestown was being shown in a reproduction of the old state capitol building, the original being located in nearby Williamsburg. An exhibit of a "baby incubator," complete with live infants, demonstrated the ability of modern science to treat prematurely born infants. Field hands from Florida rode ostriches around the grounds. A horseback rider re-enacted Paul Revere's ride in an "ingenious" arrangement involving a moving panorama of background art and photos. The 1906 San Francisco earthquake and fire could be viewed in panoramic photographs that were enhanced with electric lighting effects. There was a Wild West show reminiscent of Buffalo Bill spectacles.[4] Native Americans, African Americans, and the U.S. military were featured groups at the Exposition; in fact, there was a sprawling "Negro Building" meant to "show the life of the colored race from the days they were brought from Africa to the present," according to the New York Times in an account which glossed over the period of slavery.[5]

Thorp must have been mesmerized, as almost anyone would be. She may also have looked around nearby Newport News and Norfolk to see whether any nickel-a-throw theaters were there.

It was likely on her way back home to Bucyrus that Thorp stopped in Richmond, though it is also possible that she stopped on the way to the Exposition, or perhaps both. Since 1901 or so, the Richmond Chamber of Commerce had been marketing Richmond with campaigns focused on the region's colonial and Revolutionary heritage to draw investors and visitors, hoping to transcend Confederate associations, although the emphasis conveyed in the marketing sometimes depended on its intended recipient.[6] She had likely come across the materials in the run-up to attending the Exposition, or maybe she had picked up some brochures while at the Exposition. Perhaps prompted by curiosity to explore what the former capital of the Confederacy was like, especially given that her (secret) husband had fought for the Union in the Civil War, she would have booked a stopover stay. Where she stayed in Richmond is not documented, but the luxurious Jefferson Hotel was charging $1.50 a night, so she may have stayed at the more reasonably priced Murphy's Hotel at Eighth and Broad, conveniently located to the train station but, probably more importantly, across the street from Richmond's flourishing theater district.

When Thorp arrived in Richmond, she found a man named Jack Jacobson showing films in a tent on a lot next to the Colonial Theater,

Fig. 16. South side of East Broad at Eighth Street, Richmond, ca. 1907. The Murphy hotel annex (to the right in the photo) was in the 700 block of East Broad. Thorp's original Dixie was nearly directly across the street from the hotel annex in the old Colonial Theater building. Her later Rex Theater was located at 700 East Broad on the same side of the street as the Dixie had been. Collection of the author.

located at 714 East Broad almost directly across the street from Murphy's Hotel Annex. Calling them "movin' figgers," he charged five cents admission.[7] In a 1923 retrospective interview, Thorp described what happened: "I came . . . on an excursion from Ohio and looked the town over. That was in 1907. Things looked good here, but there was no 'picture parlor' as they were then called. Broad Street looked like it had great possibilities for a theater and I opened a parlor at Seventh and Broad. . . . We called it the Dixie. That was a name which ought to go well in Virginia and it did."[8] In another retrospective interview in 1926, she added that the Dixie had been located in a "rather obscure part of the old Colonial (Theater) Building."[9] Thorp acted extraordinarily quickly on the opportunity she saw. In a matter of possibly only a couple of days, she arranged to take over Jack Jacobson's concession, rented a room for showing films, equipped it, set up financials, and hired a manager to run it. A news article at the time confirmed some of the details: "The Dixie Theatre will open its doors to the public this afternoon [May 4]. . . . Decorators and carpenters have been busy transforming the old Bijou annex into a miniature theatre, and the task has been performed remarkably well. Mr. Pink McCarver is the manager of this enterprise and the attractions offered will be moving pictures and illustrated songs. The price of admission will be 5 cents. In the event that this effort meets with success, it is intended to put on vaudeville acts at the same price of admission."[10]

Even though Thorp started the business "in a small experimental way,"[11] it is daunting to think that she believed she could run a theater in Richmond from 500 miles away in Bucyrus. On the other hand, she could have believed she had nothing much to lose. In truth, her investment was fairly negligible compared to the potential return in a city with no dedicated movie parlor but which was said at the time to have been the second most-densely populated city in the United States.[12] Though no documentation about McCarver can be located, he had to have had some skills in showing films as well as having an understanding of how the film exchanges worked; perhaps he had worked for Jack Jacobson. He also had to have had personal attributes or a verifiable reputation of some kind which led Thorp to believe she could trust him with a potentially large number of nickels. In a stroke of luck, or maybe it was planned coincidence, Thorp would have been able to communicate with McCarver just about as directly as was possible in those days: in Richmond, Murphy's Hotel across the street housed a branch of the Postal Telegraph Company, and back in Bucyrus, the telegraph company was only four blocks' walk from Wonderland. Telephone lines were accessible in both telegraph offices, although Thorp may have had a telephone line installed in the Wonderland itself as she had done a couple of years earlier in her Hotel Franklin in Newark.

Perhaps Thorp had intended to extend her time in Richmond before returning to Bucyrus, at least to be present for the Dixie opening, but on Friday, May 3, she received word that her mother had died.[13] Amanda was in Newark, Ohio, for the funeral on May 6. Waldo and his wife left Bucyrus for the funeral as well, and Wonderland was closed for a few days.[14] Waldo's wife, unnamed in the newspaper article that told of their plans to go to Bucyrus, apparently was the Ethelda Schmutzler of the 1905 elopement scandal.

Thorp must have been very discreet about her Richmond venture, as not a word appeared in any newspaper, whether in Ohio or in Virginia, about the Richmond Dixie being associated with her in its early days. The *Richmond Evening Journal*, however, did a short follow up a few days after the opening, noting it was already a success: "The new pictures being shown at the Dixie Theatre this week are pleasing large audiences at each performance. The interior decorations of the little playhouse are also attracting much favorable comment from the many patrons."[15]

Bucyrus newspapers reported several trips by Amanda or Waldo to Washington C.H. after the opening of the Dixie, but it can be speculated that at least one or two of those trips might have been cover for making a (relatively) quick trip to Richmond by either of them.

In June, in Bucyrus, Thorp was once again trying to arrange an Easter passion play showing, this time a series of films of the live production put on every ten years since 1634 in the village of Oberammergau, Germany.[16] The passion play films would be complex showings at the Wonderland. For the first time, there were too many reels to be seen in a single thirty-minute showing, so anyone who wanted to see the entire play had to return the subsequent night. Thorp heavily advertised the films, emphasizing their exclusivity as "the only original hand-colored films" of the German production. Her advertisements also gave instructions on how they would run, since Bucyrus audiences were unfamiliar with the two-day concept.[17]

Though it was two months past Easter, almost uncannily the Theatorium advertised films on the same subject that they were planning to show.[18] Thorp had managed to get a couple of days' advance start as the two theaters prepared to compete head to head. The *Evening Telegraph*, whose offices happened to be located about a block's walk from each of the two theaters and received advertising from both of them, tried to be diplomatic in their coverage of the dueling amusements: "Those who saw the passion pictures at the Wonderland speak in very high terms of them and those who have seen the films at the Theatorium speak of them as a really artistic production."[19]

It was likely just a short time after this that Thorp may have heard the news that the Theatorium, while not closing entirely, would be changing direction—it would no longer be a nickelodeon but rather would be renovated to include a stage and opera seats in order to focus on showing vaudeville acts instead.[20] Though the press announcement noted that the picture machine would be retained at the newly-named Orpheum for occasional film showings, it would be a higher-priced theater and thus would no longer be direct competition for Wonderland. Thorp had competed against another five-cent theater and had won. She may have been celebrating this achievement when she took a weekend trip to the amusement park at Cedar Point, located then as it is today in northern Ohio, on a narrow peninsula that juts out into Lake Erie. A near disaster occurred on her return: she was caught in a dangerous crush of people who had tried to board a ferry at Cedar Point to go to Sandusky where they would take the train onward to their destinations—in her case, Bucyrus. At the boat landing, Thorp told the *Bucyrus Evening Telegraph*, she "stood for two solid hours, unable to move forward or backward, wedged in by the crowd," remaining on her feet only "with the utmost difficulty." She noted that a number of people climbed the high fence at the dock and leaped over to a space on the bay side to escape being trampled. Dozens of women and children fainted, and there was "much confusion." Thorp had been among the 45,000 people who had visited the park that Sunday, a very large number even for an attraction as big as Cedar Point.[21] There is no indication that Thorp had a companion on this trip; in fact, the implication was that she was traveling alone. This seems to be a not-unusual case for Thorp.

On the same day that the paper published the account of Thorp's harrowing trip to Cedar Point, the paper published a note saying that she and Waldo would take (another) vacation for a few days as a "needed rest."[22] Waldo's wife, Ethelda, was not included in the news of the vacation. It is likely they were divorced by this time as she was living at home with her parents in Newark.[23] Wonderland was to be run by the Hart Brothers while Amanda and Waldo were gone.[24]

The following day, on the anniversary of the Wonderland opening, an ad in the *Evening Telegraph* from Thorp thanked the people of Bucyrus for the support shown to her during the preceding year: "One year ago today, we [she may have been speaking for Waldo as well], as strangers, opened the doors of Wonderland in this city. That fact recalls the many pleasant associations, the many friendships formed, . . . [and] the many smiling faces seen . . . [that] thrill our hearts with good will toward those who have shown such friendship for us."[25] The ad's sentimental wording seems to foreshadow a good-bye.

Most assuredly, Thorp went to Richmond on this "vacation," taking Waldo with her, to look over the city and vicinity in more depth in order to make a more informed decision as to where her future lay. On September 11, 1907, the *Evening Telegraph* reported that she had returned to Bucyrus. The Hart Brothers had done so well taking care of Wonderland in her absence, the paper noted, that Thorp planned to leave again for an extended trip in the South, with the "intention of starting Wonderlands in several towns in Virginia," leaving the Harts once again in charge of her Bucyrus movie house. She also made a quick trip to Washington Court House at the same time, perhaps to tell Walter Coulter of her decision and to begin the process of closing down the theater there.[26] The following February, Coulter left the Washington C.H. theater to take a new job in Newark for the American Amusement Company, running their theater there for "a nice increase in salary."[27] No mention of Waldo's whereabouts was made; perhaps he was already in Richmond.

Amusements at an Affordable Price

Though Thorp's Dixie theater in Richmond was the first indoor venue there to be dedicated to showing films at a low cost, she would have learned

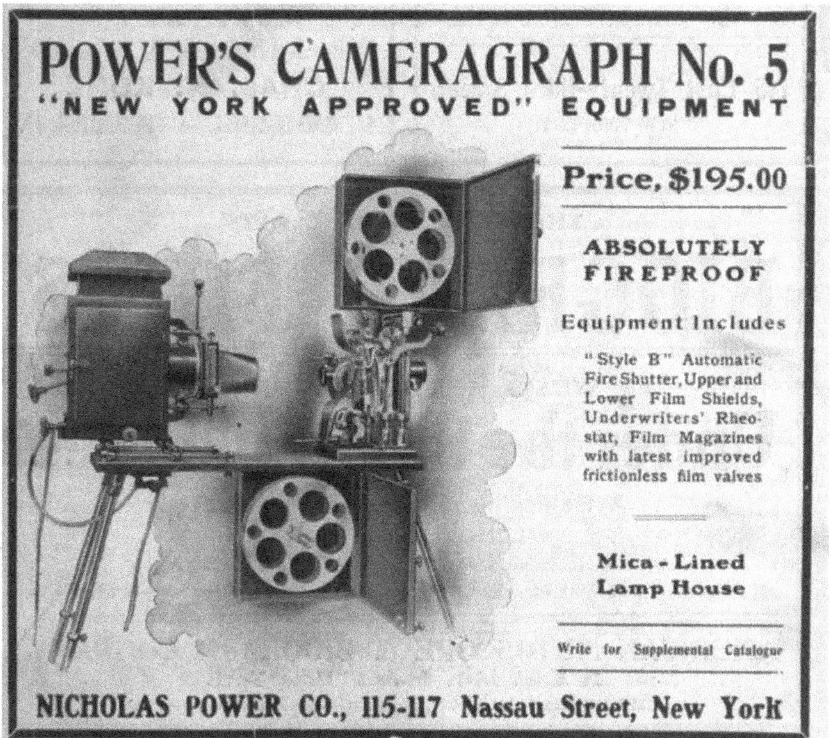

Fig. 17. Ad for the Power's Company Cameragraph No. 5 projector, likely the machine that Thorp was using at the Dixie. The weight and bulkiness of this projector shows that technology was moving toward serving fixed movie houses rather than the itinerant shows that had preceded them. *MPW*, Nov. 9, 1907.

early on that she wasn't completely without competition in the city, even though she had bought out Jack Jacobson. For one thing, Richmond already had a rich legitimate-theater history stretching back 200 years,[28] and these traditional playhouses proliferated along Broad Street in the early 1900s, offering their audiences plays, musicals, vaudeville acts, and even a "moving picture" now and then. In fact, Jake Wells, a well-known, White, Richmond entertainment empresario who owned the Colonial Theater (where Thorp rented the room for her Dixie), the Bijou, and several others, had on occasion himself shown films at those theaters as well as regularly to patrons at his Idlewood Amusement Park near today's Byrd Park, probably in the open air but possibly also indoors at the skating rink or other park buildings.[29] In addition, Charles W. Moseley, a Black man recently out of Atlanta and likely a few months before Thorp's arrival in Richmond (when she was passing through on the way to or from the Jamestown Exposition), was also showing at least the occasional film. Moseley, 40, had opened a hotel and café in the segregated area of First and Charity streets when he first came to Richmond in 1907. In March he then quickly expanded his investments

Fig. 18. Charles W. Moseley, the Black man who tried to make a go of movie theaters in Richmond at the same time that Thorp was getting into the business there. Moseley was forty-four at the time this image was published. N.d. *IF*, Dec. 23, 1911.

to a skating rink nearby where now and again he utilized the large space there to show films or host early Black vaudeville acts and even a wild animal show.[30] Operating under Jim Crow laws and customs, theater patrons of Wells and other White theater impresarios were White, of course, and Moseley's customers were Black. Churches and fraternal organizations of both races would also procure the occasional so-called educational film, brought in by itinerant film exhibitors, to show their respective White or Black target audiences and raise money for their respective charities.[31]

Thorp's business model was different from the others in that her house focused on the showing of moving pictures at a consistent, very affordable price, although she might bring in an occasional vaudeville act for variety or as a filler. As had been the case at her Bucyrus Wonderland, patrons at the Dixie were paying only five cents—in Richmond the cost of a pound of blackberries[32]—and nickels poured in by the thousands. Nearby saloon owners would not have looked at her success without viewing it as an attractive way to make some money without a lot of capital investment. They found they could renovate their back rooms, set up a few kitchen chairs and a projector, show films, and make more profit than they could by selling liquor, especially after Richmond instituted an increased tax on booze to raise revenue.[33] Richmond had a lot of saloons in those days, and so competition arose quickly for Thorp and her Dixie storefront.

In November 1907, the Dixie offered the *Oberammergau Passion Play*, Thorp no doubt realizing from her prior experience in Ohio that it was a good money-maker.[34] And later that month, as she had noted in Bucyrus that she planned to do, Thorp bought from "Mr. Jenkins" what was described as a theater at 1435 Hull Street in Manchester, across the river from Richmond but still relatively close by. She temporarily closed it for repairs and alterations, and then on November 22, "assisted" by Waldo, had an "auspicious" opening of "the New Wonderland."[35] Thorp apparently sold the New Wonderland in Manchester shortly after she bought it, and its name was apparently changed by the subsequent owner.[36]

Thorp may also have been in the process of opening other Wonderlands in Virginia. The publication *Moving Picture World* stated in a 1920 retrospective article that Thorp had gone from Bucyrus to Newport News and then later to Richmond, when she first went to Virginia to open playhouses, but this seems likely to have been misreported.[37] It is more likely that she opened a Wonderland movie house in Newport News at 2703 Chestnut Avenue after moving to Richmond to personally manage the Dixie and after opening the New Wonderland in Manchester. At any rate, there was a Wonderland Theater in Newport News by at least June 1908 although documentation has not been found which definitively points to her as its owner (Wonderland was a fairly common name for an amusement house in the early 1900s).[38] She is known to have opened a movie house in Norfolk around this same time as well, but again, the question about when she did so is up for debate. The 1907 Norfolk City Directory lists a Wonderland movie house at 62 Granby Street and though information of that period in city directories is often a year behind in publication, it is also possible that the information on the theater was collected concurrent to 1907.[39] A location on Granby would match what Thorp described in a 1926 retrospective interview, when she said she had opened a theater in Norfolk in a "galvanized iron building on Church Street, using one-half of the theater for white patrons and one-half for colored patrons."[40] Granby today is an extension of Norfolk's Church Street, and so 62 Granby would have been located right at the end of the latter and the start of the first.

Meanwhile, at her Dixie storefront in Richmond, as in Bucyrus, Thorp made a special effort to bring women through the Dixie's doors. On December 31, 1907, she ran several classified ads encouraging women to visit for the "special music" she was sponsoring for New Year's.[41] In January, she again sponsored "special concerts by one of Richmond's best orchestras."[42]

In March 1908, just about a year after Thorp opened her movie house in the Colonial Theater building, a Richmond city board composed of the chiefs of police and fire inspected the rooms and saloons on Broad Street that were showing films.[43] They had good reason to do so: early movie film was made of nitrocellulose and was highly flammable. Not only that, once it caught fire, it was difficult to put out. To make matters worse, it burned with a hot, intense flame and emitted poisonous gas in the resultant smoke. Newspapers across the country frequently ran articles about fires having started on a rickety projector or in film storage areas where movies were being shown. In fact, a fire caused by a projector "explosion" had broken out in September 1907 in Richmond's Empire Theato, an African American variety show house on North Second Street, creating a panic among the audience that was packed inside.[44] Back in Ohio, the Bucyrus Wonderland, which may have still been in Thorp's portfolio, was preemptively advertising that smoking was "positively prohibited" in the theater. Even so, in late December 1907, two months after the start of that safety campaign, a fire broke out there as well, though no other information about its cause or severity is known.[45] Even beyond the dangers posed by the flammability of film, Richmond authorities were, and still are, particularly sensitive about fires in theaters: on December 26, 1811, an historic fire at the Richmond

Theatre killed seventy-two people, including many prominent residents who were gathered to see a benefit double-billing of two plays. Newspapers across the country reported that it was the worst urban disaster in U.S. history at the time. Not due to flammable film, of course, the fire started after a curtain fell on a chandelier.

Because there were no other exits for patrons to leave the Dixie in the event of a fire other than the main entrance, Thorp was told by the inspectors to seek other quarters.[46] Likely part of the reasoning as well was that audiences at the Colonial, where the Dixie was located, were also at risk. She had sixty days' notice to find a new venue, and the "best place she could find" was a building about seven blocks west—at 18 West Broad, on the corner of Brook Road and Broad Street.[47] The Brook and Broad building itself was three stories tall; her Dixie Theater would occupy approximately the front third of the first floor, formerly a grocery.[48]

Planning to open a proper movie theater in Richmond all the while balancing the management of multiple Wonderlands, Thorp may have felt the need to bring in someone she could trust to help her manage her holdings, even if it were the case that Waldo was helpful now and again. The logical person to bring in was Walter Coulter, and so she brought him from Ohio to Virginia sometime after February 1908, sending him to manage her movie house in Norfolk. Keeping the theater open in Norfolk and having Coulter run it was likely a decision made not only on the basis of making sure the theater was run competently but also good business strategy: the Warner Brothers, who would go on to become the famous, major Hollywood moguls, operated a film exchange in Norfolk. "Naturally," Coulter said in an interview in 1929, "I was thrown into more or less intimate contact with [them]," and thus he was perfectly positioned to ensure that Thorp got the best pictures, both in Norfolk and in Richmond.[49] Whereas Thorp and other exhibitors basically took what the exchanges sent them in the early years (or more likely, months) of the industry, the nickelodeon boom of the early 1900s brought with it an intense rivalry among exhibitors to book the latest and biggest productions, and personal relationships would have been key to success in that process.[50]

18 West Broad

In Richmond, the location at 18 West Broad at the intersection of Brook Road and Broad Street, was a perfect fit for a bona fide, permanently-located nickelodeon theater. As Russell Merritt notes: "The thirst for

Fig. 19. An electric streetcar on Richmond's Broad Street that would have passed in front of Thorp's permanently located Dixie Theater on Brook and Broad. The photograph was taken at the corner of Foushee and Broad Streets toward the east, and the photographer would have been standing nearly directly in front of what would become the Dixie Theater. Postcard, ca. 1905. VCU Libraries, Digital Collections.

affluence and respectability helps explain the curious locations of the original nickelodeons. Even when they were working-class entertainment the most important nickelodeons were seldom built in the worker's community or in his shopping area. Instead, they customarily opened in business districts on the outer edge of lower-income residential neighborhoods while also fringing white-collar shopping areas; thus they were accessible to blue-collar audiences but were located even closer to the middle-class trade."[51]

In 1908, Brook and Broad was a busy intersection; street cars and trains stopped there to deliver and pick up passengers. The massive Masonic Temple had recently been built across the street; large public events were hosted on the upper floors and retail space was rented out on the bottom two. Another huge six-story building was on the opposite corner, housing Jurgen Furniture Store in the retail space on the bottom floors with offices above. In addition to its role as a center of retail trade in the city, the three-street intersection (Adams Street triangulates there as well) also served as the staging area for huge Broad Street parades that brought in thousands of participants and tens of thousands of spectators. Richmond's Chamber of Commerce often featured the intersection in publicity materials in its efforts to recruit tourist trade and business to the city. Broad Street itself, downtown Richmond's main artery then as it is now, was thoroughly modern, representing prosperity and a progressive spirit. Attracting the coveted foot-traffic that Thorp sought would not be a problem for the Dixie in this location, the "best place she could find."[52]

As a relative newcomer to the city, however, when Thorp moved her Dixie Theater to Brook and Broad she may not have fully appreciated that population demographics had changed. Although the new Dixie was not strictly within the designated confines of Richmond's predominantly African American Jackson Ward, it was very close to it, and several of the Dixie's neighboring businesses—on the north side of Broad where the Dixie was

Fig. 20. The Dixie Theater interior, likely photographed after it opened in 1907 or in 1908. *RTD*, Jan. 10, 1926.

located as well as on the Brook side running north toward Jackson Ward's acknowledged boundaries—were run by African American shopkeepers. On the other hand, across the street on the south side of Broad where there was shade in the hot summers, the shops and businesses catered mostly to White patrons. Still, despite being several blocks farther away from the already established, generally White-patron-only theater district centered around the Colonial, Thorp likely designed the posh new Dixie Theater with White audiences in mind. While it was the case that Black patrons were sometimes admitted to the galleries of some of the theaters in Richmond's traditional theater district, the Dixie was located all on one level and therefore would have no gallery available for African American filmgoers.

Determined to make her movie theater stand apart from her competition in Richmond, many of which were gussied-up saloon spaces, Thorp traveled to Brooklyn, New York City, Jersey City, and Atlantic City to "educate herself more thoroughly" in the moving picture business. When she returned to Richmond, she brought with her "all the latest improvements necessary for a first-class show."[53] A photo of the interior of the Dixie at Brook and Broad, likely taken shortly after the Dixie was completed and ready for occupancy for the first time, shows the theater seating bolted to the floor in neat, permanent rows of five seats each, a total of about 100, lining both sides of a wide center aisle; they appear to lack any padding. The theater's several ceiling fans would move the heavy humidity around during Richmond's sultry summers and circulate the stale and odiferous air otherwise. The metal ceiling tiles, still in the building today, are light in color, but the side walls, disappearing into the vanishing point at the back of the theater, are dark, inset with what probably were brocade fabric panels. The screen, about seven feet in width, large by the day's standards, was permanently affixed to the wall. Curtains—they can be imagined to be red velvet—contributed an elegance to the setup and framed the screen on both sides with a café-curtain detail along the top. To the right of the screen was a space where perhaps posters to advertise the next film would be affixed. Almost certainly there were no available restrooms.[54] During her remodel of the space at Brook and Broad, Thorp of course also had to follow the new rules just promulgated for fire safety in Richmond's "cheap amusement houses": in addition to fastening the chairs to the floor, she also had to ensure that "the picture machines [were] surrounded with fire-proof materials, and there [was] a back or side entrance in case of fire."[55] In the photo, a door to the left side of the screen can be seen, which would have permitted emergency exit at the back of the building outside to Marshall Street, making Thorp now fully compliant with fire laws.

Thorp's new Dixie Theater debuted on May 16, 1908, showing the moving picture *Great Paris Fire Scene* and also featuring illustrated songs.[56] A small newspaper article marking the occasion noted that Thorp was promising "a clean show" at the Dixie, and an ad assured a comfortable experience with "ocean breezes by ice-cooled fans."[57] She advertised fairly regularly in Richmond's evening newspaper through the end of the year though it was rare that her ads were as effusive in nature as those she had placed in Bucyrus for her Wonderland. (See Appendix 2 for her offerings at the Dixie.) Still, in addition to promoting the films or illustrated songs that would be shown, she would occasionally market movie-going in general, target women as audience members in particular, or tout her theater's qualities over others:

> In your struggle to find a suitable place to spend your time, these two things must be borne in mind—first, the Dixie, corner Brook Avenue and Broad Street, is the coolest place in the city; second, in the Dixie Theatre, for 5 cents, you can see the wonders of the world, the streets of Paris, the canals of Venice, the icy fastness [sic] of Arctic regions, the darkest jungles of Africa, and biblical and historical subjects, [all] reproduced while seated in a comfortable chair providing not only relaxation and rest for the body, but education and enjoyment. We want the Dixie to have the endorsement of every mother and every minister of the gospel, and the support of every newspaper in Richmond. If you have never paid our little theatre a visit, do so tonight. If you have and enjoyed yourself, come again. We always offer the glad hand, a pleasant smile, and a good show. The picture is but a nickel, five cents.
>
> Get the habit,
> Dixie[58]

The Gem movie theater which opened on June 4, just a couple of doors down Broad from the Dixie, volleyed back: "Illustrated Songs and Moving Pictures. Coolest, cleanest, safest place of amusement in Richmond. Five Exits."[59] Like the Theatorium in Bucyrus, rivals could not match Thorp's gift of marketing language.

Though Richmond's traditional playhouses, with their emphasis on showing live theater, generally were a different kind of competition to the movie houses, they also on occasion offered films. A few days before the new Dixie opened, the Colonial advertised it was showing "two reels of pictures" and a "great" illustrated song for an admission of ten cents, although matinee price was five cents for ladies and children.[60] In addition, some saloons and other store-front types of venues seemed to have slipped past fire code compliance and were still operating—notably the Theato located at Fifth and

Broad streets about six blocks west of the Dixie. Charging ten cents a head and more often offering vaudeville acts and speakers than films, the Theato had been operating out of a room above an old store since April 12, 1907.[61] The entire building was condemned by the City of Richmond in September 1908 but was rebuilt by December that year when the Theato re-opened as a full-fledged nickelodeon in direct competition with the Dixie.[62] On June 11, 1908, the *Evening Journal* noted the Ideal Theater, for Black audiences, would be opening, fulfilling a "long-cherished" wish of Richmond African Americans. The Ideal was located at 700 West Broad.[63]

Richmonders were "moving picture mad" during that summer of 1908 according to the *Journal*. Despite the heat and humidity, "thousands of pleasure seekers" promenaded up and down the seven blocks of Broad where the picture show houses proliferated, picking and choosing which amusements to attend. The paper noted there were six movie theaters along that stretch of Broad, book-ended by the Majestic at one end about a block west of the Dixie, and by the Colonial at the other. Three more theaters were under construction.[64] There were 16 nickelodeons in Richmond by the end of that year.[65]

What's On at the Dixie

Most of the films Thorp screened at the Dixie were not unlike what she had shown previously in Ohio, and in fact she repeated some of them in Richmond—and some of those were of comparative blockbuster caliber. In June 1908, for example, she again showed films of the Oberammergau Passion Play but combined them all into a one-hour show, still only charging five cents admission. The theater was "packed."[66] In August, she showed the movie *Damon and Pythias*[67] which told the story of the mythical beginnings of the Knights of Pythias, a fraternal, benevolent association; the *Evening Journal* noted that more than 1,500 people had attended the showing in one night.[68] But Thorp picked a "gold mine" when in late July she screened the four-reel film of the 1906 Gans-Nelson world lightweight boxing title fight,[69] the last fight-to-the-finish bouts in boxing history. Joe Gans, the reigning six-year world lightweight champion and the first African American to hold a world title in any sport, had roundly defeated Oscar Matthew "Battling" Nelson, a White Dane. The strong attendance at the Dixie for the 1908 showing of the 1906 fight was probably due to hype generated a few weeks before when Gans and Nelson had fought in a re-match, this second time with Nelson winning. "From the time the Dixie Theater opened until midnight a crowd greater than the capacity of the house stood outside waiting for the next show," a reporter gushed about the film's reception.[70] Showing the film was so profitable, in fact, that Thorp did it again on August 7. She later recalled in 1920, "I certainly reaped a harvest in those days."[71]

Thorp immediately began plans to build on her success. By late July 1908, just a couple of months after the Dixie had opened at Brook and Broad, she signed a contract with William Zimmerman, specifying a two-year lease with a five-year privilege for an "up-to-date" moving picture theater at 700 East Broad. The building was to be built purposely as a theater, and she would have overseen construction to make sure it met her specifications.[72] In late November 1908, she opened the Rex Theater there, also a nickelodeon, only steps away from the Colonial Theater. Thorp was re-claiming her territory: she already knew from experience with her original storefront Dixie that this location in the heart of Broad Street's traditional theater district was a good one for attracting a film-going audience. She pulled out all the stops for the grand opening, bringing her good friends the Hart brothers and their orchestra from Bucyrus to play music for the inaugural week.[73]

Amanda left Waldo to manage the Dixie on Brook and Broad, while she herself moved to the Rex.[74] A few months later, perhaps surprisingly, she turned at least briefly to an entirely different business model, although it wasn't completely unlike the Jacobson show she had seen in Richmond when she first arrived in 1907. In June 1909, an ad appeared for the Airdome, an open-air theater located at Jake Wells' extravagant Idlewood Amusement Park in Richmond's Byrd Park area, and noted that Thorp "wishes it distinctly understood that she manages both the Airdome and the Rex, and the programs at each theater are selected and arranged under her special

Fig. 21. Drawing of a typical airdome theater. David S. Hulfish, *Motion-Picture Work: A General Treatise on Picture Taking, Picture Making, Photo-Plays, and Theater Management and Operation*. Chicago: American School of Correspondence, 1913:195.

supervision."[75] Another manager identified only as Kendler, though often named along with her in the ads and articles about the theater that year, always received second mention; his first name was never even provided. No photograph or detailed information about the facility itself is known to exist, but airdomes, today thought of by some as the predecessor to drive-in theaters, were popular in the United States at the time Thorp was associated with the one at Idlewood. David S. Hulfish, in his 1913 book, *Motion Picture Work*, described the basic concept: "A fenced enclosure is chosen (and) a canvas 8 to 10 feet high is erected upon stakes to form an enclosed yard. At one end a projection house or even a projection platform is built; at the other end, a picture screen of usual theater size is erected. Chairs are arranged before the screen as in any motion picture theater, and the entire conduct of the airdome is quite the same. A platform may be built before the screen for vaudeville. The airdome is for fair weather only."[76]

With the park conveniently located at the end of a streetcar line that ran from downtown, the seasonal aspect of the open-air Airdome (hopefully) with its summer breezes, in theory, would have offered Richmonders a much cooler location to watch movies than the claustrophobic, air-starved theaters three or so miles away in town, even should those theaters happen to be equipped with the ice-cooled fans that Thorp advertised at the Dixie. The Airdome at Idlewood opened for the first time on May 22, 1909, and its last ad during that first year was published on September 15. Films were often shown, but the main selling point seemed to be the "polite vaudeville" acts, so called because they were deemed suitable for women and children. The venue likely was restricted to White patrons, and performers almost certainly were most frequently, if not always, White. For the closing nights, Thorp advertised "cakewalking and minstrels," the latter term likely refer-

Fig. 22. First known ad for Thorp's Airdome Theater.
REJ, May 22, 1909.

encing Whites performing in blackface.[77] Cakewalking was a kind of dance that had its roots in slavery. Paired as it was with minstrels, it might have been a caricature.

Vaudeville acts at the Airdome included athletic boxers, novelty acrobats, "equilibrist unicyclists," singing comedians, roller skating, and "eccentric monologists" (probably what were also known in the era as "humorists"), among many others. The Airdome also occasionally hosted an "amateur night" where locals could get up and present their talents after the last vaudeville performance. Films would not have started until dusk, not only because the temperatures would have begun to drop by then, but also because the light would have faded enough so that the films could be seen. Bad weather, of course, could at the least interrupt and even suspend plans to put on a show in the open air—especially one involving electricity to run projectors and the electric lights needed to illuminate vaudeville acts at night. Admission was always five cents, but showings may have been limited to two a day, a "matinee" at 4 pm and an evening show that started at 8 pm.[78]

Thorp, who likely had leased the Airdome space from Wells, must not have found the venture as profitable as she envisioned; she appears to have been associated with it only in its first year (1909). Idlewood Park itself went belly-up in 1914.

Black Patronage at the Dixie

Contrary to her experience at the Airdome, Thorp was having a highly successful run with the Rex and may have been mulling over how to maximize profits at the Dixie. At some point, although the exact date is unknown, a changeover in patronage was made, converting the Dixie to an all-Black clientele. The January 10, 1926, *Richmond Times-Dispatch* interview with Thorp notes that the shift was made soon after she moved the Dixie from the Colonial to Brook and Broad,[79] and it seems likely that she made the change at the time of the November 1908 opening of the all-White Rex, which occurred about seven months after the new Dixie opened. This would have allowed her to have two separate theaters in Richmond, one for White patrons and one for Black patrons.

As a matter of course, Thorp would have closely followed the national trade magazines where she would have learned about new technology, new films coming out, and all sorts of information regarding movie-industry trends. While still in Bucyrus, she would have come across a June 1907 article in *Moving Picture World* talking about moviegoing among African

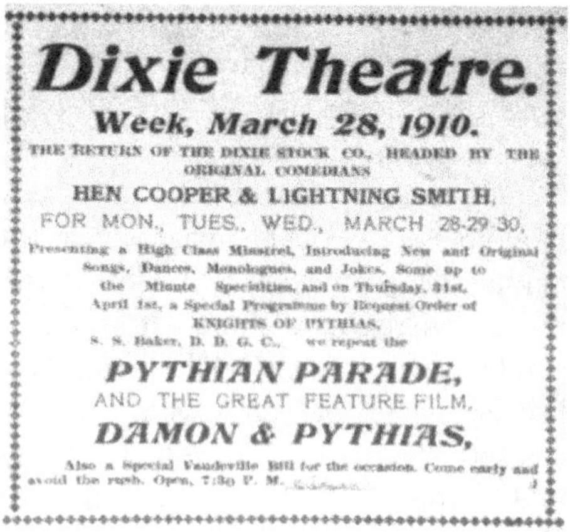

Fig. 23. Likely the first ad for the
Dixie placed in the *Richmond
Planet*, the city's influential African
American newspaper, and therefore
the first time the Dixie reached
out specifically to potential Black
patrons. *RP*, Mar. 28, 1910.

Americans. An unnamed theater owner, peppering his ideas with the racist assumptions and tropes that White people were accustomed to at the time, wrote, "Strange that moving pictures do not appeal to the masses of negroes" while also admitting that "of course, a moving picture show exclusively for negroes has not yet been tried."[80] By the time of the early 1900s, while leisure time available to African Americans compared to their White counterparts had evolved in substantially different ways, they too, in general, had more of it. Also like their White counterparts, African Americans had more spending money (again, nearly always relatively speaking).[81] Given the effects of increasing segregation and the resultant diminishing access to many "public" spaces in cities like Richmond, African Americans were in many cases a ready audience, willing and prepared to spend their money should amusement establishments recognize them as a patron base.[82] In Richmond, the potential for African Americans as customers was significant: about 40% of the population was Black.[83]

Thorp at least once claimed that she was the first to open an all-Black-patronized theater (presumably in the United States).[84] Gregory Waller, an influential authority on the African American experience in all aspects of film and theater at the turn of the twentieth century, notes that the earliest motion picture theater which existed for the exclusive entertainment of African Americans that he could find opened in Evansville (probably Indiana) at some point in summer 1908. He apparently (logically) was unaware of Richmond's Black-patronized Ideal Theater which opened on June 11, 1908, which may or may not have pre-dated the Evansville theater. The Dixie, in the meantime, had converted to Black patronage probably around November 1908. The changeover admittedly may have occurred earlier, but still after August 1908 because the review of her showing of the *Knights of Pythias* film had appeared in the White press with no mention of Blacks having attended.[85] The fact of the Ideal Theater's existence surely would not have escaped Thorp's attention, however, as she was running ads for the Dixie in the same newspaper that had reported on the Ideal. Consequently, if Thorp had converted the Dixie to all Black patronage after November 1908 when she opened the Rex, then she was not the first ever to open an exclusively Black-patronized theater as she later asserted in the 1926 *Times-Dispatch* interview, not even in Richmond, though at least part of this debate could turn on what actually constitutes a "theater." Nevertheless, it can be safely said that her Dixie was ground-breaking in the fact of its longevity for serving Black customers as well as because of its impact on Black entertainment in Richmond and even regionally, as will be seen.

Though by all accounts Thorp was able to fill her all-Black-clientele theater regularly, there were, nevertheless, reasons why some African Americans did not always find going to see a picture show a pleasurable experience: two being that, first, there were few Black actors in early films—only a handful of "all-colored" movies were produced before 1916—and second, because story lines of African Americans were often stereotypical at best and perverse at worst.[86] As late as 1920, John Mitchell, Jr., the influential editor of Richmond's African American newspaper, the *Richmond Planet*, published a guest editorial noting that Black leaders in Washington D.C., "appreciating the importance of moving pictures," encouraged production of "the kind of pictures . . . which will have an uplifting influence instead of those which are a travesty on the race."[87]

Black vaudeville acts in the early 1900s, however, had the potential to provide a different kind of experience to Black patrons than did the early films of the sort Thorp and other exhibitors across the country were screening in their theaters. A reviewer writing in the African American newspaper *Indianapolis* (Indiana) *Freeman* explained, "you can enjoy yourself better because the average colored performer can say things in that [Black] theater that place him three times funnier than he would be at a White [amusement] house . . . every slang phrase we understand, and of course he opens his heart to us because he is among his own people, enjoying himself and trying to make those likewise enjoy (the performance)."[88]

The Dixie's First Black Vaudeville Acts

Whether or not Thorp understood or even cared about such concerns of her potential Black patrons—though certainly her underlying motivation would

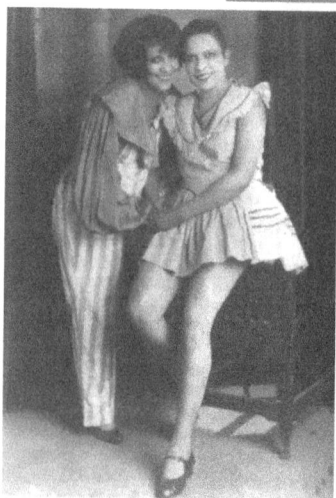

Fig. 24a–g. African American vaudevillians who performed at Thorp's Dixie Theater. *Clockwise from top left*: Buster and Rockpile; The Whitman Sisters (*from left*: Alberta, Alice, Mabel, and Essie); The Arntes (Billie and Grace); Ulysses "Slow Kid" Thompson; Henry Jines; Lottie King and Effie Gee; and The Griffin Sisters (Mabel and Emma). Photo credit: Henry T. Sampson, *Blacks in Blackface: A Sourcebook on Early Black Musical Shows*, second edition; Sampson's private collection.

have been to increase profits—it is clear from existing documentation that she was not opposed to the Dixie becoming less and less a moving picture palace and more and more a theater which emphasized vaudeville acts. The first Black vaudeville act at the Dixie may have been The Clarks, a magician duo who in February 1910 performed "feats apparently supernatural."[89] A second act, this time definitely at the Dixie, perfectly exemplifies how vaudeville could serve the Black patron in ways that film, produced and acted by Whites, could not. The husband-and-wife singing and dancing duo known as Bradford and Bradford "opened Monday, March 14 [1910], at the Dixie Theater, Richmond, Virginia, and made a decided hit singing their own songs—'Savannah Jane' [and] 'Take Me Back to Dear Old Georgia Where I'se Born.'" When Perry Bradford sang, "When Jack Johnson Wins the Championship of the World," he "set Richmond wild."[90]

The lyrics to the Jack Johnson song are lost, but singing a song in a Black-patronized, White-owned theater in Richmond about a Black man winning the world heavyweight title against a White fighter was nothing short of daring. Johnson, from Texas, had soundly defeated Canadian Tommy Burns in a December 1908 Australian contest for the title. News about the 1908 fight and its aftermath had been carried worldwide, including in the several White Richmond papers and the Black *Richmond Planet*. As he prepared for future matches to defend his title, Johnson became an ever more admired role model for many Black Americans. Ken Burns, in publicity for his 2021 film about Johnson, "*Unforgivable Blackness*," said this about the Black pugilist: "Johnson in many ways was an embodiment of the African American struggle to be truly free in this country—economically, socially, and politically. He absolutely refused to play by the rules set by the white establishment, or even those of the black community. In that sense, he fought for freedom not just as a black man, but as an individual."[91] Perry Bradford's song, in that it "set Richmond wild" in a Black theater, shows that at least some African Americans in Richmond did, indeed, find a glimmer of promise in the example Johnson set.

Another early performance at the Dixie was announced in an ad published in the *Richmond Planet* on March 28, 1910. Ben Cooper and Lightning Smith, "a high-class minstrel [act], introducing new and original songs, dances, monologues, and jokes, some up to the minute," was coming to the Dixie; the ad noted that the performers would be a team from the Dixie Stock Company.[92] Little information is known about Ben Cooper or Lightning Smith, but what little can be found seems to indicate that Lightning Smith was a Black performer, meaning Ben Cooper would have been also. It would seem logical that they were African Americans; the Dixie by this time seems to have committed to Black vaudeville and was not bringing in White acts. The ad, appearing as it did in the *Richmond Planet*, also is a strong indicator that these performers were African American. There was a well-known, White, Dixie Stock Company out of Biloxi, Mississippi, that was touring the South during the same time frame, but it cannot be evidentially linked to the company mentioned in the ad, and it is just as possible that there was either another Dixie Stock Company altogether that was composed entirely of Blacks or that the Mississippi company had a Black troupe in addition to its White one. Whatever the case, the presence of "minstrels" meant almost by definition an appearance of performers in blackface who would feature comic routines based on stereotypical ideas of African Americans. That the players were performing in blackface, however, is not necessarily an implication that these performers were White. For complex reasons, African Americans sometimes did perform in blackface. It is easy to say, in retrospect more than a century later, that the planned performance of a racially derisive art form at a Black-patronized theater—even potentially by Black actors—seems, at the least, insensitive. But there are complications and contradictions that arise from looking at a late-nineteenth and early-twentieth century phenomenon from the vantage point of the twenty-first century. This was the entertainment that existed within the times, for better or worse.

On the same bill with the Dixie Stock Company, listed secondarily, were two films, *Damon and Pythias* and *The Pythian Parade*. John Mitchell, Jr., publisher of the Richmond *Planet*, was a vocal supporter and leader of the Pythians, at the time an important Black fraternal organization in Richmond which was formed after the controversial 1880 segregation of the national organization into Black and White groups. The *Damon and Pythias* film was probably the same one Thorp had screened at the Dixie for White patrons in August 1908; but because Mitchell promoted the films within the pages of his newspaper, it may have been that the subject of the Pythian parade film was of the regional meeting of the Black Pythians which was held in June 1909 in Richmond.[93]

It is not known how Thorp felt about Perry Bradford's song or the Pythian films, but the presence of this kind of entertainment at the Dixie does seem to provide some evidence of an apparent willingness on her part to deliver a custom experience to the Dixie's African American audience. She may have been playing both sides of the coin: just a week or so before the Pythian films were shown at the Dixie, her Rex theater screened a locally filmed production which brought the White audience "to cheering" when the Stuart, Lee, and Davis Confederate monuments were shown.[94]

The Dixie continued to bring in independent Black vaudeville acts (See Appendix 3). By 1912 it had committed to the theater as a showcase for Black vaudeville to the point that twenty-four-year-old Walter Coulter, who Thorp by this time had brought to Richmond from Norfolk, met with Sherman Dudley of Washington, D.C., to discuss including the Dixie in Dudley's just-formed, and first ever, Black-operated vaudeville circuit. In fact, Dudley secured from Coulter the right to furnish all of the acts for the Dixie. The contract with Coulter, and a couple of others in Virginia (likely Black-owned theaters) that Dudley was able to negotiate, allowed Dudley to significantly expand the opportunities for Black vaudeville on the East Coast.[95] For Thorp and Coulter, it meant the facilitation of bringing in vaudeville acts on a regular basis without the need to handle the myriad details of booking each one separately. Through its contract with the Dudley Circuit, the Dixie was able to bring in two to three and sometimes even four vaudeville acts at a time, ranging from singers and dancers to magicians, comedians, ventriloquists, banjo players, animal acts, contortionists, and much more. Films quickly became secondary to vaudeville acts.[96]

Fig. 25. Advertisement for the pony contest jointly sponsored by the Dixie Theater and *Richmond Planet*. RP, May 16, 1914.

Fig. 26a and b. Editorial drawings by the *Indianapolis Freeman* showing early theaters of the Dudley Circuit including the following: Dudley Theater, Washington, D.C.; Dixie, Richmond; Globe, Norfolk; Dudley, Newport News; West End Theater, Washington, D.C.; and the Circle in Asbury Park, New Jersey. *IF*, Aug. 24 and Dec. 28, 1912, respectively.

The Dixie was a prosperous venture from its earliest (film) days forward, and so to accommodate the increasing number of patrons, by this time all African Americans, Thorp expanded the Dixie to seat many more theatergoers, up to 250 by at least 1913.[97] The timing of the last expansion may have coincided with the temporary closure of the theater following a visit by a city building inspector who found that the floor had reached "a stage of decay which placed it in a most dangerous condition," said disrepair being a testament to the many thousands of footfalls of those who had attended performances there. She had the floor rebuilt by pouring a concrete foundation and providing "substantial" underpinnings. In its report of the floor's deterioration and repair, the *Richmond Virginian* described the Dixie as "the elite theatre of its class," the term "class" being a reference to its all-Black patronage.[98] During the remodel, Thorp would have included more space to accommodate the vaudeville acts Coulter had already been bringing in as well as carved out more room at the side for musicians who would either accompany the acts (or the films) or who might perform as standalone entertainment themselves.

As she had done with the Wonderland back in Ohio, Thorp indulged in at least one promotion to market the Dixie to its (Black) patrons. The "Dunlap Pony, Buggy, and Harness" contest was intended to last four months in 1914 and was sponsored jointly by the *Richmond Planet*.[99] All children eight to sixteen years old were eligible to enter to win a Shetland pony and other grand prize accoutrements, and children would receive "votes" when they or others attended shows at the Dixie or took in newspaper subscriptions for or delivered print-job materials to the *Planet*. The program was frequently hyped in the *Planet* in articles and advertising, but something went wrong. On August 15, one month before the contest was to end, the *Planet* noted that the pony (and presumably the buggy and harness as well) would no longer be available as a prize for the contest. There had been "some misunderstanding with the Dunlap Pony people" on the part of the Dixie Theater management who were the ones offering this prize, the *Planet* reported, carefully noting it had not been the *Planet* that was at fault. Within days, the *Planet* re-invented the contest, throwing out all "votes" which had been cast at the Dixie and offering new prizes for prospective winners that included the choice of a diamond ring, gold watch, or a boy's or girl's bicycle. The termination of the contest was extended to November 1, and then again until December 1. Finally the prize winners were announced in the paper on December 5. Ruby L. Peyton was declared the winner of the top reward with 18,470 votes. There was no word as to which prize she claimed, nor was any information provided regarding how the participants or their parents viewed the moving goalposts for winning the contest.[100] And though the *Planet* went to great pains to blame the Dixie for the pony prize debacle and though the *Planet* seemed righteously upset at the Dixie for its part in the fiasco, there does not seem to have been lingering bad feelings between the paper and the theater management as they continued to cooperate in business deals over the years.

"Dixie"

It's perhaps time to talk about the name of Thorp's theater, the "Dixie," because it is an uncomfortable name, particularly when referencing a theater that served African Americans. In 2020, a "year of racial reckoning," the African American community in Richmond led protests in the city against the many vestigial reminders of the Confederacy that were—and in 2023 some still are—highly visible and sometimes celebrated.[101] The monuments lining the center of Richmond's park-like, centrally located Monument Avenue were a focal point for those protests. The Robert E. Lee monument was painted over with graffiti that called for racial justice and police reform; in its graffitied state, the *New York Times* called it the most influential piece of American protest art since World War II.[102] The African American community in Richmond is central to the national conversation on racial reckoning for many reasons. The city, after all, was the location of one of the most notorious slave markets prior to the Civil War, it became the capital of the Confederacy, and it was centered in a state which excelled, in the worse possible sense, in instituting Jim Crow laws to enforce segregation after the war.

At the time Thorp decided to name her theater "Dixie," she was a recent transplant from Ohio, a state that had supported the Union in the Civil War. As previously noted, her husband had fought with Union forces during the Civil War though he later signed the petition saying he had done so only because he supported the conservation of the Union and that he unequivocally did not fight for civil rights of African Americans. In 1923, Thorp briefly described how she chose the name of "Dixie" for her theater and implied she likely understood the nuances of the word, saying, as mentioned earlier, it was a name that "ought to go well" in Richmond (because she surely would have had no inkling that her theater would become a Black-patronized-only establishment).[103] Today, though some people may argue that the word merely refers to America's South, for many others it romanticizes deep injustices done to African Americans through the institution of slavery. In Richmond during the early twentieth century there was not a lot of debate about the connotations of the word; indeed, a great many White southerners in general were untroubled by its association with the Confederacy's unofficial anthem. Some celebrated the word and the song not only despite their racist undertones but because of them. The *Richmond Times-Dispatch* in February 1908 reported an instance of a juxtaposition of a person seemingly innocent of the song's nuances with people who were not:

> Never, perhaps, before an audience of culture and refinement has the South-land's famous war song, "Dixie," been received with a greater demonstration of enthusiasm than that manifested last night at the Academy when the incomparable [French singer] Madame Calve sang the words that cheered the armies of Lee and Jackson. Not only was there such a handclapping as is seldom heard in the Academy, or any playhouse, but there were cheers, one after another, until Madame Calve almost became disconcerted. As she expressed it afterward behind the scenes, she was for a moment terrified at the enthusiasm which swept over the house. Madame Calve . . . was very much affected by the outburst which greeted her rendition of the battle song of the South.[104]

4

THE COST OF SUCCESS

Theater Proliferation on Broad

In early 1909, Richmond city police complained that the area along Broad Street was so congested with people congregating outside of the theaters to await their turns to go inside that the officer stationed near them had little time to attend to other work.[1] The *Times-Dispatch* reported that overcrowding was a nightly problem: "Crowds assemble early, and to gain admittance at the earliest possible moment, the throngs surge toward the entrance doors until those in the middle can move neither backward nor forward, thus making an accident always imminent." Women had fainted from the press of people, the paper said, "and police officers who went to their rescue had the greatest difficulty in securing for them a breath of air."[2] Merchants in the area also complained about the large numbers of people gathering on the streets.[3] Accounts of disorderly conduct arrests, many if not most of which seemed to target Black Richmonders, filled the papers, and many of these reports told of people being detained specifically at or outside the Dixie.[4] Meanwhile, theater owners may have taken shortcuts with safety issues in order to fill theaters with as many patrons as possible. In the charges, which may have been at least partially racially motivated, the Dixie and the Pekin, the latter also a Black-patronized (but Black-owned) film and vaudeville venue nearby, were specifically singled out in January 1910 for being in "unsafe condition" with exits claimed to be blocked by stages that had been put in without required building inspection permits. Sanitary conditions in both theaters were also reported at the time to be "appalling."[5]

On a Wednesday evening in May 1910, a *Mathews Journal* (White) reporter from Gloucester, Virginia, found himself with some 15,000 other people gathered along Broad in the "balmy and inviting air of an ideal spring night" to catch a show at one of the many theaters. "Every house," he noted, specifying the Dixie as one of them, "has all the business it can handle."[6] A few months before, Jake Wells was already of the mind that the area was saturated with theaters: "I don't see the opening of another house. The vaudeville and moving picture field is taken," he told the *Times-Dispatch* in August. The traditional playhouses were even experiencing decline, he felt: "The patronage neither at the Bijou nor the Academy would justify another house in either class. The Academy was dark last winter more than half the time. . . . When the best performances we can get at the Academy do not crowd the house, I should not say that there is an opening for another first-class theatre."[7]

Amanda, Motion Picture Queen

Thorp had a high profile in Richmond. Her name often appeared in the press, though admittedly not always in ways she would have considered particularly flattering. Still, it had to have been clear to even a casual observer that she was in a very good financial position. In January 1909, Mrs. Sadie L. Skeggs filed suit against Thorp for $10,000—about $325,000 in 2023 spending power—for damages for the alleged alienation of the affections of her husband, John Franklin Skeggs. The scandalous nature of the lawsuit along with the huge sum of money involved ensured local press coverage as well as the affair being passed on to regional media by the wire services. "It does not happen frequently anywhere that one woman is sued by another for such a cause," mused the *Richmond Evening Journal*.[8] The *Baltimore Sun* was one of several newspapers in different states that picked up the story. It noted with some hyperbole that Thorp "owns and conducts a chain of moving picture theaters in Virginia and is said to have amassed a fortune by her operations"—in other words, that she had ample resources to pay such an award. The *Sun* further reported that Sadie had claimed she and her husband had lived happily together until the "motion picture queen" became attached to him and had "thusly sought to win him from her."[9] He was easy prey because of the "pretty Mrs. Thorp," Sadie told the journalist interviewing her, adding that Thorp had been "attracted by the handsome face and manly form of [her] husband."[10] Employing a "Who me?" defense strategy, Thorp claimed that she did not actually own any theaters; she only managed them, and even then merely received a salary (implied to be meager).[11] The lawsuit came to an ignoble conclusion about five months later, when it was dismissed because of the supposed reconciliation of Mr. and Mrs. Skeggs.[12]

Though a bit of a sleazy story, the accounts of the lawsuit are interesting because it is the first known time that Thorp is referenced in print as "the motion picture queen." The catchy moniker subsequently was applied to her in various iterations over the years, particularly after she died, as a shorthand way of describing her power and influence in the motion picture industry—in Richmond specifically, but also in the wider regional arena as she worked and negotiated with representatives of the industry in many cities inside and outside Virginia.[13] Because of her gender, she was a rarity not only in Richmond but also across the country as a whole. When one thumbs through archival issues of national trade magazines of the era, such as *Moving Picture World, Billboard, Motion Picture News*, and others, with only notably uncommon exceptions one sees articles about men written by men, pictures of men in the industry, and advertisements directed at men: the pronouns "he/him/his" are used exclusively. At the time of the lawsuit, Thorp had been in Richmond just over a year but had already earned a reputation for being a leader in the field (which at this point, much to her chagrin, ironically worked against her).

Mrs. Skegg's lawsuit is also noteworthy because it shows Thorp's willingness to bend the truth when it benefitted her. Even before her arrival in Richmond, she had been maintaining the fiction that she was a widow, a scenario which, among other things, probably facilitated her ability to do business as a woman. But bending the truth as a movie impresario was not restricted to Thorp; nearly all of those involved in the early motion picture business in Richmond were occasionally less than honest in their descriptions over the years as to their part in the history of its early beginnings.

Waldo, in Trouble Again

Waldo, since he and Amanda had left Newark in 1907, and through 1911, had pretty much stayed out of trouble, or at least he'd managed pretty much to stay out of the newspaper. He'd once been charged with and fined $20 for being disorderly in Richmond in 1909 after assaulting Lillian Barnett on Mayo Street, Richmond's sex-worker area.[14] A dust-up was reported in September 1910 when, during a city inspection at the Rex, Waldo got upset at the electrical inspector who criticized Waldo for improper film storage and for allowing smoking in the projection room: Waldo called the inspector a liar and then punched him. The chief of police was also present and so Waldo was immediately arrested; no information could be found about the legal outcome of the skirmish.

Not long after that, however, in April 1911, he managed to get into a sensational mess which for him was déjà vu, all over again. Details were covered in the *Baltimore Sun*, the *Washington Herald*, the *Washington Times*, the *Washington Post*, and the *Free Lance* of Fredericksburg, Virginia, but notably less so in the Richmond papers. Waldo had tried, once again, to elope with a young woman who may have been underage. With differing but damning information, the newspapers reported:

> Julia (also reported as Julie and as Susie) A. Blankenship (also reported as Blackenship) of Richmond, 15 (also reported as 16 and also reported as 18) and Waldo F. Thorp (also reported as Thorpe and Tharp), 28, twice divorced, and proprietor of a moving picture show in Richmond (all the newspapers agreed on his age, marital status, and occupation though he technically wasn't "proprietor") were foiled in their attempt to be married at the home of a Washington, D.C., pastor where they had gone to get the deed done. They had taken a train from Richmond to Washington but had missed the train they had intended to take, apparently giving the girl's mother, who had somehow learned of the plot, time to raise an alarm. The girl's parents objected to the marriage due to her age (objections were also variously reported as having been due to his age, as well as because she was a Catholic while Waldo was a Protestant). After literally being stopped at the altar from getting married, the girl was "arrested" and held in Washington until her parents arrived to take her back home, at which point Mrs. Blankenship fainted. After the marriage was thwarted, Waldo was said to have ridden around Washington in a taxi (though one of the reports claimed that he also had been arrested), apparently deciding at some point to return to Richmond the same day—though it is hoped not on the same train—as Julia/Julie/Susie and her parents. The *Washington Post* had apparently originated the reporting of the scandal; local Richmond papers may have been reluctant to cover it with pressure from the young woman's parents, although the *Richmond Virginian* did report some details, quoting the *Washington Post*.[15]

Just three months later, a sensational scandal hit Richmond that dwarfed any that either Waldo or Amanda ever had been in. On July 18, 1911, Henry Clay Beattie, Jr., described in the press as a spoiled South Richmond playboy from a very prominent family, murdered his much younger wife by shooting her in the head. The murder, subsequent arrests, and court cases were highly publicized, and the story was carried on front pages of hundreds of newspapers across the country. The media demand for wire services was so great that, during the trial, the Western Union Telegraph Company took over an entire store building adjacent to the Chesterfield County courthouse square for its operators.[16] In November, in Newark, Ohio, an enterprising reporter for the local paper learned that Waldo happened to be back in town and interviewed him for a local angle on the story which had just culminated in Beattie being electrocuted in Richmond for the crime. It is easy to imagine Waldo blowing smoke, both literally from his Richmond cigarettes and figuratively, as the two men talked in the hotel once owned by his mother Amanda and as the reporter probed for any juicy details that could liven up the *Advocate's* coverage. Waldo claimed to have known the slightly younger Beattie, though not intimately acquainted with him.[17]

Waldo also told the reporter that Amanda was at that moment in Chicago Junction, Ohio, a place nothing much more than a road-crossing about thirty miles north of Bucyrus, where she was visiting with the family of friends they had known previously in Newark. He said they had come back to Ohio to explore possibilities of opening a theater there "if an opening presented itself." There may have been some grain of truth to Waldo's comment, because the *Evening Herald* of Norwalk, Ohio, noted that Amanda had been involved in a real-estate purchase in Chicago Junction, today known as Willard, involving a paid price of $2,200 (about $69,000 in 2023) to Eva Windisch.[18] Although what the purpose or what became of the purchase is unknown, it is very unlikely that Thorp would have considered putting in a theater in that very remote location.

While Amanda had been in Chicago Junction, Waldo himself had just been in Columbus visiting his father in a "joyful reunion" since they had not seen each other for five years.[19]

Running the Rex

Theater owners faced growing public scrutiny from church ministers, legislators, and others who expressed concern about purported moral hazards posed by watching moving pictures.[20] It almost seemed as if Thorp was pressing the issue when, at the Rex in August 1910, she scheduled *Uncle Tom's Cabin*, a film that had just been banned in Atlanta. The 1852 publication of the book of the same name by Harriet Beecher Stowe is often considered to be among the successive events which led to the Civil War, though Stowe's abolitionist account of the fictional Uncle Tom ironically perpetuates a number of stereotypes about African Americans. Some patrons who had seen the movie at the Rex—remember, these are White Richmonders—complained about the film, which the *Times-Dispatch* described breathlessly in racist tropes and Lost Cause language as "true to the book," a bad thing because the book had "painted such a dark and untruthful picture" of slavery: "For two hours yesterday afternoon, those harrowing

Fig. 27. Men, at least some of whom are probably Thorp's employees, lined up in front of her Rex Theater. The year 1908 is noted in the 1926 *Times-Dispatch* photo caption and it is probably accurate. If so, the photo could be of the grand opening, and some of the men, perhaps those in uniforms, could be members of the Hart Brothers Orchestra, her friends that she brought to Richmond from Bucyrus to provide special music for the occasion. *RTD*, Jan. 10, 1926.

but unreal scenes were depicted [at the Rex] from that ancient bit of fiction written by Mrs. Harriet Beecher Stowe more than 50 years ago. Uncle Tom was there, and Simon Legree, with his big bloodhound and his blacksnake whip, as he clapped irons on Uncle Tom's wrists and gave him a love tap with the butt of the whip. . . . Uncle Tom died in his cabin on a pitchfork full of hay, an instant after Simon Legree had struck him on the neck with that ever-present blacksnake whip." Responding to complaints, Richmond Mayor David Richardson visited the theater, watched the film, and suggested it would be "a good idea" to stop showing it, "which was done."[21] Since the Rex changed films every two or three days anyway, withdrawing film by that time would have had little impact.

As has already been seen, Thorp was not known, particularly, to steer away from controversy if there were profits to be made. In another example, though the Rex most often functioned as a nickel-a-throw movie theater, she would also occasionally rent it out to host a speaker, at least one of whom was well-known for his tendentious remarks. John Armstrong Chaloner, an infamous New York socialite who had settled near Charlottesville in Virginia's Albemarle County, visited the Dixie fairly often to deliver his peculiar lectures. Perhaps best known for his catchphrase, "Who's looney now?", his talks at the Rex were covered at length by the local press which noted, among other things, his tendency to wander from the scheduled topic.[22]

On March 18, 1911, the Rex caught fire. Although according to the *Times-Dispatch*, it had been "ablaze," Thorp minimized the scare: it had been "small," had been confined to the projection room, and the wide aisles and many exits of the Rex had afforded "ample time and space" for patrons to leave "before they were really even aware that there was a fire in the building."[23] A few days after that, the city building inspector ordered the theater closed until "certain unauthorized wood partitions," alleged to have been built without a permit under the main auditorium and front doors and being used to store "large numbers of reels" of film, were removed. There was, again, a difference in opinion: Thorp claimed that no films had been stored in the makeshift room except for the ones that were in daily use and even those, she said, were kept in an approved metal box. The partitioned area was, she said, simply a men's dressing room and an area for storage of tickets and printed matter. But, no matter, she added, the theater was undergoing extensive alterations because of the fire in the projection room and when reopened would be as "nearly fireproof as possible."[24] The theater did resume operations about a week later "notwithstanding the alarming and fictitious reports concerning guncotton, nitroglycerine, and other explosives being stored in the building all of which were utterly absurd and without the least foundation in fact," reported the *Times-Dispatch*, innocently not finding any irony in publicizing the non-facts. Rex fans weren't worried, however; the paper noted the theater was fully packed for reopening performances during the entire afternoon and night.[25]

Thorp had another run-in with authorities a couple of months later at the theater. The incident involved an acrimonious conversation with a police officer about the Rex's cellar which was, he alleged, in disrepair. Though the press reported slightly different versions of what was told in court regarding what occurred, the gist seems to have been that Thorp told the policeman at some point in the dispute, "You are no gentleman," and in so doing was charged with having impugned his character. Thorp might have been saved from trouble, the officer testified, had she simply apologized to him as he had requested. She told the court that in response to the request for apology, she had told the officer, "if anyone apologized it would be [you]." She told the judge, "He shook his mace in my face and said, 'I wish you were a man.' To that I replied that as he had talked to me like a man, he might as well treat me as one.'" "Policemen must be protected from abuse," Judge Crutchfield concluded, and fined Thorp $5 (about $150 in 2023).[26]

Signs of Personal and Professional Success

Except for the occasion of the Skeggs lawsuit, when Thorp presented herself as practically broke, all accounts are that she was doing extremely well for herself financially. In early 1913, the *Richmond Virginian* reported that she had bought for herself a snazzy electric brougham-style vehicle. "Finished in dark blue with blue leather trimmings" at a time when most vehicles were black, it was "one of the smartest cars of its kind in Richmond."[27] Broughams like this were marketed especially to women because they were said to be easy to drive. Henry Ford's wife Clara had a 1914 Detroit (of course) version and liked it because it started instantly without hand-cranking and the transmission was not difficult to shift.[28] Thorp's brougham, sold to her by a Richmond dealership which had Rauch and Lang vehicles in its inventory, may possibly have been manufactured in Cleveland, Ohio, one of her old haunts.

Thorp was also at the top of her game professionally, and to her credit, she did not let her gender isolate her. She attended the first organizational

Fig. 28. A Rauch and Lang electric brougham vehicle which would have been similar to Thorp's car. *Brooklyn Daily Eagle*, Jan. 12, 1913.

Fig. 29. Thorp, seated far left, at the 1913 Virginia Motion Picture Exhibitors' League meeting. *MPW*, Jul. 12, 1913.

meeting of the Virginia branch of the Motion Picture Exhibitors' League of America held at Richmond's swanky Jefferson Hotel in 1913. Most assuredly the only woman there in a professional capacity, it is easy to imagine that she drove herself to the meeting at the Jefferson in her new blue car. At the meeting, she received a nod from her peers to represent them as a delegate to the Exhibitors' League national convention to be held later that year in New York.[29] In a rare photograph (counting this one, only two photographs of Thorp are known to exist, both published in periodicals and thus poor reproductions), Thorp sits as the lone woman among the eighteen men who were officers or members of the League, several of them fellow theater owners from Richmond.[30] She sits at one end of the front row, leaning not in but rather somewhat away from the others; her left hand is on her hip, the other in her lap. She wears typical early-1900 women's business attire: the skirt of her light-colored dress reaches the floor, the blouse has contrasting dark epaulets at the shoulder, and her dark, oversized, shawl collar stands in for the ties that her male colleagues are wearing with their suits. She wears a dark hat which appears to have a dark feathery plume protruding out over the front, a trendy choice for a woman in a group of men who mostly wear their own nod to fashionable headwear: straw boaters. As most of her male colleagues do, she looks directly at the camera, her expression enigmatically perfunctory. She is there for a picture, her purpose neither to stand out nor to blend in.

Other than Thorp and the very few, if any, others of her gender who were at her level in business of exhibiting movies at the time, the place for women in the nascent industry was not as owners, managers, or projection-ists, but rather in jobs that were unlikely to provide upward professional advancement, much less increase wealth. Thorp herself had advertised once for a "girl" to work her ticket booth in Bucyrus[31] and likely continued to see women employees through the same sort of business lens that male exhibitors would have: as unskilled, temporary workers. Her views on (other) women as leaders in the theater industry are unknown—certainly she did not mentor any women to do what she did. But, as is seen from the advertisements in Bucyrus she specifically directed at women, she did see them as patrons, realizing that targeting them successfully would essentially double her potential customer base and possibly more, since they hopefully would also bring their children. Thorp's gender most definitely set her apart as a theater operator and may have made her seem an easy mark for the husband-stealing lawsuit of Mrs. Skeggs. The fact that she didn't appear to have been targeted more often is noteworthy; the conclusion that could be drawn is that she inherently was either very strong or very wily, or both—and people pretty much knew it.

Other Theaters

It is difficult to know for certain how many theaters Thorp herself owned, when she opened them, where they were located, or when she sold or closed them (Appendix 4—Known Theaters of Amanda Thorp). The documented record is incomplete, and circular reporting has resulted in many errors be-ing repeated over the years in publications and on the internet where she is mentioned. But it is clear that as much as she can be considered an exhibitor, she was also an adept deal maker: she would sell a theater to others, make a profit, and then invest in the development of other theaters which were bigger and better and would bring in more cash.

Some writers give Thorp credit for opening the theater in Richmond called the "Theato" at some point after opening the Dixie and before opening the Rex.[32] The confusion probably arises from a contemporaneous misprint or two in the *Richmond Times-Dispatch* which called the Dixie Theater the "Dixie Theato,"[33] but she never appears to have been associated with a Richmond Theato theater. There was a Theato at 500 East Broad in the news on July 11, 1907, when a patron was charged with being disorderly after threatening to hit the proprietor, L. E. Lucas (not Thorp), with a brick; as a side mention, at some point in the fracas, Lucas hit the patron in the head with a chair.[34] On February 26, 1908, that same Theato was in the news because it had just gone into receivership[35] and then again on September 26 because the city had declared the building to be in a dangerous condition; the building owners listed then were John and Emannual (*sic*) Robinson.[36] The Richmond City Directory for 1911 shows the Theato at 500 East Broad as owned and operated by D. L. Toney,[37] a middling figure in Richmond's movie theater history. There was a Black-patronized storefront movie house, the Empire Theato, in existence in September 1907, but names of people associated with it were never that of Thorp.[38]

Some references claim she also had a theater in Charlottesville. The first known instance of the possible existence of a theater of hers there was a report during the Skeggs lawsuit, appearing in the *Baltimore Sun* newspaper.[39] The claim was repeated without attribution in retrospectives published after Thorp died, but no information can be found to confirm it; in fact, an investigation into theaters of the era in Charlottesville reveals no connections to Thorp.

Her friend Earl Hart was quoted once as saying that after leaving Bucyrus, Thorp "migrated to Cleveland where she opened the first picture houses in that city"—the word Cleveland clearly being a discombobulated misprint for Richmond.[40] The incorrect information that she had theaters in Cleveland was repeated in later accounts of Thorp's impact in the motion picture theater industry.

In 1909, Thorp did lease the Cockade Theater in Petersburg, Virginia, with the intention of showing films there, but how long she kept it is unknown.[41] It may well have been only a storefront house of the common sort with kitchen chairs, and it may have been from there that Walter Coulter was coming when he was stopped for speeding on the Petersburg Turnpike in June 1911.[42]

5

BLACK VAUDEVILLE AT THE HIPPODROME

Richmond's Hippodrome

Once the popular Dudley Circuit vaudeville acts started playing at the up-graded and expanded Dixie, it didn't take Thorp long to realize she could make more profit with an even larger theater devoted to Black vaudeville. By 1913, she embarked on her riskiest endeavor yet, but the September 1, 1912, *Richmond Times-Dispatch* only gave a curiously mysterious hint about what it was in a published drawing of the theater that carried this minimal caption with no accompanying story: "Hippodrome Theatre, North Second Street, being erected solely for colored people."[1] The *Richmond Virginian* filled in some of the blanks a couple of weeks later when it published the same drawing, noting the theater would be the sixth in "Mrs. Thorp's chain," but erroneously said the theater would be located on Brook Road.[2] The newspaper back in Bucyrus in January 1913 provided still more details: In Richmond, Thorp had purchased a $9,000 building site and would be building a $40,000-$50,000 moving picture house.[3] A 2013 comment on a website available in 2022 claims that a Richmond building permit names the architect for the project as Charles H. Fisher of Fisher and Rabenstein.[4] Few details are known about the Richmond architect or firm.

The news of Thorp's plans apparently prompted the *Virginian* to publish a short feature about her on the same day it published the Hippodrome drawing. The article in "Progress," the paper's business section, was head-lined, "Woman's Success an Object Lesson":

> There are many women in Richmond actively engaged in business but none have attained greater success than Mrs. A. E. Thorp who has devoted her time and talents to the theatrical field. In fact, Mrs. Thorp's advent into the commercial world here and her subsequent success in her chosen field of

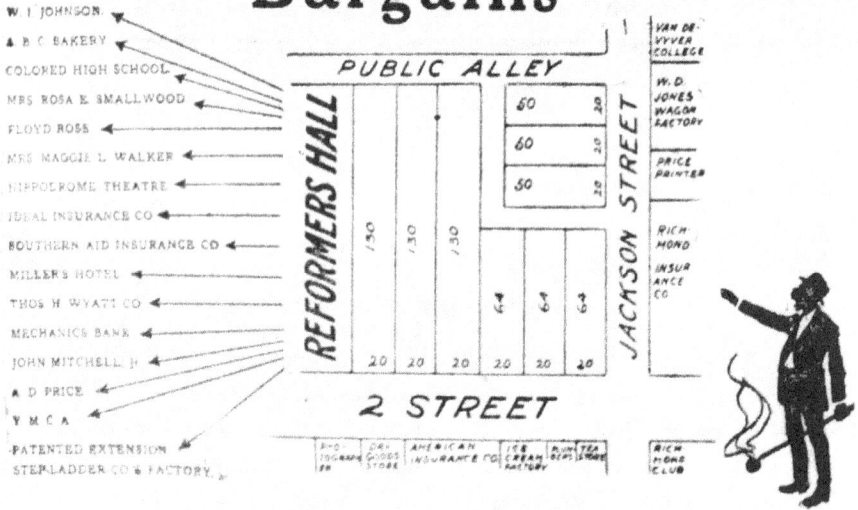

Fig. 30. Detail from a 1913 *Richmond Times-Dispatch* full-page ad which contained a map of Jackson Ward businesses including Thorp's Hippodrome which had opened only six months before. The ad touts real estate in the area to potential investors—the White readers of the newspaper—and shows the rich variety of business already there. In addition to the businesses shown on the map, the caption notes that nearby there were also three dry goods stores and "among many other enterprises, four house furnishings stores." *RTD*, Aug. 17, 1913.

endeavor reads like [a] romance. . . . It only goes to show what opportunities there are in Richmond for anyone, man or woman, with the proper energy, nerve, and perseverance, backed by a little capital. Mrs. Thorp has just and appropriately been crowned the "Theatrical Queen of the South," and her host of friends in this and other cities wish her all the success that her energy, courage, and perseverance deserves. If nothing else, it is at least an object lesson of what the fair and gentle sex can do in a field entered for the first time by a woman.

She is the owner of a chain of five picture shows and vaudeville theaters. Her circuit at one time included ten different theaters but was so exacting upon her she was forced to relinquish five and is now devoting her time to the five others. Among these is the Rex ... and the Dixie.... The [Hippodrome] building will cost at least $20,000, which together with the $8,000 cost of the lot and the equipment of the new theatre, will represent an investment of over $30,000.⁵

It is noted that the cost of the Hippodrome differs in the Ohio and Richmond newspapers, but the bottom line is that it was a significant investment. The *Virginian* reporter had other details in his article that were likely incorrect. For example, three of the five theaters claimed to have been in Thorp's portfolio at the time of the article were not mentioned; the reporter listed only the Rex and Dixie. The number could have also included the Airdome and perhaps the Cockade in Petersburg, but that leaves one still unaccounted for. The reference to ten theaters on her circuit implies concurrent ownership, but it instead may have been a reference to how many she had owned during the course of her career overall, and at that point in time, ten seems like a reasonable number.

It should also be noted that the *Virginian* reporter, when considering who had prospered as a woman working in Richmond at the time, had overlooked the existence of Maggie L. Walker, a Black woman in Richmond who was very successful in business as well as in her humanitarian work.⁶

Fig. 31. Hippodrome Theater grand opening advertisement. *Richmond Planet*, Jun. 27, 1914.

"Hippodrome" was a cheeky name, copied from the famed theaters of New York and London which would be well known among well-heeled White Richmonders. Perhaps applied, as it was in Richmond, to a Blacks-only patronized theater makes up a bit for naming the previous theater "Dixie." The *Virginian* described the building plans for the Hippodrome: "The style of this attractive theater will be Roman-Grecian in architecture with decided classical cutlines embellished with Corinthian columns, ornamental grille work, etc. [The theater], together with the two attractive plate glass-front stores on each side, will about cover the 50-foot lot. It will have a seating capacity of at least 900. . . . The situation of the building is most desirable, being [at] the center of the business negro enterprises in the city such as Miller's Hotel, Mechanics Savings Bank, Reformers Hall, and the YMCA."[7]

The Hippodrome, built specifically for the entertainment of the Black patron, was a unique, first-of-its-kind venue in Richmond. Theaters in the city up to this time for the Black patron, even the Dixie, had been buildings re-purposed for entertainment, not designed exclusively for it.

The building itself was meant to be "refined," and the entertainment would be too. The *Virginian* reporter explained, using racist tropes and prejudices of the day: "Nothing but standard high class road shows of the very best class of negro artists will appear at this theater, it being the intention of the proprietress to considerably elevate the tone of the exhibition usually patronized by the race."[8] The description of the stated aim of the theater references a supposed innate difference in "class" of African Americans, a notion commonly held in the early twentieth century. Calling the idea an "image of a bifurcated Black community," Gregory Waller speaks of it in his 1992 *Cinema Journal* article "Another Audience: Black Moviegoing, 1907–1916,"[9] but many other social scientists have acknowledged its existence as well. As it was used at the time in the *Virginian*, the idea was to legitimize the Hippodrome's existence: since the theater would be serving an "upper class" of African Americans, concerns of the average White newspaper reader would be allayed that the theater would somehow encourage a scourge of "lower class" Black delinquency. The *Virginian* writer went on to note that Thorp did not plan to abandon the Dixie, but rather would enlarge and improve it, but with "the idea of the [Hippodrome] being to take care of the high class and expensive road shows which could not be accommodated in houses of less size."[10] The irony, of course, is that the Dixie is implied to be a "lower class" theater.

Once built, the theater seemed to have met expectations. The *Richmond Planet* oozed in May 1913: "The Hippodrome, near the corner of Second

Fig. 32. Drawing of the Hippodrome Theater. *RTD*, Sep. 1, 1912.

and Leigh streets is a place of beauty. The magnificent building fitted up for the colored people is one of the most palatial ever erected in this city. The electric sign on the front is a marvel, [with its] flood of light illuminating the neighborhood and telling the whereabouts of this modern playhouse as far as the eye can reach. The program each night with its many variations is on modern lines and will continue to induce patronage."[11]

Thorp's conscious decision, as a White woman, to expand business into Black Richmond is all the more remarkable because Richmond's White businessmen were instead expanding their ventures into higher-priced, White areas of the city.[12] Even so, the problematic fact of White ownership of theaters in the Black diaspora, even by a woman, is complicated. Unquestionably, Black leaders in the business, Sherman Dudley included, would have agreed that if there were going to be segregated theaters, then Black owners would be the preferred case. Still, as Dudley himself noted in July 1915, the reality was that there were White owners of Black theaters and that while on its face that might be undesirable, the end result still meant support for Black-centric entertainment. Dudley specifically mentioned the

PAMPLIN

MISS LULA
TOO SWEET,
CROWN

DEMON OF THE TROPICS

Fig. 33a–f. African American vaudevillians who performed at Thorp's Hippodrome Theater. *Clockwise from top left*: John Cooper with ventriloquist dummy; Muriel Ringgold and unidentified performer; Lula/Lulu and John Willie Too Sweet; Tim Moore; Alberta Whitman; and John Pamplin. All photos from Sampson, *Blacks in Blackface* except for Tim Moore, from Billy Rose Theatre Collection, Digital Gallery, New York Public Library, NYC, www.nypl.org; and John Cooper, from www.blackpast.org.

Hippodrome, saying: "White capital may be largely enlisted in making these [Black vaudeville] ventures a 'go,' but as the ultimate result is the widening of the field for the Negro performer, . . . they may be counted as assets for the race. There is logically no color-line in the work of entertaining the public, and White and Black managers and artists must labor, hand in hand, to raise the plane of popular amusements and divide the profits that accrue therefrom." He continued, "We are embarrassed by the [large] number of [Black] performers and the scarcity of [Black] houses which, on the one hand, means long jumps and much idle time for everybody. . . . [In addition,] inadequate houses restrict the activities of novelty performers and prevent the satisfactory placing of road shows in but a few of the good cities. This deters the development of the novelty act requiring a large and high stage and discourages the formation of road companies carrying 20 to 40 people."[13] In addition to providing a cost versus benefit analysis of White ownership of Black-patronized theaters, Dudley had *de facto* explained Thorp's motives for opening the Hippodrome, located only a few blocks from the Dixie: to bring in bigger acts and in so doing, bring in more money.

The Hippodrome was Thorp's largest theater to date: with a seating capacity of 700 when it was completed, it could accommodate four times more patrons than that of the Dixie and double that of her Whites-only Rex. The 1915 Richmond City Directory listed the Hippodrome as a vaudeville and moving picture house with continuous performances from 7:30 to 11 pm.[14] The price for regular shows at the Hippodrome (vaudeville with films or vice versa) was generally kept at five cents, but special events could be more costly with tiered pricing. On May 5, 1913, the program for a group billed as the Society Minstrels cost patrons twenty-five, fifty, or seventy-five cents with box seats going for $1. On March 28, 1914, evening performances for a bill of well-known early Black vaudeville stars were advertised as having ten and twenty cents admission; only two showings a night were offered, indicating they were longer programs. In March 1915, "a week of movies" was advertised with matinee costs for children at five cents and adults at ten cents; nighttime shows were ten cents for general admission or fifteen cents for reserved seats.[15]

Walter Coulter was put in charge of managing both the Hippodrome and the Dixie, and he continued to utilize Dudley Circuit vaudeville performers at both theaters. The first known show at the Hippodrome featured The Griffin Sisters, a very well-known duo who sang and performed comedy, and who had appeared the year before at the Dixie. (See Appendix 5 for a list of Black vaudeville and other offerings at the Hippodrome.) They apparently performed at the Hippodrome for a six-week gig, from early March to mid-April 1913. In August 1913, the Hippodrome reserved Richmond's

Fig. 34. Special reservations were made
available to White people when the Frogs came
to segregated Richmond. *RTD*, Aug. 12, 1913.

City
Auditorium

Thursday Evening, August 14,

Under Hippodrome Theatre
Management,

The FROGS, Inc,

OFFER

BERT WILLIAMS,

Permission Klaw & Erlanger,

AND

50 Musical Comedy, Vaude- **50**
ville, Minstrel Stars

Never Again a Night Like This.

Price: 25c, 50c, 75c, $1.00, $1.50.

Special Reservations for White
People.

City Auditorium, a venue with a seating capacity of 3,000, and sponsored the Harlem-based variety show "The Frogs, Inc." Richmond was one of only four cities outside of New York that hosted this program: it had been showing annually in Harlem for the past seven years or so and was one of the biggest yearly social events there, drawing huge crowds.[16] Prices for The Frogs show in Richmond ran from twenty-five cents to $1.50. In a reversal of traditional segregation norms, there were "special reservations" available for White people.[17]

Sherman Dudley himself, returning to his vaudeville roots, performed at the Hippodrome in December 1913 and then again in August 1915.[18] Another show, advertising in the *Times-Dispatch* that it would have "a section of the theater set aside for White people," was a wrestling match to be staged at the Hippodrome on November 6, 1914. It featured Akri Sikaso, the "Liberian cyclone," and Billy Brandon of Norfolk.[19] Thorp and Coulter occasionally also brought stock companies to the theater which would stay for longer engagements, continuously presenting different entertainments.[20]

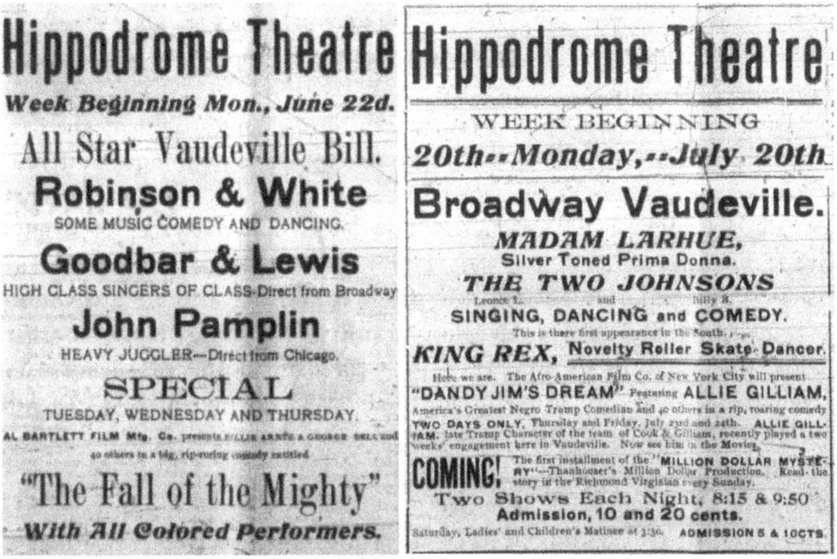

Fig. 35a and b. Two ads in the *Planet* advertising rare all-African American films as well as Black vaudeville acts. *RP*, Jun. 20 and Jul. 18, 1914, respectively.

They also allowed the Hippodrome to be used for Black community meetings, though likely for a fee. The *Times-Dispatch* reported in June 1914 that the Black Pythians of Virginia would hold one of their statewide meeting sessions at the Hippodrome, and the *Richmond Planet* reported on an anti-segregation meeting held there in March 1915.[21] And in one last, if odd, detail about running the administrative side of the Hippodrome, the July 1914 *Motion Picture News* noted Thorp had bought a drumona, a purchase so unusual that the magazine added a parenthetical expression to explain that it was a "(musical instrument)."[22]

Though Black vaudeville acts were the mainstay at the Hippodrome, films were shown in good number, the vast majority being White-produced reels with White actors. But occasionally under Thorp's ownership, rare all-Black production films were screened. In June 1914, *The Fall of the Mighty*, a "big rip-roaring comedy" produced by Al Bartlett Film Manufacturing Company, was shown, featuring Billie Arnte, George Bell, and forty more African American performers.[23] Just over a month later, the Hippodrome showed *Dandy Jim's Dream*, produced by the Afro-American Film Company of New York. It featured Annie Gilliam, "America's greatest negro tramp comedian," and, again, forty other Black performers.[24] Arnte, of the *Fall of the Mighty,* had appeared live at the Dixie in late 1912, and Gilliam of *Dandy Jim's Dream* may be the same Gilliam who appeared live at Thorp's Hippodrome in late 1913.

Despite Thorp's efforts in 1910 to show *Uncle Tom's Cabin* at the Rex when she had been threatened with closure for showing a much watered-down version of the story, she showed a later version of the film in September 1914 at the Hippodrome. Advertised in the *Richmond Planet* as being a five-reel version of "America's most famous play," the film was described as using "real negroes, real actors, real scenes from real life as it really was in the antebellum days."[25] This almost certainly was the version released earlier in 1914 which featured Sam Lewis, the same African American actor who originated the role of Uncle Tom for the New York stage in 1879. Despite the many societal and cultural issues of the film and the book it was based on, all-told, the screening of this film at the Hippodrome could be considered very much a progressive move at the time. Once again, however, it is not likely that Thorp's motives were altruistic but rather she very probably had her eye on the theater's receipts.

Williams, the Funny Man

When Black vaudevillians performed at a White-owned versus a Black-owned venue even in the Dudley Circuit, they probably understood there were certain measures of care involved. This was perhaps evidenced in at least one 1914 incident at the Hippodrome when Walter Coulter fined a Black performer "for telling a funny story in the dressing room."[26] The fact that it was reported in the *Indianapolis Freeman,* which at the time extensively covered Black entertainment news across the country, indicates the episode was troublesome, and its publication perhaps was intended to serve as a heads-up warning to those who would be playing there later.

The anecdote about Coulter assessing a fine against one of the performers is one of few known direct accounts about the experience of Black vaudevillian performers at the Thorp theaters. Another, this time without negative connotations, was hinted at in September 1912, when the Indianapolis *Freeman* published a small ad placed by a Mrs. Rosa E. McKenzie of New York thanking Coulter, then at the Dixie, for helping her (unnamed) husband during his illness and subsequent death in Richmond. There is no McKenzie known to have played at the Dixie, but since the ad appeared in the *Freeman* entertainment section, her husband would have been associated with Black vaudeville there in some capacity, perhaps as an accompanying musician

Fig. 36. Bert Williams, funny man. Photo, n.d., Harvard Theatre Collection, Harvard University, Cambridge, Massachusetts.

who may not have been included on the bills.[27] Another *Freeman* anecdote related that Coulter had sponsored a special program at the Hippodrome in December 1914 as a benefit for Henry F. Watterson, a well-known local Black pianist who had been seriously ill for about four weeks. A musical theater number was performed at the benefit by some fifteen or so Black participants, including male and female actors and singers and a three-piece orchestra composed of a pianist, traps player, and violinist. The matinee door receipts of $40.05 were turned over to Coulter to pay Watterson's expenses which were otherwise undescribed.[28]

Outside of the theaters, Black vaudeville performers in Richmond would have been subject to police and judicial harassment as they would have been in any American city, especially in the South. In one such incident in Richmond, a performer with The Frogs was arrested when the show had returned for at least the second time in November 1915: Bert Williams, a very well-known comedian to both Blacks and Whites, and later credited as being the first Black man to have the leading role in a (White) American film, got choked up while laughing with other performers after the show and spit on a sidewalk. He was arrested by a passing "ubiquitous" police officer. The conversation in court with (White) Judge Crutchfield the next morning went like this, according to the Indianapolis *Freeman*:

> Judge: What is your name?
>
> Williams: Williams, your honor.
>
> Judge: Williams! Williams! Williams William, or William what?
>
> Williams: Bert Williams, your honor.
>
> Judge: Umph! Humph! and where are you from, Bert Williams?
>
> Williams: My theatrical business makes it imperative that I reside in New York, your honor.
>
> Judge: Oh, yes! You're Williams, the funny man! Are you funny?
>
> Williams: Some people think so, your honor, and I have heard of people who think otherwise.
>
> Judge: Umph! Humph! Well, Williams, did you think it funny to come all the way from New York to spit on our clean sidewalks?
>
> Williams: Your honor, the spitting was purely accidental. I had just finished the night show and was on my way home—
>
> Judge: And thought you would give a little matinee by spitting on our sidewalks. Well, Bert Williams, that little performance will cost you $5.
>
> Williams: All right, your honor (fishing in vest pockets), I happen to have that little amount in my vest pocket.
>
> Judge: All right, Bert Williams. Fish in your pants pockets and see if you can find 10 days.

The paper noted that the sentencing of confinement was the result of the judge evidently not being impressed with Williams' "droll talk," although it is noted that the judge demonstrated he was not above some of his own. It took considerable "wire pulling" (likely by Walter Coulter) to lift the jail sentence.[29]

Onward

Perhaps being theater-rich and cash-poor, at about the same time Thorp started construction of the Hippodrome, a classified ad appeared in the *Richmond Times-Dispatch*: "For Sale. Richmond, Va.: oldest and best located colored vaudeville and picture theatre in the city: now running and making money: manager wishes to retire. Address or call on W. J. Coulter, Hippodrome Theatre, City."[30] The unnamed theater was the Dixie.

As is often the case with press items having to do directly or indirectly with Thorp, there is a lot to parse from what amounts to only a little information. Probably more than anything, the ad likely reflected her desire to leave the Dixie behind and move on, not necessarily to actually retire. The description in the ad of the Dixie as a vaudeville and picture theater deserves attention in that it shows that the Dixie was no longer merely a nickelodeon which sometimes also offered vaudeville acts, but rather that the two types of entertainment were at least equally important at the Dixie, or perhaps even that vaudeville had grown to be the more important one. Finally, the

Fig. 37. Detail from earliest known photograph of 18 West Broad, Richmond, taken in the early 1920s. The ghost sign "Dixie" is barely visible on the front façade. The rounded arch in front may have been part of the original Dixie nickelodeon. From "Broad Street Old and Historic District," September 1986, Historic Richmond Foundation, VCU Libraries, Digital Collections.

instruction for interested buyers to contact Coulter at the Hippodrome gives an indication of his rising level of responsibility in Thorp's organization.

Thorp sold the Dixie to Charles Somma, a twenty-five-year-old White Richmonder, who by February 13, 1915, was advertising as proprietor of the Dixie in the *Indianapolis Freeman*, looking for "good (vaudeville) acts."[31] The sale of the Dixie to Somma was the initiation of a relationship among Thorp, Coulter, and Somma which would significantly impact the experience of moviegoing in Richmond for decades.

6

LIFE HAPPENS

Waldo, Again in Trouble

In the initial report of Waldo's most scandalous and violent escapade yet, the lengthy, multi-level headline on the front page of the August 22, 1915, issue of the *Richmond Times-Dispatch* read, "Pulled Girl out of Bed for Morning Auto Ride; Police Arrest Waldo F. Thorp on Four Warrants Arising from Escapade; Ran Car into a Tree; Charged with Being Drunk, Recklessly Driving Car, Threatening to Kill Miss D. C. Baker and Abusing and Beating Miss L. C. Walker." With the headline pretty much summarizing what had happened, the story itself, running the entire length of one column from top to bottom, simply provided additional details. Amanda tried to afford cover for Waldo, telling the press that he was "doped up" (she probably meant drunk) and was not responsible. She said that "Miss Baker" (Faun) was a friend of the family from Cleveland, "an exceedingly nice girl," who had stayed with the Thorps for a while before moving in with her roommate Miss Walker. Amanda said Faun desired as little publicity as possible, which is no doubt what both Amanda and Waldo wanted as well, especially because the actual relationship between Waldo and Faun Baker was more complicated than they probably wanted anyone else to know. An article which appeared a few years later in the *Buffalo* Courier shed some additional light on the identity of Miss Baker: she was the estranged wife—she was alleged to have abandoned her husband and young son in 1910—of Waldo's first ex-wife's (the former Della Baker) brother.[1]

Justice was quick in the Richmond affair. Two days after the wild car ride, in a "lively" police court trial featuring "several tilts" between the prosecutor and Waldo's lawyer—and apparently no details about the familial relationship of the parties involved—Waldo was sentenced to seven months in jail and fined $250. "Miss Baker" did not appear at the trial: "it was said that she had left town." Waldo appealed the conviction.[2]

Waldo failed to appear in the subsequent trial held four months later. Amanda told the court that Waldo had been in ill health since he was sentenced and that he had only recently returned to Richmond after an absence in the West (probably a reference to Ohio). His lawyer asked that the case be continued in order that further (probably knowingly-futile) efforts could be made to find Waldo, but the judge refused to grant a postponement and instead issued a warrant for Waldo's arrest, declaring the $500 bond which Amanda had put up, the cost of 2,000 admissions to a nickelodeon theater, be forfeited.[3]

A half-year later, the Ohio paper *Newark Advocate* reported that Waldo had been visiting there after several months in Canada, possibly an indication that Waldo had fled to Canada to escape a Virginia jail term, an echo of what his unnamed partner in crime had done back in Newark in 1904. Though the *Advocate* noted that Waldo bragged he was making a "princely salary" at his job in a munitions plant in Canada, he had been denied entry when he had tried to return. Canadian law required non-residents to be in possession of at least $50 when they entered the country; Waldo said he had been short $7 because he had paid that amount for his return railroad ticket. No matter, the paper said, Waldo had been able to secure the money needed while back in the Newark area and was once again preparing to go back to Canada.[4] Probably not coincidentally Amanda was also in Ohio at about the same time as Waldo. She and Walter had "motored back" there together—perhaps the first time they had driven the route instead of taking the train. It would have been a long and arduous trip; Virginia roads in particular were notoriously bad. In Bucyrus, they stayed at the home of Walter's parents,[5] but it is not hard to imagine that Amanda probably also visited in Newark on this trip back to Ohio and was more than glad to help Waldo out financially with the cost of a train fare, especially if his plan was to go back to Canada.

Pulling Out All the Stops at the Bluebird

At this point in her career, Thorp, now 55, was between theaters: about three weeks before, on May 15, 1916, she had sold the Hippodrome Theater, along with the seats, fixtures, furnishings, and piano, for $40,000 to Charles Somma.[6] Though a precise date is unknown for when she sold the Rex, the 1916 City Directory noted W. H. Hoover was proprietor,[7] so it most likely sold sometime in 1915.

The lengthy trip to and from Bucyrus would have given Thorp and Coulter plenty of time to bounce ideas around about what another new theater in Richmond could be like. Running the Hippodrome, with all the complex administrative work of bringing in the larger vaudeville acts, may have led Thorp—perhaps encouraged by Coulter who had likely done most of the groundwork in that area—to develop a desire to return to earlier roots where movies were the main attraction. They may have reminisced about the old days of the nickelodeons and talked about how the movie experience was no longer about watching a series of shorts, but rather multiple-reel features. They would have talked about how the trade magazines were reporting on the development of much larger and more elegant theaters. Technology would have been under discussion: what were the latest trends in projectors and how much did they cost? Should music be considered merely as accompaniment to film or as special in and of itself? They might have talked about how the social stigma of going to the movies had all but vanished, and that film patrons now included both men and women of higher socio-economic status who would pay more for a quality experience.

Despite the cash Thorp may have had upon the recent sales of her remaining theaters, and whether or not Coulter had significant influence on her decision-making, she needed more capital to open the kind of theater she next envisioned. The 700-seat Bluebird Theater opened on Friday, March 2, 1917, at 620 East Broad, and was the result of a partnership with Walter P. Klein, forty-seven, the only time she admitted having partnered in business with anyone.[8] How Walter Klein entered Thorp's orbit, or even how he became prosperous enough to jointly open a theater with her is largely unknown. In 1918, the Richmond City Directory shows him somewhat abruptly emerging as secretary-treasurer of the Bluebird Theater Company,[9] therefore seemingly describing his role in the partnership of the company on the financial side. The *Richmond Times-Dispatch* described him as "lessee" while Thorp was described as "president."[10] Twenty-nine-year-old Walter Coulter was to manage the theater[11] which would accommodate White patrons only.[12]

The *Richmond Times-Dispatch* described the Bluebird thus: "The new house is one of the prettiest in the South and comprises every known feature for the comfort of its clientele. The exterior and interior decorations are harmoniously carried out, and there is a marquee projecting over the street as a protection to waiting patrons in bad weather. In the rear of the lobby is the foyer, and from the foyer a stairway leads down to the ladies' retiring room. The auditorium floor is so graded that from any part of the house a good view is obtained of the picture, thus eliminating the necessity of looking up at the screen. The lighting is indirect throughout, and fresh air is forced into the building through mushrooms under the seats."[13] ("Mushrooms" were mushroom-shaped metal duct openings through which air would flow.) The *Richmond Virginian* added even more details: "[The theater] was designed by Henry T. Barham [of Richmond]. The exterior and interior are harmoniously carried out in L'Art Nouveau [*sic*]. The floor of the lobby is of red brick tile, while the walls are decorated with plaster lattice, foliage, and bluebirds. The operator's room is above the foyer and connects with the generator room, both being well ventilated and dust proof. The heat and ventilation system is the most modern, producing 3,400 cubic feet of fresh air per minute, and is warmed in winter and cooled in summer. Special attention was given to the music with the selection of a style Z Hope Jones unit orchestra [organ] consisting of 25 instruments, made by the famous Rudolph Wurlitzer Manufacturing Company of North Tonawanda, New York.[14] S. H. Spafford, an expert assembler and setup man, installed the instrument which, the *Virginian* noted, "is the newest and most up to date of its kind in the country. In volume and variety, it will surpass any twenty-five piece orchestra, and because of flexibility and instantaneous responsiveness is ideal for the cueing and playing of motion pictures." Professor Henry F. Houston, of the Strand Theater in New York and Cedar Theater, Philadelphia, gave daily recitals on the Hope-Jones through March 15, a two-week engagement.[15]

Though the term "unit orchestra" seems odd today, it was well-known among movie-goers of the time because its presence signaled, as the *Virginian* article mentioned, a "special attention" to music in a given theater. Developed in 1895 by a British man whose last name was Hope-Jones, the organ for the first time mimicked orchestra instruments (hence the term), allowing owners of medium- and smaller-sized theaters to provide a supposed reasonable facsimile of orchestra music with a single instrument and a single musician. The *Virginian* provided additional details about the instrument several days after the opening of the theater:

> This organ, which is the only instrument of its kind in the country . . . is a mammoth instrument and has on its tabulation fifty-six different instruments, including the only set of magnetic chimes. The chimes echo throughout the house and they are placed so that you hear their tones coming from all parts of the house. Three motors are used to put the magnetic control under [the player's] direction. The organ has a full set of English oboes, very seldom heard, and a family of six saxophones, also a new feature. [It also has] clarinets, hautboys, diapasons, horns, flutes, cellos, [and] piccolos; in fact, the whole instrument takes the place of a twenty-five-piece orchestra.

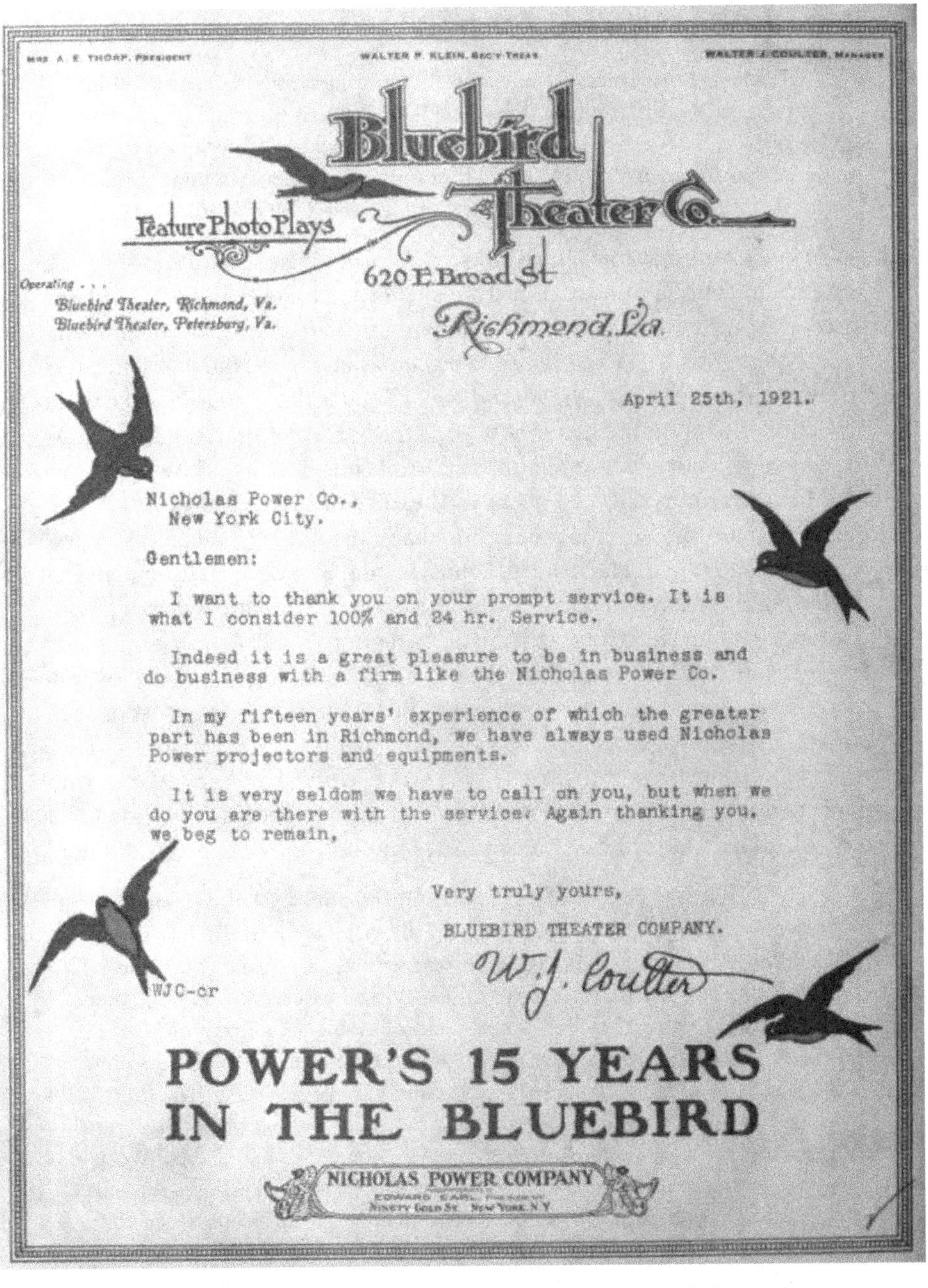

MRS. A. E. THORP, PRESIDENT
WALTER P. KLEIN, SEC'Y-TREAS.
WALTER J. COULTER, MANAGER

Bluebird Theater Co.
Feature PhotoPlays
620 E. Broad St
Richmond, Va.

Operating . . .
Bluebird Theater, Richmond, Va.
Bluebird Theater, Petersburg, Va.

April 25th, 1921.

Nicholas Power Co.,
New York City.

Gentlemen:

I want to thank you on your prompt service. It is what I consider 100% and 24 hr. Service.

Indeed it is a great pleasure to be in business and do business with a firm like the Nicholas Power Co.

In my fifteen years' experience of which the greater part has been in Richmond, we have always used Nicholas Power projectors and equipments.

It is very seldom we have to call on you, but when we do you are there with the service. Again thanking you, we beg to remain,

Very truly yours,
BLUEBIRD THEATER COMPANY.
W. J. Coulter

WJC-cr

POWER'S 15 YEARS
IN THE BLUEBIRD

NICHOLAS POWER COMPANY
NINETY GOLD ST. NEW YORK, N.Y.

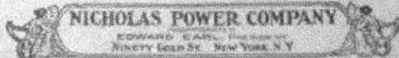

Fig. 38. Letter written by Thorp's protégé Walter Coulter on Bluebird Theater letterhead. It mentions that Thorp and Coulter had been using Power's projectors the entire time they had been in Richmond. The letterhead is beautiful and shows the level of detail Thorp considered in all aspects of her business. The letter was reproduced in *Moving Picture World* as a Nicholas Power Company advertisement. *MPW*, May 28, 1921.

Besides the three motors, nine fans of large dimensions are used to pump air into the six different sections of this wonderful instrument. The last feature of this instrument is in its wonderful attachments. Attached to the organ console are bird notes, Indian tom-toms, bells, castanets, tambourines, horns, train effects, snare drum, kettle drums, and a Turkish crash.[16]

Articles and ads for Thorp's theaters in the past often described the presence of "special music," a feature she deemed vitally important to the success of her theaters. Theatergoers apparently agreed with her assessment: a patron upset with changes in music protocols in one of Jake Wells' theaters wrote to the editor of the *Richmond News Leader* that "[music] is the main attraction in a movie no matter how good the particular movie may be."[17] At the Bluebird, Thorp was going full out. While it is unknown how much she paid for the organ, it wasn't cheap: a theater in El Paso, Texas, advertised that theirs had cost $10,250, one in Spokane, Washington, had paid $15,000 for theirs, and one in Harrisburg, Pennsylvania, $25,000.[18] The expense of the unit orchestra might explain why she had agreed to a partnership with Walter Klein, whose extra financing he brought to the deal may have made the installation of the organ possible. Though it was extravagant, the overall cost for the movie house was reported to be $100,000, and the cost of such an organ would have been well within the budget.[19]

F. H. Richardson, a representative from *Moving Picture World* who happened to be in Richmond at the time of theater opening, provided still more details about some of Bluebird's technology and operations design:

> The Bluebird . . . just opened and managed by Walter J. Coulter, a manager with ideas, is a pretty little house with a really excellent operating room and new Power's 6B projectors taking current through an AC/DC Fort Wayne Compensarc.[20] The only criticism on the Bluebird operating room is that the walls are light; also the operator had three big incandescents blazing away full blast. There is a wash basin with running water. In the auditorium, Manager Coulter had installed an odd and very pretty thing. The ceiling is flat but joins the walls in a graceful curve at the bottom of which, about three feet below the ceiling, is a cove. In this cove are concealed lights one about every three feet, alternately red, green, and white. The lights send up a pointed flare of light on the curve and the effect is decidedly good. The auditorium is long and narrow. . . . The house is a pretty one, but the front rows of seats are entirely too close to the screen. Patrons occupying any of the first three or four rows of seats will strain their eyes severely. Aside from this there is very little to criticize and much to praise in the Bluebird.[21]

The descriptions of the Bluebird theater and its accoutrements illustrates how far movie theater development had come since Thorp had started in

Fig. 39. The Richmond Bluebird Theater in 1922. The photo shows the marquee including the bird-shaped sign which, as its lights sequentially blinked, gave the appearance of a bird in flight. Valentine Museum, Richmond.

the business only a dozen years before. Lobbies and restrooms had been added; there was a sloping floor to give moviegoers a better view of the screen (as opposed to the back of other patrons' heads); consideration was paid to ventilation which would not only help keep customers cool but also ameliorate disagreeable odors they left behind; and the attention to music came at great expense. But the descriptions of the theater are as interesting for what they leave out. The Bluebird Theater today is remembered most for the large, illuminated sign it had at the top of the facade of the building, lit up in blue and white light bulbs. The lights, mounted on a frame in the shape of an enormous bird, flashed in an alternating series, giving the illusion of flapping wings.[22] It's hard to believe the reporters missed that detail, but the sign was there in the earliest known photograph of the building in 1922 while Thorp still owned the theater; if it wasn't there originally, she added it shortly afterward. With the installation of the organ, the electric sign mimicking the flight of a bird, and the state-of-the-art ventilation system and other amenities designed for customer comfort, Thorp had set a new standard for movie theater design in Richmond.

The March 2, 1917, opening feature at the Bluebird was the "gripping story" of the 1906 San Francisco earthquake, *Hell Morgan's Girl*, with Dorothy Phillips.[23] The feature was special, too, consisting as it did of five reels lasting fifty minutes and telling a single story. In the coming weeks, newspaper ads enticed patrons with puffed-up descriptions of other films that were being offered, like: "fascinating romance of a queen and a cowboy," "full of romance and thrills," a "powerful drama," a "remarkable production," and an "amazing adventure." Names of emerging movie stars, such as Harry Carey, Frank Keenan, Elizabeth Risdon, and Cleo Madison, were included to help draw in the audience.[24] Reminiscent as it was of the kinds of taglines she used to put in her ads for the Wonderland back in Ohio, it was likely Thorp who came up with the clever if cheesy slogan that appeared atop the theater's ads in the press: "Visit the Bluebird for Happiness."

In the meantime, Thorp's success, and that of other Richmond moving picture exhibitors who had moved into the territory, had not escaped the notice of Jake Wells. Wells, a powerful man not only in Richmond's entertainment industry, but, in fact, regionally, had been running traditional playhouses in the city for the past twenty years. It had not been lost to him the money being made by the moving picture houses. A reporter estimated that in 1916, movie houses in Richmond were counting some 100,000 admissions each week[25]—at a time when Richmond's population was about 150,000. In fall 1915, Wells had converted his traditional playhouse at Richmond's Bijou to run films. He went on to flip more of his chain of legitimate theaters to movie houses and purchased others, controlling six moving picture theaters in Richmond by summer 1916, presenting formidable competition to Thorp. He eventually mapped out a rank and order for his theaters: the larger, more elegant theaters—the Colonial, Bijou, and Strand, which held close to or a little more than 1,000 patrons each—were first-run houses which would show better quality pictures and charge higher patron prices. His smaller theaters, such as the Odeon and Isis that sat close to 500 patrons each, were second run houses showing lesser quality pictures for cheaper ticket prices.[26] (See Appendix 6 for a list of movie theaters in Richmond ca. 1917.)

The capacity of Thorp's Bluebird—700—lay right in the middle of the seating range of Wells' theaters. Low ticket prices indicate that she was most likely showing second-run pictures, but even so, the Bluebird marked a definite end to the nickel theater among Thorp's holdings and may have been the end of nickelodeons in general in Richmond. When it opened, cost to adult patrons was ten cents, though children would still pay only five cents for matinee performances until 6 pm. Continuous performances were held at the Bluebird daily (except Sunday) from 10 am to 11 pm, but it is not known whether film sessions were still routinely at thirty minutes long or whether they had increased to an hour. By 1919, the cost to attend a show at the Bluebird was eleven and fifteen cents.[27] Whether or not it was always Thorp's intention to run the Bluebird as a second-run theater is unknown; however, the elaborate scale of the Bluebird and the expensive organ tend to belie such a plan. Her hand might have been forced by Wells' maneuvers at the time that she built the Bluebird.

1918: World War and the "Spanish Flu"

U.S. Congress declared war on Germany on April 6, 1917, and U.S. troops began major combat operations on the European Western Front in late spring 1918. Richmond theaters, including Thorp's Bluebird, assisted the effort by supporting bond campaigns, and they suffered equally with other businesses by enduring the effects of fuel shortages and other wartime sacrifices.[28] Theaters showed news reels from the war, carefully edited by producers for positive propaganda value. Few of these aspects of the European war, however, significantly impacted Richmond theaters' bottom line; and in fact, though fuel shortages caused intermittent closures, people flocking to theaters to see news reels of wartime action may have actually more than made up for them. But, in fall 1918, a new threat began emerging that would definitely have a negative impact on theater financials. Mingled with news about the war and on the same page with ads and other theater news, a worrisome article on September 18 in the *Richmond Times-Dispatch* talked about concerns about the spread of the so-called "Spanish" flu. Dr. Roy K. Flannagan, chief officer of the Richmond Health Department, told the paper that the city was "threatened with an epidemic. I would not be surprised if we were visited by the most widespread epidemic of grippe [flu] the city has ever seen. In Camp Lee [in Petersburg] a few days ago there were just a few cases of Spanish grippe. Today there are 500."[29] The flu had been epidemic in Europe for some time, and the movement of soldiers back and forth across the Atlantic was thought to be one of the causes for the rapid toehold of the disease here in the United States. "Persons should avoid crowds and ill-ventilated places," Dr. Flannagan warned.

Two weeks later, the *News Leader* reported that the flu had made gains in Richmond, keeping doctors busy. "So far as I can understand," Dr.

Flannagan told the paper, "there is no quarantine at Camp Lee. Hundreds of soldiers from that camp daily visit Richmond and these must, to a greater or lesser extent, spread the disease."[30] Flannagan was talking about the propensity of Camp Lee soldiers for taking the train into Richmond for R&R, which very often would have involved catching a movie. A few days later, the *Times-Dispatch* reported that theater attendance was declining precipitously. "Efforts are being made locally to avoid closing if possible," the paper noted, "The theatres are being sprayed with disinfectants," and exhibitors were also employing other ventilation and sanitary measures. Managers of many of the movie houses were reporting that business was so light they would not lose much even if there were a closing order. Other aspects of daily life were being affected: a hospital in the Westhampton area announced plans on September 30 to increase capacity from 1,000 to 2,000 beds to handle the influx of patients.[31] On October 5, officials said schools, considered to be well ventilated, would not be closed because they were considered a means by which to disseminate information to the community about how to live under the epidemic.[32] The very next day, however, the city issued orders to close all public and private schools, churches, theaters, motion picture houses, dance halls, poolrooms, and side shows, and to forbid all other public gatherings. Two thousand cases of the disease had developed in Richmond in just a few days. A desperate appeal was put out for nurses. Visitors to hospital wards were prohibited with some exceptions made for those who wore masks.[33] On October 8, the *Times-Dispatch* reported 10,000 cases of the flu in Richmond, and a prediction was made that some 900 to 1,400 Richmonders would die in the next two months. Concern was raised that there were not enough coffins to bury the dead.[34] Theaters remained dark for four weeks, resulting in an estimated loss of weekly gross receipts for all theaters of between $35,000 and $40,000. The papers reported that "most of the houses" (it is not known whether Thorp's Bluebird followed suit) were still paying sixty percent of their employees' salaries to lessen the economic impact on them, a policy which resulted in further financial hardship for the owners.[35]

On November 4, despite signs that the epidemic was not waning significantly, Richmond's Administrative Board voted to withdraw its prohibition of public assemblies, specifically mentioning that motion picture theaters could open. The theaters opened their doors immediately and were met with "heavy patronage" of Richmonders "who had been deprived of their favorite entertainment, turning out to view again the doings of film heroes."[36] Thorp ran an ad in the November 5 *Virginian* touting the ventilation features of the Bluebird, which included a photograph of its huge rooftop "typhoon

Fig. 40. Ventilation apparatus that was installed on
the Bluebird Theater roof.
RV, Nov. 5, 1918; originally
from *MPW*, Jul. 31, 1915.

twin blower." The ad claimed that the air taken from the roof and distrib-
uted through the mushrooms in the floor under the theater seating made
the Bluebird "fresh as the outdoors."[37] Though the Bluebird ad asserted the
blower was "our" system, and it probably was the brand installed on the
roof, the ad itself used a photograph of a blower which had appeared in a
Moving Picture World article three years before after being installed on the
roof of a theater in Brooklyn, New York.[38]

Statistics of the number of cases and of deaths from the flu epidemic
ebbed and flowed over the next several months in Richmond. Even when
there were spikes in the number of cases, generally less aggressive measures
were taken in efforts to moderate its impact. One, however, was an order that
all persons affected with colds must carry handkerchiefs so that they could
cover their sneezing. Failure to comply with the order in theaters (specifically) would "cause the sneezer to be ejected."[39] The epidemic was largely
considered ended by summer 1919 as it was thought that most people had
been exposed to the disease and had either developed immunity or died.[40]

Perhaps realizing during the 1918 ordeal that soldiers were lucrative
patrons, Thorp and Klein expanded their holdings in September 1919 by
taking over a theater at 145 North Sycamore Street in Petersburg, the closest town to Camp Lee. They gave it also the name Bluebird.[41] Walter and

Bob Coulter were sent to the theater, previously operated as the Lyric, to spruce it up for its late 1919 opening, although Roy Holstein would manage it.[42] In 1922 the theater underwent another extensive renovation which involved strengthening the roof, renewing the floors, and covering the boiler room with fireproof material.[43] To accomplish the 1922 theater overhaul, the Petersburg Bluebird was moved for a week into another theater house in town, known as the Columbia. At the time of the renovation, the Petersburg Bluebird's earlier BarckHoff organ was reportedly replaced with a Wurlitzer.[44] An elaborate sign, such as that on the Bluebird in Richmond, does not appear to have been installed.

On January 2, 1922, Thorp's husband Frank, seventy-nine, died at his home in Columbus, Ohio, as the consequences of a fall (though he also had cancer), officially making her the widow she had claimed to be in every known newspaper article, census, city directory, and legal document (including real estate transactions) since 1904 when she was still living in Newark. Waldo, who may have never gone back to Canada in 1916 as the Newark paper had assumed he would, had been moving around in Ohio and was in Columbus at the time of his father's death.[45] At Frank's death, Waldo listed Frank's occupation as retired baker though Frank had been employed at least part-time from about mid-1909 to September 1915 at Ohio's State Capitol building as custodian of the flags and relic room, losing the job when he was fired for being a Democrat by the newly-elected Republican governor who was "cleaning house."[46] Waldo took his father to Newark for burial; in 1965 Frank's grave was marked with a military headstone noting his Union Civil War service.[47] No obituary for Frank can be located, and it is not known whether Amanda traveled to Newark for the funeral. On January 16, 1922, she filed for the widow's pension that was her due as the widow of a soldier who had fought in the Civil War.[48] Six months later, her Bluebird Theater in Richmond gave free admission to all Confederate veterans who were attending a reunion being held in the city that week.[49]

Real Estate and Living Arrangements

In addition to land and building transactions associated with her theaters, Thorp dabbled in other kinds of real estate over the years. As noted, she had apparently purchased a house (or perhaps a farm) in rural Ohio in 1911; for reasons unknown, she later bought at least one or two houses or lots in Bucyrus as well, long after she was established in Richmond. Buying the land in August 1912 where she would build the Hippodrome was one of her earliest purchases in Richmond, but she had also bought three residential lots in the city in a bit of a buying binge the month before. Later on, she bought several more lots in addition to the Hippodrome's, and possibly also houses, in Jackson Ward and other parts of Richmond, apparently for investment or speculative purposes, especially after 1915. Among her largest purchases was a smallish apartment building on Monument Avenue near today's Virginia Museum of History and Culture as well as some apparent single-family residences on Grace Street. In January 1915, she sold a sixty-acre farm located five miles out of Richmond on Midlothian Turnpike. She apparently had, for a while, actually engaged to some degree in long-distance farming there, as classified ads on various dates show her offering for sale a two-year-old jersey bull, four "nice" pigs, four hogs, three cows, a "family horse," team of six-year-old mules, two-horse farm wagon and harness, and a 100-egg Buckeye incubator which had been used to hatch only three times.[50] Perhaps not coincidentally, the sale of the horse, farm wagon, and harness in late 1914 seem to occur at around the dates of the evaporation of the same items from the "Dunlap Pony, Buggy, and Harness" promotion the Dixie was running with the *Planet* at the time, and may explain what actually had happened to them.

Some of these real estate purchases and sales involved her current or former business associates: she and Walter Coulter together bought property in what today is known as the Museum District as well as in Barton Heights; Walter Klein and Walter Coulter sold their stakes in the apartment building on Monument Avenue to her in 1924; and in 1926, the three of them (Thorp and the two Walters) were noted as delinquent on taxes for a property in Madison Ward.[51]

In a variety of housing arrangements unusual even for the time, Amanda and Waldo Thorp and Walter Coulter not only worked together, they also lived together (when Waldo was in town), although "living together" given the nature of the hours they would have kept, running multiple theaters as they did, might be an exaggeration. They moved often, with at least some of the homes being properties that Thorp owned. In 1910, they all were residing at 611 East Broad (located across the street very close to the Rex); around 1911, all three had moved to 314 East Clay, and around 1913, they all lived together at 2207 Stuart Avenue. The first two homes were more likely small, walk-up apartments, but the home at Stuart Avenue was a spacious rowhouse. By 1916 Waldo had fled Richmond, but Amanda and Coulter continued to share housing arrangements, living together around 1916 in a home at 2205 Stuart, then around 1917 likely sharing a residence at 414 North Seventh and from about 1918–1919 living at 411 East Cary. Coulter may have moved out on his own for a time around 1919 (the city directory has him at 620 East Broad while Thorp is still shown at 411 East Cary), but around 1920–1921 they were living at the same address at 2518 West Grace, and around 1922–1923 they were once more shown as living at the same address at 105 South Boulevard.[52]

In about 1919, Coulter, then thirty-one and possibly suffering from an unspecified illness, brought his brother Robert, twenty-three, from Bucyrus to help out in the business; Robert had just returned from serving in World War I.[53] Robert initially joined Thorp and his brother Walter at the home on 2518 West Grace, where they all were living around 1920, but by around 1921, he had moved into his own place at 1710 Hanover Avenue. He does not appear to have shared living arrangements with Thorp except for that brief period.[54]

We Are OK

After selling the Hippodrome and before starting construction on the Blue-bird, Thorp told the publication *Moving Picture World* that she was think-ing about retiring in order to travel throughout the country, visiting places which she had "heretofore only seen on screen."[55] Thorp's love of travel is well documented: she had indulged herself many times over the years in taking lengthy vacations (even though we do not always know where she went), traveling by train in the days before there were automobiles and later traveling by car once she had them.

So, whenever there was an excuse for business travel, Thorp would take it. As noted, in 1908 before opening the Dixie Theater at its permanent location at Brook and Broad, she had gone to Brooklyn, Jersey City, New York City, and Atlantic City to learn about new trends in film exhibition. In 1910, she sent Coulter to Pittsburgh, Baltimore, and Washington, D.C., for the same purpose, apparently on his own,[56] but after that, Coulter, who seemed to share her love for travel, sometimes accompanied her. In 1913, the two went together at least to New York, where they arranged to book new vaudeville acts for her theaters.[57] In 1915, Thorp went to Washington, D.C., for an invitation-only World Film Corporation exhibition that was given to a select group of theater exhibitors.[58] In 1916, she travelled to Charlotte, North Carolina, "[to] arrange for service and to secure equipment" for a new theater she was planning to open, which would be the Bluebird.[59] She had been a member of the Virginia Exhibitors' League since 1913, necessitating travel to state, regional, and national meetings—her work with the League culminated in 1918 when she became the League's vice-president (with Jake Wells as president).[60] In 1923, both Thorp and Coulter attended the meeting of the recently-formed, Washington, D.C., unit of the Motion Picture Exhibitors' Alliance.[61] These are the known documented examples of Thorp's excursions to keep abreast of the rapidly evolving motion picture exhibitor business, but it is likely there were many more instances that were not documented.

Thorp and Coulter also traveled together for personal pleasure, one of those being the automobile trip back to Bucyrus in 1916. But one of their traveling adventures turned perilous in May 1923. Along with Coulter's mother, they had gone to the resort city of Hot Springs, Arkansas, and were still there when a severe storm came through, spawning at least one tornado as well as floods and fires. News of the natural disaster hit the national press, including the *Richmond Times-Dispatch* which reported the event on its front page: "Hot Springs, its business district swept by flood and flame, tonight was slowly recovering from the effects of the storm which late yesterday sent a torrent sweeping down from the mountainside, leaving in its wake a trail of destruction. . . . Store fronts smashed, bath houses wrecked and debris strewn about stood as mute evidence of the fury of the elements . . . . Tonight a company of Arkansas National Guard was on duty patrolling the area wrecked by the storm and fire. Some placed the toll at 17, one said 50 people had been killed."[62]

Fortunately, Coulter got a telegram off to his brother back in Richmond as soon as the lines were open: "Horrible flood and fire. We are O.K. Town a complete wreck." As it turned out, the early reports of the number dead were exaggerated; only one woman died in a car that was swept down Hot Springs' main avenue.[63] In an instance of art imitating life, on May 24, Thorp's Bluebird Theater in Richmond showed patrons a newsreel on the Hot Springs flood and fire.[64]

Professional Press

Amanda Thorp was known to keep up with all aspects of the movie theater business—she once advertised in Bucyrus that "not being up to date is like riding a dead horse."[65] In addition to traveling to cities far and wide to personally observe the trends of her business, she also would have pored over the several trade magazines in existence at the time and that carried articles not only about new technologies but also new films, emerging actors with

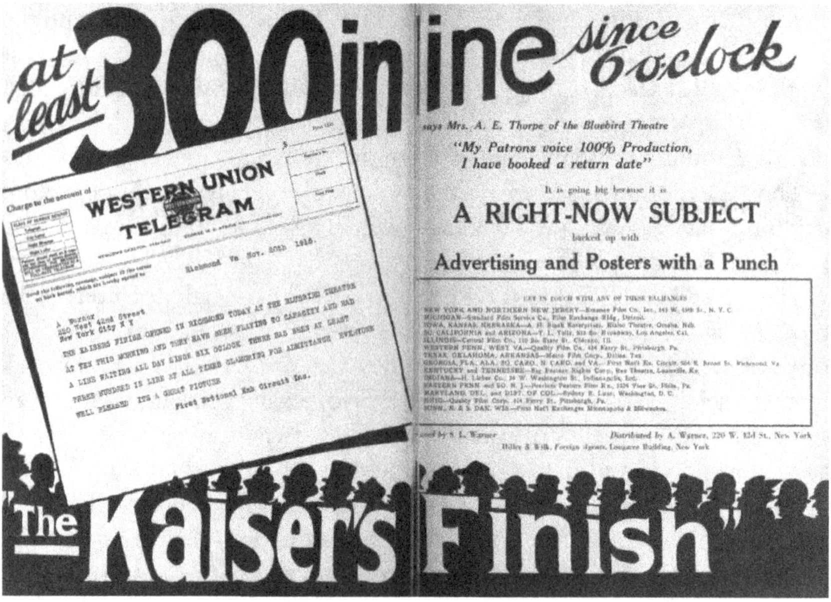

Fig. 41. A two-page ad in *Motion Picture News* showing a telegram sent by
Thorp to the Warner Exchange in New York saying their film, *The Kaiser's Finish*,
had been so popular at her Bluebird Theater that it was playing to full capacity
and had 300 in line every day and for every showing after 6 pm "clamoring for
admittance." *MPN*, Dec. 7, 1918.

star quality, and industry gossip. She even warranted the occasional mention in the magazines, making her first appearance in late 1906 in *Billboard
Magazine*, as the owner of Wonderland in Bucyrus, on a list of about 300
"electric theatres and nickelodeons" in the United States.[66] In an early assessment of her personality, an unnamed film sales representative who was
traveling through Richmond in 1910 told the *Film Index* this: "[She is] a
very agreeable lady of good business judgment—popular with her patrons
and has a large following. She says, 'politeness doesn't cost anything and to
be nice is the cheapest sport in the world.'"[67] Her plans to open the Hippodrome as an African American theater were mentioned in 1912 in both the
Tradesman and *Moving Picture World*.[68] In 1918, *Motion Picture News* ran
an ad running across two full pages for a Warner film entitled *The Kaiser's
Finish*, along with a reproduction of a telegram from Thorp in which she
said the movie had been so popular at the Bluebird that it was playing to
full capacity, with 300 people in line every day after 6 pm "clamoring for

admittance." She continued to be of interest to the national trade magazines as more people were getting to know of her. The trade magazine *Moving Picture World* in 1920, taking note both of her success and her gender, asked her what would be her advice "to other members of the fair sex" in regard to successfully conducting a moving picture house. She answered, "I would tell them this: Study your territory and your patrons. The rest will come."[69] No doubt the formula would have been equally applicable to men such as Walter Coulter, who aspired to become successful movie theater moguls.

Moving On

Sometime after October 1923, Thorp and Coulter took another quick trip together to Washington, D.C., for the regional Motion Picture Exhibitors' Alliance meeting.[70] It was perhaps on that trip that the two of them had serious discussions about her next plans and how he would fit in with them. At the end of 1923, Thorp and Walter Klein sold their interests in the Bluebird Company (the theaters in Richmond and Petersburg) to Charles Somma and

Fig. 42. Postcard showing the big theaters (formerly "legitimate" theaters which were changing over to movie houses) at Seventh and Broad in Richmond in the early 1920s. Thorp's Bluebird, at 620 East Broad, is just out of sight to the left. VCU Libraries, Digital Collections.

Walter Coulter,[71] marking the first time that Coulter had a stake in a theater other than as an employee. At about the same time, he brought the rest of his family—his father, mother, and sister—from Bucyrus to live in Richmond in a small apartment at 3014-A Park Avenue.[72] Then, on March 24, 1924, the thirty-six-year-old Walter Coulter married the twenty-four-year-old Clarice MacDonald of Columbus, Ohio.[73]

The business of showing films was going through some radical changes: efforts by national chains to put local movie houses out of business, changes in the distribution of films that put movie house owners at odds with one another, fights with lawmakers about the legality of theater closures on Sunday (blue laws), threats of onerous government censorship procedures, litigation by music publishers over copyright violations of music used in the silent theaters, and, not least, incredible talk of coming technology claiming that movies would have synchronized dialogue.[74] On the same day that Thorp sold both her Bluebirds, she announced her retirement from running movie houses.[75] This was at least the third time she had contemplated retirement: the other two were after selling the Dixie and then after selling the Hippodrome. This time she really meant it, turning the reins over to Walter Coulter as the person she most respected, and to Charles Somma who could afford it.

Three months later, Thorp announced that she was planning a new theater in Richmond's Southside.[76]

7

THE THEATER BEAUTIFUL

Possibly part of the deal in selling the Bluebirds to Somma and Coulter was an agreement that Thorp would not compete with them with another theater in the area. She could offer daunting competition, and they knew it. If that were the case, then it could explain why Thorp looked southward, across Richmond's James River, for her next venture: perhaps the river had been an agreed-upon dividing line, or at least that is where Thorp felt it was fair game for her to build. Her main competition in Southside would be Jake Wells, who owned the smallish Victor movie theater as well as an even smaller movie theater called the Shirley.

Before Thorp turned to building the new theater, she decided for the first time to build herself a home. She bought property at 7204 West Franklin Street in Richmond's Near West End neighborhood of Duntreath, and hired prominent Richmond architect, L. T. Bengtson, to draw up plans. Perhaps not surprisingly, Thorp chose a less common architectural style for her home, eschewing the traditional Americana designs that were, and still are, the norm in the area. But even so, she chose a more subdued plan than her taste in theater design might have predicted. A drawing of the home was published in the December 23, 1923, *Times-Dispatch*, revealing an "adaptation from the Italian." To be built at an approximate cost of $15,000, it would have a sleeping porch, four bedrooms, two baths, a sunroom, breakfast alcove, living-porch, and a paved terrace. The main entrance arch would have an ornamental mosaic treatment. In the rear of the house would be a detached garage with a servant's room and bath. The plan was grand, but not ostentatious. The house still exists today, and almost exactly matches the drawing which the newspaper published in 1923.[1]

Once the house was underway, Thorp turned her attention to her new theater in Southside, which the *Times-Dispatch* in a back-handed complement noted would be the "third finest" cinema palace in the Richmond area.[2]

NEW $15,000 HOME BEING BUILT
    FOR MRS. TRORP IN DUNTREATH

—L. T. Bengtson, architect.
The beautiful new home of Mrs. A. E. Thorp, in Duntreath, which is
being erected at a cost of approximately $15,000, is shown above. The
plans, drawn by L. T. Bengtson, the architect, call for a sleeping porch
and four bedrooms, two baths, a sun room, breakfast alcove, living-porch
and paved terrace.
The building's main entrance arch is in ornamental mosaic treat-
ment. The entire building is an adaptation from the Italian. In the rear
of the house is a garage and servant's room with bath.

Fig. 43. Architect's drawing of the house Thorp was building for
herself in Richmond's Near West End. *RTD*, Dec. 23, 1923.

Petersburg architect Fred A. Bishop had been hired to design the new $75,000
theater, located at 1414 Hull Street.[3] Though primarily designed for showing films, it would be equipped with a stage and scenery loft for presenting
"legitimate drama," should it "ever be found convenient to do so." It would
seat a thousand people, Thorp's largest theater yet. The interior would be
made of ornamental plaster, and the Typhoon ventilating system would keep
the air flowing, warming the space in the winter and keeping it as cool as
possible in the summer.[4] The building would be three stories in height and
would include office space, presumably for Thorp and theater managers.[5]

By the end of the year, Thorp was pressing the builders to finish construction for an early 1925 opening, and she had christened the theater "The
Venus." Before it opened, she added Jake Wells' tiny theater, the Shirley, and
another Wells theater nearby, the Victor, larger than the Shirley but much
still much smaller than the Venus, to her Southside portfolio. In so doing,
the press noted, Thorp got full control of all movie theaters in Southside.[6]

Adding to her plate of responsibilities, Waldo was back—and living with her at 105 South Boulevard.[7] Waldo's return to Richmond, perhaps not coincidentally, occurred at about the same time that Walter Coulter left Thorp's employ. Waldo's latest wife, the former Lulu (Lesley) Irene Cordell of Toledo, Ohio, who at the time of their marriage in 1920 was only a year younger than Waldo, may have come to Richmond with him.[8] Lulu was the seven-year-older step-sister of Clarice MacDonald whom Walter Coulter had married in 1924, meaning that Waldo and Walter were brothers-in-law (with a step relationship) by marriage.[9]

It may have been risky for Waldo to come back to Richmond; it doesn't appear that the warrants for his arrest for the 1915 violent attacks on Faun Baker and her friend had ever been sorted out. More than ten years had passed, however; Faun was no longer in Richmond, and the other young woman had likely left as well, leaving (Waldo undoubtedly hoped) no one particularly interested in pursuing the case. If Waldo could rise to the occasion, Thorp could use his help running the Venus and the two smaller theaters. For the first time in about twenty years, Walter Coulter was no longer helping her; he was starting to build his own theater empire across

Fig. 44. Thorp opened her Venus Theater on March 18, 1925, showing the film *Janice Meredith*. This image is of a collectible "lobby card" of the film and pictures actors Holbert Blinn and Marion Davies, the latter of whom portrayed the titular character. www.commons.wikimedia.org.

the James River, and employing his brother, Bob, to do many of the things Walter once did for Amanda.

The grand opening of the Venus was March 18, 1925, and the event garnered a full page of advertisements in the local paper from companies that had helped build and furnish it. The ads, in turn, no doubt inspired the accompanying flamboyant editorial coverage in the *Times-Dispatch*. A photograph was published of the crowds, "virtually the entire population of Southside," that were gathered outside on opening night hoping to score one of the 900 available tickets. The theater itself was "modern in every aspect," and the electric sign with its "Venus de Milo—armless and everything," helped generate buzz. William Loeffler was seated at the organ console, and native son Thomas M. Bullock was engaged to sing several solos. Willis Pulliam, a Chesterfield County Commissioner and Commonwealth Attorney, made an extemporaneous speech. *Janice Meredith*, a melodramatic love story set during the American revolution starring Marion Davies and also the lesser-known W.C. Fields, was the feature offering, and "as though nine reels were not enough," a comedy and a cartoon specialty were also included

Fig. 45. Grand opening of the Venus Theater. Image quality is poor, but it shows the crowds and façade of the theater. *RTD*, Mar. 29, 1925.

for the undisclosed admission price. Music that played for the silent film was a score created especially for it, with thematic melodies accompanying the scenes of Paul Revere's ride, Washington crossing the Delaware, and "all the [other] echoes of the Revolution, not to omit the Spirits of '76." The *Times-Dispatch* faintly praised actress Davies as "a factor to be reckoned with" but was somewhat more enthusiastic about the effect on moviego-ers of the scene with Patrick Henry delivering his (intertitled) "give me liberty or give me death" speech, noting it made the "more impressionable movie fans groggy with excitement." The organ was an instrument of the Robert Morton Company, the next most prolific builders of pipe organs in the country after Wurlitzer, a sign that Thorp was being cost conscious. The press noted that the Venus, her "Theatre Beautiful" as she coined it (though misheard once as the "Theatre Butterfly" by a reporter writing about it), was trying out a new schedule for Richmond: one program would be shown on Mondays and Tuesdays; a different program would be shown on Wednesdays; still another program on Thursdays and Fridays; and yet another on Saturdays. [10]

In June 1926, Thorp traveled to Charlotte, North Carolina, to visit E. F. Dardine, manager of the Charlotte branch of Universal Film Exchanges, and his wife who were holding a dinner dance at Darvilla, their suburban estate there. [11] And then, less than a month later and just over a year after the Venus grand opening, she sold her theater beautiful to a small group out of North Carolina (not associated with Jake Wells). [12] It may have been for that reason that Thorp had traveled to Charlotte. Waldo became manager of the Victor, but the Shirley, at 1224 Hull Street, had already been sold in March 1926 when it was turned into a used car lot. [13]

On July 7, 1927, Amanda Thorp, sixty-four, died at the home she had built for herself in the Near West End. As Waldo had done for his father, he served as the informant for his mother's death certificate. He noted her occupation as proprietor of motion pictures and listed her marital status, truthfully now, as widow. Her doctor indicated the cause of death as stom-ach cancer and noted he had been treating her for one year, which was about the time she sold the Venus. She is buried in River View Cemetery in Richmond. [14]

CODA

In the archives of the Albert and Shirley Small Special Collections Library at the University of Virginia, there is an extraordinary document that describes an alleged scheme to put an ignoble end to Thorp's theater legacy.[1] In an undated affidavit that was written circa January 1927, Thorp describes a conspiracy by the Jake Wells organization, in possible collusion with Walter Coulter and Charles Somma, to establish a monopoly of first-run theaters in Richmond and put her out of business.

According to another document in the archives, the legal court case started on November 27, 1925, when Thorp had agreed to take over the lease for the Southside Victor Theater building from Jake Wells. At the same time, she had agreed to purchase the physical property of the theater for $16,500 due to be paid in installments with interest over the next three years, effectively purchasing the theater. Thorp was either late or failed to make one of the installments and was sued by Wells' Richmond Theatrical Operating Corporation.

In response to the lawsuit, Thorp described the alleged conspiracy. She began by noting that she had opened the Venus Theater in Southside as a "first class" moving picture theater, "designed for a high-class patronage and for the exhibition of only high-class pictures." At the time, Jake, his brother Otto, and other associates were operating as several corporations in Richmond, among them the Wells Amusements Company and the Richmond Theatrical Operating Corporation. Jake had purchased the Victor Theater shortly before the Venus, only a couple of blocks away, opened. The purpose of Jake's purchase, according to Thorp, "was to put his interests in a position where they could control the picture business in the City of Richmond including South Richmond, which they had not done theretofore by reason of the fact that they had not been operating a theatre in South Richmond."[2]

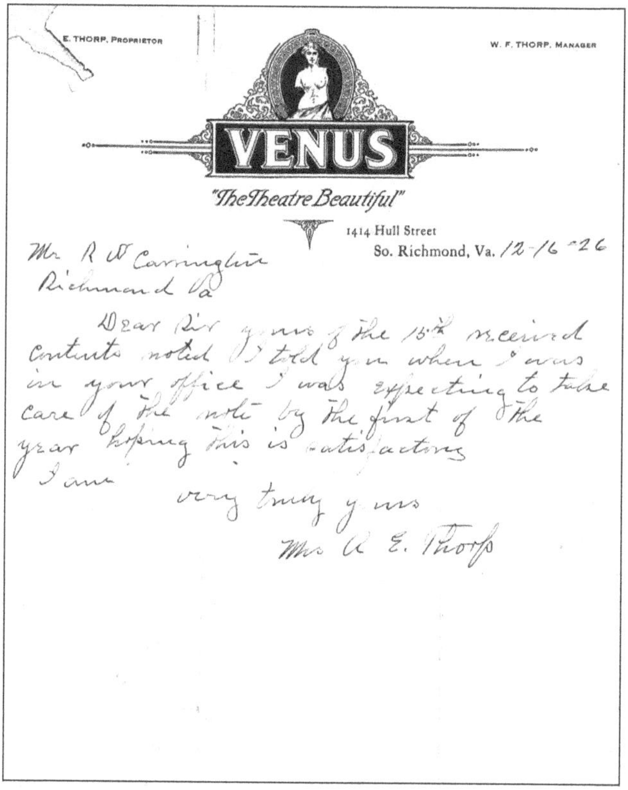

E. THORP, PROPRIETOR

W. F. THORP, MANAGER

VENUS

"The Theatre Beautiful"

1414 Hull Street
So. Richmond, Va. 12-16-26

Mr R W Carrington
Richmond Va

Dear Sir yours of the 15th received contents noted I told you when I was in your office I was expecting to take care of the note by the first of the year hoping this is satisfactory
I am
very truly yours
Mrs A E. Thorp

Fig. 46. Letter, on Venus letterhead, Dec. 16, 1926, from Thorp to the Jake Wells organization after receiving a collection notice regarding payments for the Victor which were in arrears. Albert and Shirley Small Special Collections Library, University of Virginia, Charlottesville.

At that point, Thorp continued, Wells' business entities "united with the owners of the Bluebird and the Brookland theaters in securing the picture rights for the City of Richmond, the entire purpose of which was to control . . . first-run pictures . . . and thus stifle the competition" that the Venus would represent. They could do this, she said, because Wells had made an agreement with the Washington, D.C., company known as Film Exchanges, which had an exclusive for the Richmond territory, that only his theaters, along with those of Coulter and Somma (the Bluebird and Brookland), would be furnished first-run pictures.

Thorp realized, at about the time she opened the Venus, that she was going to have a problem procuring pictures because she had approached Film Exchanges to obtain "first class pictures" for her new theater and was told none were available, all of them having been contracted by Jake Wells and his associates. If she wanted to obtain pictures for the Venus, they told her, she would have to make arrangements through Jake Wells' companies. She was then referred to Harry Bernstein at the Colonial who, she was told, was representing Wells' business in Richmond. In her affidavit, she quoted what Bernstein had told her when she contacted him: "You know we have bought all the pictures for Richmond." She said he further told her that unless she "turned her Venus over to Jake," she would not be allowed to have any films. Another option he proposed, however, would be that she take over their Victor Theater. Bernstein put the cost for the Victor at $6,500 (about $110,000 in 2023).

Thorp then set in motion the requirements to buy the Victor, only to be told later that Wells had changed his mind and would not make a deal. Fortunately, Thorp had already purchased several "quality" pictures in anticipation of the Venus opening, and so she commenced operations at the Venus, believing that she would eventually be able to procure more good films, and in particular, that she might be able to obtain second-run but apparently still high-quality pictures from Richmond's new National Theater which had just been opened on Richmond's Broad Street by interests adverse to the Wells' companies. But then the Wells organization also acquired the National Theater, foiling Thorp's plans to do even that. Thorp said at that point she faced either going out of business or selling her Venus, but quickly realized that selling was not an option since there was no market for the Venus because of the Jake Wells monopoly. And so she found herself in the position of having to look for yet another solution.[3]

She said she approached the Wells organization once more, and was again offered the original deal: in other words, if she wished to procure pictures she would have to do so from Wells and she would have to lease the building which housed the Victor Theater as well as purchase its physical assets (Appendix 7—Inventory of the Victor Theater, 1926). But then the Wells organization nearly tripled the price for the Victor's physical property from $6,500 to $18,000 ($18,000 is about $300,000 in 2023). Thorp said she agreed "under compulsion" to their terms rather than sacrifice her large investment in the Venus.

The bottom line of Thorp's argument, then, was that she should not be held liable for the payments for the assets of the Victor Theater since they had been inflated and she had been coerced into the contract. Thorp may have been very ill at the time; as may be recalled, she died only six months later, on July 27, 1927, with her doctor noting he had been treating her for stomach cancer for a year.[4]

Jake Wells committed suicide on March 16, 1927, in North Carolina where he had moved several years before to manage his burgeoning regional business concerns. The matter of the debt for the purchase of the Victor had not been settled by the time of Thorp's death, but it is of note that the Wells organization's lawyer handling the case, attorney Richard W. Carrington of Richmond and a good friend of Wells, did not dispute the matter of coercion as presented by Thorp. He instead countered that her arguments that the purchase price had been inflated were moot: among the several Virginia court cases he cited to make his case was one in which the court decided that, even though a price contracted had been double its value, the purchaser had been fully competent and so the contract was judged enforceable.

After Thorp died, the Wells organization, Richmond Theatrical Operating Corporation, again represented by Carrington, sued the estate for payment of the Victor debt.[5] Waldo and State Planters Bank, which was a trustee under the will, were parties to the suit as estate executors. Carrington quickly took over the lead role in settling the estate since the money owed to the Corporation was substantial and the Corporation by far and away had the largest claim against the estate which did not otherwise, Carrington showed, have other significant financial assets.

The estate took a long time to resolve. It was a very long and complicated affair involving multiple attorneys with multiple interests, multiple suppliers who asserted varying amounts of claims against the estate, possible failure on Thorp's part to have collected rent on some of her properties, and an apparent lack of and disarray in financial paperwork, particularly regarding the multiple second mortgages that Thorp had taken out for the purposes of building the Venus. One note in the estate files contains an interesting tidbit: one of the properties Thorp had mortgaged to raise money for the Venus had been jointly held by Walter Coulter, although she had mortgaged only her half.

Thorp's allegations of extortion never surfaced during the legal procedures for settling the estate. Waldo and State Planters Bank may have believed it was futile to pursue her claims, and, anyway, the bank, which was merely acting as trustee, had little motivation to fight for Waldo's interests. At one point during the estate resolution, Carrington noted without irony that personal property from the estate (which would have included that of the Victor) was "entirely insufficient to pay off the creditors."

In October 1928, Carrington was able to notify the Wells interests that the estate finally had been settled, with the decree "paying us out in full," including "principal, interests, and costs." His relief that the ordeal was over was palpable: "Literally, I did not know that we would be successful in our contentions until the minute the decree was entered. Every conceivable trouble arose; numerous new and unexpected claims were continually cropping up." Even after the decree was filed, Carrington continued to act as *de facto* negotiator for resolution of the estate, putting out fires which had to do with relatively minor demands against it. The last document in his files, dated February 21, 1929, dealt with the closure of an unsuccessful apparent attempt by Waldo to walk off with a check for $5,000 which was meant to go for estate settlement purposes.

Though what Waldo may have ultimately received from the estate is not known, Carrington had managed to stave off foreclosures of Thorp's real estate properties because he believed the estate would not have reaped sufficient monies under those conditions to pay off debts, including those for the Jake Wells interests Carrington himself represented. In the end, Waldo may have received those real estate properties as his inheritance in the estate, but it is likely, as Carrington implied, they would at minimum have required very skilled managerial effort to have provided any financial gain. It is not known how many debtors other than the Wells interests were paid for their claims against the estate: at one point Carrington estimated they would receive about seventy-five percent of what they were owed.

What ultimately happened to the Victor's assets or to the theater itself is not known; an article appearing in the February 29, 1928, *Richmond Times-Dispatch* indicated the theater was still in operation[6] but it was not mentioned again until July 11, 1931, when the paper noted that the theater, "which has for some time been unused" was being re-opened, after renovation, by a Danville theater exhibitor.[7] One other curiosity remains unsolved: why Thorp bought the tiny Shirley theater from Jake Wells in December 1924.

In the unfortunately short interview with Thorp that appeared in the January 10, 1926, *Richmond Times-Dispatch* about six months before she sold the Venus, interviewer Virginia Lee Cox wrote: "In the days when Mary Pickford appeared absolutely incognito on the screen, when even two-reel pictures were unknown and the great features were trick pictures, when the moving picture industry was not even beginning to lay aside its swaddling clothes, Mrs. A. E. Thorp came to Richmond from Ohio and opened here the first movie theater Richmond ever had."[8] But that only touches on her accomplishments: Amanda Thorp went on to become one of the earliest film exhibitors in the South, if not the nation, to operate a theater exclusively for Black patronage, and then to create there an important venue for early Black vaudeville. Seeing the success the Dixie was having in presenting Black vaudeville, she went on to build Richmond's original Hippodrome, another theater exclusively for Black patronage but one capable of featuring larger Black vaudeville acts. After selling the Hippodrome, Thorp returned to the movie theater business, building the beautiful and fantastical Bluebird. She then went on to develop the Venus in Richmond's Southside that, although it didn't eclipse the Bluebird, was a very pretty theater in its own right.

Thorp herself never spoke of the early Black vaudeville offerings that she had brought to the Dixie and the Hippodrome, and neither has any retrospective article which mentions the Dixie nor those that describe the early years of the Hippodrome (in general, she is absent from early histories of the Hippodrome). Thorp's failure to mention this area of her contributions may reflect her own and others' internal racist attitudes that see the Black experience as lacking importance in our history. She may have also been concerned—within the paradigm of living in an era of Jim Crow—that awareness of her work in that area might even have damaged what she considered to be her legacy as an early developer of affordable entertainment venues in Richmond. Whatever the reason, this oversight has resulted in the fact that the presence of early Black vaudeville in Richmond has been largely, if not wholly, omitted in otherwise rich retellings of its theater history.

Another contribution never attributed to her is the bringing of Walter Coulter to Richmond. Richmond today would not have the beloved Byrd Theatre without his presence and the lessons she taught him that he applied to its construction and management. Thorp's struggles with her son, on the other hand, which continued well into Waldo's adulthood, show a woman who was conflicted in doing what she could to help him while surviving on her own in the face of his problems. It feels apparent that Waldo from an early age suffered from alcoholism; today she might better understand that much of what she did to help him may have instead enabled him.

There can be no question that Thorp was passionate about all things having to do with movie theaters. No detail went unnoticed by her, whether it was the projector, screen, music, seats, ventilation, the lights out front, or the theater letterhead. In a 1939 retrospective, written at the height of importance of motion pictures in the United States and more than a decade after Thorp's death, a *Times-Dispatch* reporter wrote, "Mrs. Thorp's houses [drew] the biggest audiences because she kept pace with the improvements in pictures."[9] But she didn't just keep pace, she pretty much ran circles around nearly everyone else in the early movie theater business in Richmond, her work attracting even regional and national favorable attention. A 1916 article in North Carolina's *Charlotte News* noted she was in town for "Electrical Week" (a gathering of moving picture exhibitors) and described her as "one of the most skilled and prominent moving picture operators in Richmond." The article continued, "(She is) a master hand in the theatre business. All moving picture operators here will be interested to know of her visit and will not lose the chance of meeting her and learning of her work."[10] Thorp's contributions to theater in both Ohio and Virginia laid a baseline for others to follow, and these she accomplished despite her gender, despite being a self-made woman financially, and despite being self-educated not only in the particulars of the film industry but also in the generalities of running a business of any kind.

EPILOGUE

Amanda

As noted, much of the published secondary information on Amanda Thorp, her theaters, and other details about the early days of her work with moving picture theaters in both Richmond and Ohio, is inaccurate. Some of the inaccuracies can be traced to an unsourced article in the now defunct non-peer-reviewed journal *Richmond Quarterly*, also known as the *Richmond Literature and History Quarterly*,[1] not to be confused with the Virginia Museum of History and Culture's *Virginia Magazine of History and Biography*. Other misinformation was published in newspapers after Thorp's death in the form of recollections of mostly Richmond residents. These recollections were often based on sketchy personal remembrances or apocryphal stories oft-repeated from second- and third-hand sources. Sometimes men well-known in the motion picture business in Richmond and Ohio told of their contributions but omitted Thorp's. These latter recollections, without exception, appeared after she had died and was unable to correct the record; it is easy to imagine that if she had still been alive, she would have had no problem letting them know the error of their ways. Some Richmond theater histories have speculated that Jake Wells helped bankroll Thorp or at least gave her advice and encouragement as she opened the first moving picture house in Richmond. This is almost certainly untrue. When she came to Richmond, she was fully capable of opening her own picture houses, having both the financial wherewithal and the experience necessary. Her early relationship with Jake Wells was more likely that she knew him as the owner of the Colonial Theater where she rented her first "room" (the original Dixie) from him. Jake likely thought, as did many others perhaps including even Thorp herself in the early days, that moving pictures were

Fig. 47. Thorp's gravesite in Richmond's River View Cemetery, May 2022. Peony blossom in front of the marker and nickel on top placed by the author. Photo by the author.

a passing fad which viewing patrons would soon tire of, and so he did not invest in theaters as moving picture houses until several years later after Thorp came to town.[2] Another bit of information which confuses issues regarding Thorp's initial investment in Richmond is the one which erroneously locates her first Dixie nickelodeon at 300 East Broad. Direct, primary source information indicates it was, rather, at 714 East Broad, the location of Wells' Colonial Theater. Her second Dixie, a "real" theater, was located at 18 West Broad at the intersection of Brook Road and Broad Street.[3]

The parting of ways between Thorp and her protégé Walter Coulter appears to have occurred suddenly at the end of their twenty-year relationship that theretofore had been extremely close. Though this biography generally makes the case that Thorp thought she was ready to retire and that's why she sold the Bluebird to him and he went his own way, there are other factors that might have been involved. These include Coulter's upcoming marriage which might have driven a wedge into the personal relationship between him and Thorp, a possible desire on Coulter's part to own theaters himself and to make his own decisions and reap his own profits, or a difference in opinion on how to finance future theaters (Coulter sold stock to raise cash but Thorp distrusted partnerships). Perhaps even the imminent return of Waldo could have caused problems between the two: it can be imagined that throughout the time Amanda knew Coulter, she had conflicted feelings about her relationships with the two men, one a faithful and enterprising employee, and the other, well, her son. Both Coulter and Waldo could have been resentful at the attentions she paid to the other, contributing to possible squabbles among them. No known documentation connects Thorp and Coulter after the time their association ended except that which was invoked in her allegations against the Wells organization pertaining to acquiring films for her Venus. Whatever the emotional fallout in the split between Thorp and Coulter, it may never be known.

Thorp's death was marked only by a three-paragraph obituary on page 3 in the *Richmond Times-Dispatch* which noted, "Movie House Owner to be Buried Today." She was survived by her son, Waldo, a sister, Mrs. Emma Hoodlet of Ohio, a brother, Stanley Baughman of Ohio, and a granddaughter, Mrs. Thelma Burnette of Charleston, West Virginia, who was Waldo's daughter with Della Baker.[4] The Associated Press, however, apparently also sent out a wire notice that was picked up by at least some Ohio papers. In it, it was reported that she had established the first motion picture theater in Richmond and had (allegedly) "amassed a fortune of more than half a million dollars."[5]

Waldo

Waldo, as his mother Amanda's heir, was likely anxious for the estate to settle, but as noted, it took a long time to resolve the many complicated issues with it. He and his wife Lulu lived in his mother's Duntreath home until at least February 1928, when Lulu died.[6] (Her death, incidentally, ended the brother-in-law [step] relationship between Waldo and Walter Coulter.) Six months later, Waldo married Elizabeth Broadnax of Richmond, likely eloping to Cumberland, Maryland, for this, his fifth (more or less) marriage. He was forty-one and she was twenty.

In 1930, he and Elizabeth lived in a home he claimed to own at 2222 Park Avenue in Richmond, likely purchased with proceeds following the probate of Thorp's will.[7] Waldo either blew the rest of his inheritance or he did not inherit as much as he thought he would once debts were paid, and then whatever remained of his fortune was further battered by the effects of the Great Depression. In July 1929, he opened a dance hall, Iona Park

Pavilion, about ten miles east of Richmond on Williamsburg Road, but it went bankrupt in September 1932.[8] In money trouble nearly constantly after his mother's death, Waldo wrote a series of alternately cloying and pleading letters to Charles Somma, who had already lent him money in the past that Waldo had not repaid. Somma refused to loan him any more. In Waldo's last letter to him, he begged Somma to give him a job of any kind and promised that he did not drink any more. Somma did not respond to Waldo's efforts to contact him once Waldo failed to repay the loan.[9]

Waldo died at age seventy-four on June 15, 1956. His obituary noted that he was a retired office manager for the O'Connor Vending Machine Company which had made news in 1952 because the owner was imprisoned for a five-year sentence on a conviction of federal income tax evasion.[10] Waldo was survived by his daughter, Thelma, then living in Richmond and married since 1940 to William Joseph Parsley, a Richmond native.[11] A graveside service was held for Waldo at Riverview Cemetery, where he is buried next to Amanda.[12] Thelma had no children, and so Amanda Thorp has no living descendants.

Walter Coulter

Coulter had been devotedly loyal to Amanda Thorp from 1905 (the approximate date when he met her in Bucyrus, Ohio) until at least 1926 when he bought, with Charles Somma, her Bluebird Theater franchise. By all accounts, he was a charming, gregarious, and popular man who, after he struck out on his own, appeared often as a man-about-town in society columns of the Richmond newspapers. His influence in the Richmond movie theater business and his financial fortunes increased quickly and dramatically after he left Thorp's employ.

Coulter and Somma added to their holdings in 1924 by building the $70,000, 574-seat, Brookland Theater in Richmond's Northside, putting into practice what they (likely mostly Coulter) had learned from Thorp—installing the latest innovations and flashy accoutrements to entice patrons. Of note at the Brookland Theater was the glass-fronted projection booth that allowed sidewalk passers-by to see the inner workings of showing a movie at the theater.[13] Their tour de force, however, was the 1928 construction of the $800,000, 1,600-seat Byrd Theatre on Cary Street, "one of the finest [movie] houses . . . in the South," where they upped their game from the use of first-class materials and current technology of the Brookland to even more luxurious materials and cutting-edge technology. Its modern

Fig. 48. Thorp's protégé Walter Coulter; photo taken ca. early 1920s. *RTD*, Jul. 14, 1929.

projection room was fully equipped with equipment to show pictures with sound (which had debuted in Richmond only the year before), it had the largest screen in Richmond, and it had a thousand-pipe organ, one of the three largest in the country. An elaborate chandelier hung in the auditorium and Italian marble was used in the lobby and other parts of the theater.[14] The lush Rococo interior included plasterwork resembling an Italian opera house.[15] For a while the lobby had a fountain, fed by natural springs that flow under the building.[16] The theater remarkably has remained largely intact through the decades and is still open to the public, showing movies and hosting weekly concerts on the original Wurlitzer that still rises dramatically out of the floor, being played by the organist as it does so.[17] Many accounts of the Byrd note its architectural references to grand movie palaces in New York, theaters Coulter would have seen with Thorp on their travels or that he would have seen while travelling there on Thorp's dime. Coulter and Somma were able to finance their very expensive ventures by creating charters and inviting investors.[18]

Shortly after the Byrd opened, Coulter bought out Somma's interest in all four theaters the two men had operated jointly: Thorp's old Bluebird theaters in Richmond and Petersburg, the Brookland Theater, and the Byrd.

He stayed friendly with Somma, however, joining forces with him in developing other popular cultural enterprises during and after 1933.[19] Coulter opened other Richmond movie theaters (none nearly as grand as the Byrd) but is particularly known for the Tantilla Gardens, a popular, extravagant dance hall at 3817 West Broad that operated from 1933–1967 and brought to Richmond nationally known entertainment figures such as Duke Ellington and his Orchestra. Coulter often contributed to charities by opening his theaters for benefit showings, and as he replaced organs in his theaters with instruments of newer technology, he donated the older ones to area churches.[20] He fought the city's censorship and laws closing businesses on Sunday (blue laws) and was known for the occasional eccentricity. In 1930, for instance, he ordered "20 feet" of (real) alligators from Florida which he placed in the Byrd Theatre lobby fountain, put them on view to the hundreds of daily moviegoers, and donated them two weeks later to the new Richmond zoo.[21] He was a member of national benevolent societies and active in their cultural and fund-raising events, whether they were held in his theater or not.[22] In 1936, he appears to have narrowly escaped possible prison time when he was indicted by a U.S. Grand Jury for income tax evasion. Excused due to alleged illness from appearing at some of the proceedings, a compromise that ended the ordeal was reached in June 1938 in which he paid a $42,000 ($885,000 in 2023) fine.[23]

Walter Coulter, at age fifty-four, died in Richmond's Stuart Circle Hospital at 1 am, May 18, 1943, of a probable stroke. His father, Mathew, died about three hours later the same day in Richmond but in the hospital at the Medical College of Virginia, of complications after an apparent fall and amid other indications of poor health. Walter's wife was with her husband at his death; his brother, Bob, was with their father (Walter and Bob's mother Sarah had died in 1930). Walter Coulter was buried on May 21, 1943, where his father was buried the day before, at Forest Lawn Cemetery in Richmond.

The *Richmond Times-Dispatch* reported on June 12, 1943, that Walter's estate was valued at $362,000 ($6.2 million in 2023); of that, most, of course, was left to his wife, but he also bequeathed $25,000 each to his brother and sister. His will directed the heirs to provide a suitable place for his father to live, but because their father was deceased, the estate instead paid for Mathew's burial expenses.[24]

In 1950, the families of the two Richmond theater magnates Walter Coulter and Charles Somma briefly united, when Walter's daughter Joyce married Charles' son Charles A. Somma, Jr. The marriage ended in divorce in 1958.[25]

Bob Coulter

Bob Coulter apparently did not possess his brother Walter's penchant for wheeling and dealing, and the fact that Walter left a bequest to him indicates that he had not experienced the same financial success in his career as his brother. When the Byrd Theatre opened in 1928, Bob became its manager, a post he filled for forty-three years until he retired in 1971 at age seventy-six. He trusted no one other than himself to shine the crystal of the auditorium's chandelier, and he intimately knew the workings of all the theater equipment, sometimes even repairing the Wurlitzer organ when necessary. By 1963, Virginia movie theaters, including those in Richmond, were beginning to desegregate, and the Byrd was no exception. Bob is said to be lovingly remembered by thousands of Richmond residents—hopefully by both races after that date—for his warm greetings at the theater door. With Bob as manager, parents were said to have trusted sending their children alone to the Byrd for the Saturday shows, as he knew all their names and where they would sit. His ghost is said to still oversee the building's care.[26]

Bob, eighty-two, died on January 27, 1978, of cerebral thrombosis and is buried at Forest Lawn Cemetery in Richmond.

Charles A. Somma

Charles A. Somma, a Richmond native, got his start in business in 1913 by taking over his father's ice cream shop located not far from Thorp's Dixie and Rex theaters. By 1915, at age twenty-five, Somma had bought the Dixie at Brook and Broad and continued to run both the family business and the Dixie until about 1917, when his father died and Charles either closed or sold the ice cream shop. In 1918, he married Caroline (Carrie) E. Rowe of Washington, D.C.[27]

After buying the Dixie and the Hippodrome theaters from Thorp, Somma continued to guide them through the early years of their heyday as venues for African American entertainers on the Black vaudeville circuit. Though there were other Blacks-only theaters owned and operated by African Americans nearby as well as on Hull Street across the river in Southside, the Hippodrome in particular continued to enjoy the most success, situated as it was in a choice location in the heart of Jackson Ward which was not only the center of Black commerce in Richmond but also important to Black commerce in the South. In September 1937, Somma leased the Hippodrome to

Fig. 49. Charles A. Somma in photo likely taken
in the mid-1930s. *RTD*, Sep. 4, 1936.

the theater chain of Washington, D.C., owned by Abe Lichtman, a prominent
Jewish man in the industry.[28] In October 1928, Somma installed a Vitaphone
projector at the theater, giving it the capability of showing "talkies." The
Hippodrome in Jackson Square today replaced Thorp's original structure
which was destroyed by fire in 1945; it can be rented as a private event space.

In a controversial move which generated many column inches of negative local press, in February 1927 Somma gained a controlling interest
in the Virginia State Fair Association as its majority stockholder. He was
largely forgiven for turning the formerly nonprofit organization into what
amounted to a moneymaking business by running it successfully and expanding its offerings.[29] In 1931, in an effort which won him accolades even
from those who still had sore feelings about his takeover of the state fair,
he rescued Richmond's Eastern League baseball club which, due to a lack
of capital, was at the brink of being moved to Portland, Maine.[30] He also
ran a trucking company for several years.[31] Somma was active in raising
money for many charitable causes through occasionally offering his venues
as sites for fundraising benefits. He stayed friends with Walter Coulter, occasionally partnering with him in the startup of new theaters, although none

were as grand as their Byrd Theatre. He died seven months after Coulter, on Christmas Day, 1943. His obituary noted many of his accomplishments, but erroneously reported that he had opened the Dixie Theater.[32]

Jake Wells

Born on August 9, 1867, in Memphis, Tennessee, Jake Wells was playing professional baseball by age 19, breaking into the major leagues in Detroit and St. Louis. In 1894, he ended up in Richmond, Virginia, as a player and manager with the city's minor league team, eventually assuming complete control over the franchises' affairs. As baseball evolved from a club activity to a mass-spectator sport, Wells became more interested in the entertainment business, moving into investing in traditional theater by opening in 1899 the 1,100-seat Bijou Theater in Richmond.[33] If Thorp did not know of Wells when she first came to Richmond, it would have taken little time for her to have learned about his status in the city's theatrical circle. She likely first met him when she rented the room at the Colonial from him for her first Dixie, and they would have have crossed paths often over the years, especially in their work with the exhibitors' associations. In addition to his work with theaters in Richmond, Wells became a regional powerhouse in the movie theater industry, by 1919 owning more than 30 theaters in several cities and states in the Southeast.[34] Though his later years were spent in North Carolina where he concentrated on real estate development, many Richmonders continued to consider him a favored native son. When, said to have been suffering from debilitating depression, he committed suicide in North Carolina at age sixty-three on March 16, 1927, his death generated front page banner headlines in the *Richmond Times-Dispatch*.

Charles Moseley

Charles Moseley had come to Richmond after being stymied at every turn in Atlanta while trying to make a living as a Black entrepreneur.[35] In early 1907, he took over management of Richmond's Northside Skating Rink,[36] located at the intersection of Jackson Ward's First and Charity streets, which initially had been opened in June 1906 by James Bahen, a White Irish immigrant and well-known Richmond City alderman; even under Bahen's management, the rink had always been for Black patronage only.[37]

Fig. 50. Today empty fields mark the site of Charles Moseley's bowling alley and later theater of the early 1900s. The image shows what happened to this part of a predominantly Black neighborhood which had once thrived as an area of homes and businesses but was divided in the late 1950s from the rest of Richmond by the building of Interstate 95. Photo by the author.

Moseley also opened other businesses nearby: a hotel (probably more like what might be thought of today as a boarding house), a café, and a saloon.[38] By September 1908, Moseley had closed down the skating rink and completely renovated it, using the space, which could seat about 1,400 people,[39] to show films, illustrated songs, and stage presentations, among other things. He called it the Globe Theater.[40] The same month, an ad appeared in the *Richmond Times-Dispatch* announcing the sale of the property by auction,[41] thus creating the conditions for the closure of the short-lived theater about a year later. Charles Moseley or his brother then took over a (likely formerly White) West Broad theater operating as the Orient, located only a couple of blocks west from Thorp's Dixie at Brook and Broad.[42] Charles Moseley's brother William then managed it as a Blacks-only theater re-named the Pekin, while Charles Moseley moved on to Norfolk and opened a successful Blacks-only theater there, also known as the Pekin, showing Black vaudeville acts and moving pictures.[43] By 1917, Moseley had moved on to Baltimore, once again opening a Blacks-only theater called the New Regent Theater.[44] That theater was sold in 1920.[45] It is unknown what happened to Charles Moseley after 1920.

Walter Klein

Little existing documentation is known for Walter Klein. Born 1869 in Richmond, his father was very active in Richmond's German immigrant community. In about 1888, Klein was working as a bookkeeper, probably at his father's tin shop.[46] City directories over the years show him working as a traveling salesman in the early 1910s, and in 1913, he was living with his parents at 1712 Hanover in Richmond's trendy (even then) "Fan" neighborhood in a 1910-built home. The fact that they owned the home in this up-and-coming neighborhood may indicate at least a degree of financial prosperity. By 1915, Walter Klein may have purchased a restaurant at 120 East Broad. He is shown as being an "agent" for an unknown company, a job that today probably would be called a sales representative, in the Richmond City Directory in 1917.[47] His wealth may have come at least partially from inheritance from his father's business. What became of him after the Bluebird Theater venture is unknown.

APPENDIX 1

*Films and Other Entertainments Shown at the Wonderland
in Bucyrus, Ohio, under Amanda Thorp's Ownership*

Source of information below is from the *Bucyrus Evening Telegraph*. The
dates are when the information appeared in the newspaper, but they generally precede the actual film by up to three days or so. The same films were
most often shown for three days in a row and then new films were brought
in. Thorp was sometimes unaware of what films she would be receiving, so
she would run ads saying a "surprise" was coming, or that there would be
a "complete change of program" but provide no other details. The names
of the films are as provided in the Bucyrus paper; there are likely inaccuracies. Many of these films are likely lost; however, the American Film
Institute Catalog (www.aficatalog.com) may provide additional information
on the individual films. When included in the ad, some other details about
the entertainment are included. The advertisements which appeared in the
Bucyrus paper for shows at the Wonderland changed in layout and tone
after the final date listed here, likely reflecting the Hart Brothers' influence
after Thorp left for Virginia.

DATE	FILMS OR OTHER ENTERTAINMENTS
1906: 08–22	*Love vs. Title* or *An Up-to-Date Elopement* and *The Angler's Dream.*
1906: 08–28	*Romance of a Gold Field* and *Funny Shave.*
1906: 09–08	*Trip through the Mining District.*
1906: 09–11	*Beware my Husband Comes* and *The Holiday.*
1906: 09–19	*The Love Letter, Angler's Dream, Love Fuller, Spontaneous Generation, A Frightful Night,* and *I Have Lost My Eyeglass.*
1906: 09–25	*Beware my Husband Comes, A Terrible Anguish,* and *The Watch Dog.*

DATE	FILMS OR OTHER ENTERTAINMENTS
1906: 10–02	*The Whole Dam Family* and *The Subpoena Service*.
1906: 10–09	*The Bigamist, The Lost Child,* and *The Holy City*.
1906: 10–16	*My Uncle's Testament* and *Escaped From Sing Sing*.
1906: 10–19	*The Art Committee, European Rest Cure,* and *The Robbers Robbed*.
1906: 10–23	*The Great Panorama of San Francisco*.
1906: 10–25	*Robbing his Majesty's Mail, The Deadwood Sleeper,* and *Dogs used as Smugglers*.
1906: 10–30	*The Miller's Daughter*.
1906: 11–02	*Child Stealers of Paris* and *A Winter Straw Ride*.
1906: 11–07	*The Lone Highwayman* and *Choosing a Servant*.
1906: 11–09	*Letters Which Speak* and *Nobody Works Like a Father*.
1906: 11–13	*American Boys*.
1906: 11–19	*The Danger of Carpet Beating, Mother-in-Law,* and *A Race for Bed*.
1906: 11–22	*Troubles of a Fireman* and *The Terrible Kids*.
1906: 12–03	*Strenusus [sic] Wedding* and *The Paris Students*.
1906: 12–07	*Automobile Thieves*.
1906: 12–11	*Love vs. Title* and *The Broken Idol*.
1906: 12–13	*Evil Day Miniature Theaters* and *Six Dragons*.
1906: 12–17	*100 to 1 Shot* and *The Tenant's Revenge*.
1906: 12–24	*Skyscrapers of New York* and *Madam Wears the Pants*.
1906: 12–20	*The Child's Revenge, Tit for Tat,* and *Cat with Nine Lives*.
1906: 12–24	*Skyscrapers of New York* and *Madam Wears the Pants*.
1906: 12–27	*The Fox Chase* and *Wonderful Bee Hive*.
1906: 12–31	*The Tramp Dog* and *The Deserter*. Illustrated song: "The Moon Has His Eyes on You."
1907: 01–03	*Dolly's Papa* and *Invisible Men*.
1907: 01–07	*Poisoned Fowl, Riderless Bicycle,* and *Midwinter Night's Dream*.
1907: 01–14	*Tom Removes* and *The Election*.
1907: 01–17	*The Female Highwayman*.
1907: 01–21	*A Voyage Round a Star, Soldier,* and the *Ingenious Dauber*.
1907: 01–24	*Who's Who* and *The Town Boys*.
1907: 01–28	*For Another's Crime* and *Please Help the Blind*.
1907: 02–01	*The Charmer* and *The Dream of the Race Track Fiend*.

DATE	FILMS OR OTHER ENTERTAINMENTS
1907: 02–04	*Trial Marriage* and *Dislocation.*
1907: 02–07	*Alice, Where Art Thou Going?*
1907: 02–11	*A Female Spy, Skating Lesson,* and *Pay Day.*
1907: 02–13	*A Female Spy, Payday,* and *The Skating Lesson.*
1907: 02–16	*The Old Masher* and *False Coiners.*
1907: 02–18	*Leaving Camp, The Village Cut Up,* and *Scales of Justice.*
1907: 02–21	*Officials, Smugglers, Bad Mother, Birthday Cake.*
1907: 02–28	*A Day in the Country* and *The Gypsy and the Knight.*
1907: 03–04	*When We Were Boys, Foxy Hobos,* and *Spot at the Telephone.*
1907: 03–07	*The Villain Still Pursued Her.*
1907: 03–11	*The Blind Girl* and *An Exciting Honeymoon.*
1907: 03–15	*Exciting Auto Race* or a *Race for Wife.*
1907: 03–19	*The Great International Cross Country* and *Hot Chestnuts.*
1907: 03–20	*Subordinate Hypnotizer, The Great International Cross-Country,* and *Hot Chestnuts.*
1907: 03–21	*A Venetian Tragedy, The Cab,* and *Burglars at Work.*
1907: 03–25	*The Sportsman, The Desperate Girl,* and *Casey's Dream.*
1907: 03–28	*The Bad Man* and *Among the Animals in the Zoological Gardens in New York.*
1907: 04–01	*Mr. Hurry-Up of New York* and *Determined Creditor.*
1907: 04–04	*Japanese Sports* and *A Wrestler's Wife.*
1907: 04–08	*Young Apple Thieves* and *Niagara Falls.*
1907: 04–11	*Magic Flute* and *Troublesome Flea.*
1907: 04–15	A show on the Thaw murder consisting of 62 slides divided into the following five sets: No. 1 *Evelyn Nesbit, Young Model* No. 2 *Blackbird Pie* No. 3 *The Millionaire's Pet* No. 4 *Courtship with Thaw* No. 5 *Shooting of White and Thaw in Prison* Next moving pictures: *The Cruise of the Gladys.*
1907: 04–19	*Humorous Phases of Funny Faces* and *The Pay Master.*
1907: 04–23	Films for the *Passion Play* were ordered but they did not arrive on time.
1907: 04–25	*A Difficult Arrest, Cavalry School,* and *The Determined Creditor.*
1907: 04–27	*Scenes of a Military Prison.*

DATE	FILMS OR OTHER ENTERTAINMENTS
1907: 04–30	*Wonderful Flames* and *Dog Catcher.*
1907: 05–03	*Picturesque Canada* and *From Jealousy to Madness.* Illustrated song: "When You Know You're Not Forgotten by the Girl You Can't Forget," sung by Miss Lucy Holm. Hart Brothers orchestra tonight from seven until ten. Tomorrow night's film: *A Nurse Wanted.*
1907: 05–06	*The Paper Factory* and *Truants.* Illustrated song: "Nobody's Little Girl."
1907: 05–09	*Mephisto's Son*, a hand-colored film.
1907: 05–11	Prof. Lloyd T. Hart will play all the latest hits of the season on the new piano. Miss Lucy Halm will sing the illustrated song, "Daddy's Little Girl."
1907: 05–14	*Marriages on Bicycles* and *Fights of All Nations.* There will be an entire change of program on Wednesday including the illustrated song, "Don't Cry Katie Dear," sung by Mr. Newman Browarsky, accompanied by Prof. Lloyd Hart on the piano.
1907: 05–15	*Climbing the Alps.*
1907: 05–17	*All for a Necklace, Transformation*, and *A Runaway Motor Car.*
1907: 05–20	*Cinderella* or *The Glass Slipper.* Illustrated song: "Somebody's Waiting for You" sung by Newman Browarsky accompanied by Prof. Earl P. Hart.
1907: 05–23	*On the Brink* and *The Electric Belt.* Illustrated song: "Star Bright" sung byNewman Browarsky accompanied by Prof. Earl P. Hart.
1907: 05–28	*The Bandit King.*
1907: 05–30	*Black Beauty* and *The Fishing Industry.* Song: "Love me and the World is Mine."
1907: 05–31	*The Pirate's Treasure is Mine.* Song: "Love me and the World is Mine" sung by Mr. James Kirk.
1907: 06–04	*The Seaside in London, At the Show*, and *Billiard Fiend.*
1907: 06–06	*Daniel Boone.* Illustrated song: "Fanella." *Passion Play* film delayed by distributor.
1907: 06–08	*Night Duty* or *Experiences of a Policeman, Willie's Day in the Country*, [and] *Peasant Girl's Revenge* or *Peasant's Life in Russia.*
1907: 06–10	*Forty Winks*, or a *Strenuous Dream* and *The Joys of Tight Boots.*

DATE	FILMS OR OTHER ENTERTAINMENTS
1907: 06–13	*The Caribou Hunt.*
1907: 06–14	*The Girl from Montana.* Illustrated song: "Little Dolly Driftwood." "*Passion of Christ* . . . will arrive in Bucyrus, Monday, June 17, and will run for one week."
1907: 06–17	*Passion Play.* [The ad listed these scenes would be shown: "Wedding Feast, where He changes water to wine; Mary Magdalene at the feet of Jesus, and His gracious forgiveness, followed by Jesus and the woman of Samaria;" also "the restoring of the dying daughter of Jarius" and "Jesus walking on the surface of the troubled waters of the sea, the draught of fishes, . . . and the raising of Lazarus."]
1907: 06–19	*Passion Play.* [The ad noted that the night's showing would be divided into seven parts: Calvary, Christ Put on the Cross, Agony and Death of Christ, Christ Taken from the Cross, Christ Placed in the Tomb, The Resurrection and The Ascension.]
1907: 06–20	*Passion Play.* [The ad noted it was the first part of the showings.]
1907: 06–21	*Passion Play.* [Comments from the ad: "Second reel of film of the Passion Play tonight. The third and fourth reels Saturday afternoon and evening."]
1907: 06–24	*To Tame His Wife* and *A Brigand Story.*
1907: 06–28	*The Kidnapped Child.*
1907: 07–02	*The Terrorist's Remorse.*
1907: 07–03	*The Village Celebration.*
1907: 07–06	*The Squatter's Daughter* and *The Green Dragon.*
1907: 07–09	*Picturesque Japan* and the *Passion Play.* Comments from the ad: "We cannot say no. We cannot, will not turn a deaf ear to the urgent request of our numerous patrons so we have decided to repeat the *Passion Play* along with our regular show. All this week."
1907: 07–10	*A Visit to the Dentist* and second reel of the *Passion Play.*
1907: 07–16	*The Corsican's Daughter.*
1907: 07–19	*A Horse of Another Color.* Illustrated song: "While the Old Mill Wheel is Turning."
1907: 07–24	*The Boar Hunt* and *Fun in the Bakery.*
1907: 07–31	*The Mountaineer's Home.* Illustrated song: "Thelma."
1907: 08–05	*A Slave's Love.*

DATE	FILMS OR OTHER ENTERTAINMENTS
1907: 08–06	*Trip Through the Alps.*
1907: 08–08	*Pompeii, Baby's Outing* and *A Roar.* Illustrated song: "Bye Bye, Fly Caroline."
1907: 08–09	*Farmers Making Bread.* Illustrated song: "There is Room in My Heart for You."
1907: 08–14	*The Revenge* and *The Seaman's Widow*, with special orchestra music. Illustrated song: "In Dear Old Fairy Land."
1907: 08–15	*The Modern Pirate* and *Wanted, 10,000 Eggs.*
1907: 08–21	*Rocksniff Fetches the Doctor* and *Police Dogs.* Song: "I Wouldn't Change Your Sweetheart for a New Girl Now."
1907: 08–21	Performance by Newman Browarsky, the Bucyrus "German Jewish" comedian and four-piece orchestra (probably the Hart Brothers).

APPENDIX 2

Films and Other Entertainments Shown at the Dixie Theater
at Brook and Broad, Richmond, Virginia, in 1908,
Before Becoming a Black-Only Patronized Theater

Sources of the information below are Dixie advertisements in the *Richmond Evening Journal*. The dates are when the information appeared in the newspaper, but they generally precede the actual film by up to three days or so. The names of the films are as provided in the Richmond paper; there are likely inaccuracies. Many of these films are likely lost; however, the American Film Institute Catalog (www.aficatalog.com) may provide additional information on the individual films. When included in the ad, some other details about the entertainments are provided. The dates span the earliest known shows when the Dixie at Brook and Broad opened in May 1908 through November 1908, which is when the Dixie is thought to have converted to all-Black patronage and began to change the offerings to better appeal to its then African American audience.

DATE OF NEWSPAPER	FILMS OR OTHER ENTERTAINMENTS
1908–0516	*Great Paris Fire Scene* and illustrated songs.
1908–0525	*My Uncle's Bulldog* and *The Animated Clock*. Illustrated song: "In Old Rhode Island Fire Away."
1908–0528	*The Merry Widow.*
1908–0602	*Circus Boy* and *Tale of the Pig*. Illustrated song: "Sweethearts May Come, Sweethearts May Go."
1908–0604	*A Lover's Hazing* and *The Rivals* with illustrated song.
1908–0610	*Oberammergau, the Passion Play*. 5,500 feet of film, hand-colored. Special today: San Juan and other moving pictures. Illustrated Song: "When Dreaming Dream of Me."

DATE OF NEWSPAPER	FILMS OR OTHER ENTERTAINMENTS
1908–0616	*Passion Play.* Also, the film and song, Holy City.
1908–0728	*Gans-Nelson Fight.*
1908–0729	*Gans-Nelson Fight* and *A Crime in the Mountains.*
1908–0801	*Damon and Pythias* (3,000 feet of film)
1908–0807	*Gans-Nelson Fight* and *It Smells of Smoke* with the comedy song, "Wait for Me at the Mulberry Tree."
1908–0826	*Nero* or *The Burning of Rome.*
1908–0828	*The Red Man and the Child.*
1908–0829	*Bluebirds* (1,000 feet of film, hand-colored).
1908–0912	*The Gambler's Fate*
1908–0929	*Cinderella* or *The Glass Slipper.*
1908–1130	*Barbara Fritchie* or *The Patriotic American Woman.* Special music.

APPENDIX 3

Black Vaudeville Acts at the Richmond, Virginia,
Dixie Theater, under Amanda Thorp's Ownership

Much of the following information about the Dixie's vaudeville schedule originated in the *Indianapolis Freeman* (Indianapolis, Indiana) (*IF*) weekly newspaper, on the dates indicated. The *Freeman* billed itself as "an illustrated colored newspaper" and was national in scope, particularly in its coverage of Black theater news. Another common source of the acts playing at the Dixie was the *New York Age* (New York) (*NYA*), an African American newspaper that also covered some national theater news. The names of the acts are listed here, although lack of punctuation in original lists made it difficult to discern them individually; this may have created errors in the names of some of the acts. Other possible errors have been left as they originally appeared in the newspapers. When information about the performers could be located, it is provided; however, many of the performers and the acts they performed are unknown today. Richmond's local African American newspaper, the *Planet* (*RP*), did not generally cover the offerings of the Dixie during this time period. (To address potential questions, it is noted here that Richmond natives who became famous Black vaudevillians and actors, notably Bill "Bojangles" Robinson and Charles Sidney Gilpin, had left Richmond to make their fortunes in New York and other large cities before Thorp arrived in Richmond and did not perform in Thorp's theaters. The same is true for Aida Overton Walker who is sometimes claimed to be from Richmond.)

DATE OF NEWSPAPER	ACTS
1910: 02–12	**The Clarks** Charles H. and Alberta E.—magician duo. Source: *BiB*, which published the text of an *IF* newspaper article on this date; the original newspaper article cannot be located.

DATE OF NEWSPAPER	ACTS
1910: 03–19	**Bradford and Bradford** Perry and Jeanette, husband and wife team—singing, dancing, and talking Source: *BiB*, which published the text of an *IF* newspaper article which appeared on this date; the original newspaper article cannot be located.
1910: 03–28	**Ben Cooper and Lightning Smith of the Dixie Stock Company** Source: *RP*.
1910: 03–31	**The Orrs** Source: *NYA*.
1910: 09–08	**Jeff de Mont** Jeff DeMont—comedy sketches, banjo Source of act playing: *NYA*; about the act: *BiB*.
1910: 12–17	**The Two Johnsons** Leona L. and Billy B.—singing, eccentric dancing. Source of act playing: *IF*; about the act: *BiB*. Article noted the Johnsons had been at the Dixie for thirteen weeks and would be there until the end of the year.
1911: 09–16	**Harry Brooks** Source: *IF*.
1911: 10–19	**Maggie Dixon** Source: *NYA*.
1911: 11–11	**The Jolly Hendersons** Billy and Beulah. Billy Henderson—singing [Beulah, unknown] Source of act playing: *IF*; about the act: *BiB*.
1912: 05–30	**Susie Sutton** character monologues Source of act playing: *NYA*; about the act: *BiB*.
1912: 06–29	**T. Spencer Finley** comedy Source of act playing: *IF*; about the act: *BiB*.
1912: 07–20	**E. Pugh and James A Lillard in their Texas Tommy act with Lizzie B. Pugh and Ethel B. Lillard** James Lillard and wife Ethel were singers. Source of acts playing: *IF*; about the act: *BiB*.

DATE OF NEWSPAPER	ACTS
1912: 07–20	**Johnnie Woods, [illegible], Minor and Minor** Johnnie (also spelled Johnny) Woods—ventriloquism, singing. His ventriloquist puppet was named Henry. Minor and Minor (husband/wife duo, names: Coleman and Ruby E.)—singing, talking Source of acts playing: *IF*; about the act: *BiB*.
1912: 07–27	**Robinson and White, Eleanor Wilson, George Harris** Eleanor Wilson—singing George Harris—musical comedy Source of acts playing: *IF*; about the act: *BiB*.
1912: 08–03	**Seminole Quartet, Love and Love, Leon** Seminole Quartet—singing (J. E. Loomis, first tenor; T. Francois, tenor; J. Bangers, baritone; W. Long, bass) Leon—magician and ventriloquist Source of acts playing: *IF*; about the acts other than Leon: *BiB*; about Leon, *NYA*, Aug. 1, 1912.
1912: 08–10	**Griffin Sisters, Lillian Bradford, The Great Mathews** Griffin Sisters—comedy, singing Source of acts playing: *IF*; about the act: *BiB*.
1912: 08–17	**Harris and Turner, Mme. Eva La Rhue, Miss Bessie Brown** Eva LaRhue—singing Miss Bessie Brown—singing Source of acts playing: *IF*; about the act: *BiB*.
1912: 08–24	**Mme. Fairfax, Billy Cumby, Ora Criswell** Billy Cumby—singing, comedy Ora Criswell—singing, comedy Source of acts playing: *IF*; about the act: *BiB*.
1912: 09–07	**King and Gee, Joe Sandifer, Charles Huggins** King and Gee (Lottie Gee and Effie King) - singing Joe Sandifer—comedy Source of acts playing: *IF*; about the act: *BiB*.
1912: 09–14	**Buster and Rockpile, Mazie Bush and Claude Williams** Buster and Rockpile—comedy, singing Source of acts playing: *IF*; about the act: *BiB*.
1912: 10–12	**Brown and Brown** husband and wife—singing Source of act playing: *IF*; about the act: *BiB*.

DATE OF NEWSPAPER	ACTS
1912: 11–02	**Peat and Hayes, Latimore Dixon, Jean Kelly** Peat and Hayes—singing and dancing Source of acts playing: *IF*; about the act: *BiB*.
1912: 11–09	**Howard and Mason, Lillian Brown, Dinslow and Dinslow** Howard and Mason—dancing Lillian Brown—singing Source of acts playing: *IF*; about the act: *BiB*.
1912: 11–30	**Davis and Rector, Nash and Carwell** Source: *IF*.
1912: 12–07	**Jeff DeMont, The Arntes** Jeff DeMont—comedy sketches, banjo The Arntes—husband and wife: Billy and Grace; singing and dancing Source of acts playing: *IF*; about the act: *BiB*.
1912: 12–14	**Whitman Sisters, Toy Comedians** Whitman Sisters (Alberta, Alice, Mabel, and Essie)— singing, dancing Source of acts playing: *IF*; about the act: *BiB*.
1912: 12–28	**Robinson and White, Miss Loretta and Company** Source: *IF*.
1913: 01–25	**King Williams, U. S. Thompson, Gertrude Williams** King Williams—"educated dogs" animal act, comedy sketches U. S. (Ulysses S.) Thompson—dancing, jokes Gertrude Williams (may have been King's wife and may have helped with the dog act)—singing, dancing Source of acts playing: *IF*; about the act: *BiB*.
1913: 02–22	**The Mississippi Trio with Tom Delaney** singing, dancing Source of act playing: *IF*; about the act: *BiB*.
1913: 02–22	**Stone and Stone, Bud Minus** Stone and Stone—comedy sketches Source of acts playing: *IF*; about the act: *BiB*.
1913: 03–01	**Molloy and Molloy, special pictures** Molloy and Molloy—singing Source of act playing: *IF*; about the act: *BiB*.
1913: 03–08	**Crampton and Banks, Cary and Cary** (Crampton may be the same individual as in the act Crampton and Bailey, who were singers and comedians.) Source of acts playing: *IF*; about the act: *BiB*.

DATE OF NEWSPAPER	ACTS
1913: 03–15	**Robinson and Randall, Leona Marshall** Leona Marshall—singing Source of acts playing: *IF*; about the act: *BiB*.
1913: 04–05	**Brown and DuMont, Susie Sutton** Brown and Dumont—singing, dancing Susie Sutton—singing, comic monologue Source of acts playing: *IF*; about the act: *BiB*.
1913: 04–19	**Peat and Hayes, Daisy Collins** Daisy Collins—singing, dancing Source of acts playing: *IF*; about the act: *BiB*.
1913: 04–26	**The Pewees, the Mills Sisters** Pewees (Charles and Sadie)—singing Mills Sisters (Florence, Olivia, and Maude Mills)—singing Source of acts playing: *IF*; about the act: *BiB*.
1913: 05–03	**Easton and Easton, The [illegible]** Easton and Easton—comedy Source of acts playing: *IF*; about the act: *BiB*.
1913: 05–10	**Florence Brooks, Russell and Caldwell** Source: *IF*.
1913: 05–17	**Closed on account of fire regulations** Source: *IF*.
1913: 06–14	**Spencer Finley and Carwell and Mason** Source: *IF*.
1913: 07–05	**Harris and Turner, Sam Davis** Source: *IF*.
1913: 07–26	**Watts and Turner, C. Hannibal Coffey** C. Hannibal Coffey—comedian Source of acts playing: *IF*; about the act: *BiB*.
1913: 07–26	**Wilson, Goff, Kitty Berry** Kitty Berry [possibly Catherine Berry]—singing Source of acts playing: *IF*; about the act: *BiB*.
1913: 08–09	**Leigh Whipler, Gertrude King** Leigh Whipler—monologue Gertrude King—singing Source of acts playing: *IF*; about the act: *BiB*.
1913: 08–11	**Frazier Brothers, Dancing Darrell** Source: *IF*.

DATE OF NEWSPAPER	ACTS
1913: 08–23	**Johnson and Johnson** singing, dancing Source of acts playing: *IF*; about the act: *BiB*.
1913: 09–06	**Perryman and Stiles, Eddie Daye** Eddie Daye—"The Boneless Wonder," contortionist Source of acts playing: *IF*; about the act: *BiB*.
1913: 09–06	**Burton and Bumbry** Source: *IF*.
1913: 09–13	**Jines and Hill, Jesse Brown** Jines and Hill (Henry Jines and Lula Hill)—comedy Source of acts playing: *IF*; about the act: *BiB*.
1913: 09–20	**Burton and Bumbry, Percy Harris** Source: *IF*.
1913: 09–27	**Stock company** Source: *IF*.
1913: 10–04	**Stock company, Stewart and Brown, Barton and Bumbry** Source: *IF*.
1913: 10–11	**Stock company** Source: *IF*.
1913: 12–06	**Earl Bolton Stock Company** In the company: Helen Bumbray, Maggie Dixon, Lena Wilson, Mrs. McNeal, Earl Burton, London Johns, and Joseph N. Fauntleroy. They were accompanied by musicians Jorand Beasley and William Beasley. Source: *RP*.
1914: 02–07	**Owens and Owens, Green and Pugh** Green and Pugh—comedy Source of acts playing: *IF*; about the act: *BiB*.
1914: 02–14	**Smith and Jones** Source: *IF*.
1914: 03–07	**Hill Sisters** Source: *IF*.
1914: 03–21	**Hill Sisters** Source: *IF*.
1914: 03–21	**George and Nana Coleman** George Coleman—comedy Source of act playing: *IF*; about the act: *BiB*.

DATE OF NEWSPAPER	ACTS
1914: 04–25	**Seals and Fisher, Jake Hellan** Seals and Fisher (Baby Seals and Baby Fisher)—singing, comedy Source of acts playing: *IF*; about the act: *BiB*.
1914: 10–03	**Scott and Simmons, Henry Jones** Scott and Simmons—comedy, singing Source of acts playing: *IF*; about the act: *BiB*.
1914: 10–24	**Terry and Terry, Hugh Turner** Terry and Terry—singing Source of act playing: *IF*; about the act: *BiB*.
1914: 10–31	**Henrick and Lee** Source of act playing: *IF*; about the act: *BiB*.

APPENDIX 4

Known Theaters (Including Storefronts) of Amanda Thorp

The end date of the theaters in this index is the date when Thorp sold the theater (the theater may have continued operation under the same or different name) or when other information indicates that it was no longer in Thorp's portfolio. Some secondary sources indicate that Thorp owned the Theato theater in Richmond, but this is inaccurate. Similarly, no primary-source evidence can be found to support secondary-source information that she had a theater in Charlottesville, Virginia. Still other secondary sources say that she had a theater in Cleveland, Ohio, but that, too, is unlikely. Sources and other details for the information in this appendix, which is meant to serve as a summary, are provided in endnotes to the book text where the information originally appears.

START DATE	END DATE	THEATER/STOREFRONT
Aug. 1906	late 1907 or early 1908	Established the store-front **Wonderland Theater** on Sandusky Avenue in Bucyrus, Ohio. Sold to the Hart Brothers in late 1907 or early 1908. A leased space.
possibly late 1906	possibly early 1908	Likely a storefront (name unknown) located in Washington Court House, Ohio. A leased space.
4 May 1907	ca. May 1908	**Dixie** in a room (storefront) at the Colonial Theater traditional playhouse at 714 East Broad in Richmond. Leased the space from Jake Wells.
Nov. 1907	late 1907– early 1908	**New Wonderland,** probable storefront, 1435 Hull Street in Richmond. A leased space.

START DATE	END DATE	THEATER/STOREFRONT
likely late 1907	Oct. 6, 1908	**Wonderland** (probable storefront) in Newport News. This likely was in Thorp's portfolio, but evidence is circumstantial. Would have been a leased space.
likely late 1907	likely 1909	**Wonderland** (probable storefront) in Norfolk. This was likely in Thorp's portfolio, but evidence is circumstantial. It is known that Thorp did have a theater in Norfolk at this time, which was managed by Walter Coulter sometime after February 1908, but it might have had another name. Would have been a leased space.
May 1908	early 1915	**Dixie Theater** at 18 West Broad in Richmond. Permanent theater with theater seating bolted to floor. Early photo and articles show capacity of 100, city directory of 1915 shows capacity as 250. A leased space. Originally an all-White theater, it was converted to all-Black patronage probably around November 1908. Charles Somma was advertising in the *Indianapolis Freeman* as proprietor of the Dixie by February 13, 1915.
Nov. 1908	ca. 1915	**Rex Theater** at 7th and Broad in Richmond, 1915. Date sold is unknown but city directory shows new owner by 1916. Seating capacity 250 people. Thorp leased the building, but it was purpose-built as a movie theater likely under her close supervision.
May 1909	Sept. 1909	**Airdome** seasonal open-air theater at Idlewood Amusement Park in Richmond. Leased space from Jake Wells.
1909	unknown, but likely only months	**Cockade Theater** in Petersburg, Virginia. The theater was likely a storefront in a leased space.

START DATE	END DATE	THEATER/STOREFRONT
ca. Mar. 1913	May 15, 1916	Thorp bought the property for the **Hippodrome Theater** on 26 July 1912. The theater was built to Thorp's specifications and opened by 15 March 1913 when the *Indianapolis Freeman* noted acts there. Sold to Charles Somma on 15 May 1916. Seating capacity 700. (The theater space which is today known as the Hippodrome at this location is not the original one built by Thorp; after burning down in 1945, it was rebuilt as the current structure.)
Mar. 2, 1917	Dec. 7, 1923	Thorp and Walter Klein open the **Bluebird Theater** at 620 East Broad in Richmond. The theater was built to Thorp's specifications; Thorp and Klein owned both the theater and the building. Seating capacity 700. It was sold to Charles A. Somma and Walter Coulter on 7 December 1923.
Sept. 1919	Dec. 7, 1923	Thorp and Walter Klein open **Bluebird Theater** in Petersburg, Virginia, likely in a storefront. It is not known if Thorp and Klein owned the building, but probably not. It was sold to Charles A. Somma and Walter Coulter on 7 December 1923.
Mar. 7, 1924	ca. 1925	Thorp owns the **Shirley Theater** by this time, having bought it from Jake Wells; the building was leased from Jake Wells. Last known mention in the newspaper as a theater appears in *RTD* ad published on 13 May 1925.
Mar. 18, 1925	Jul. 1926	Thorp opens **Venus Theater**. She sells the theater to Goldberg and Rosser in July 1926.
Nov. 1925	owned at the time of her death in 1927	Thorp buys **Victor Theater** from Jake Wells; the building was leased from Jake Wells.

APPENDIX 5

*Black Vaudeville, Benefits, or Speakers at the Hippodrome Theater,
Richmond, Virginia, under Amanda Thorp's Ownership*

Much of the following information about the Hippodrome's vaudeville
schedule originated in the *Indianapolis Freeman* (Indianapolis, Indiana)
(*IF*) weekly newspaper, on the dates indicated. The *Richmond Planet* (*RP*)
also covered some shows at the Hippodrome either in ads or in articles,
particularly when they were deemed particularly important. An effort has
been made to list the names of groups where lack of punctuation in original
lists made it difficult to discern them; this may have created errors in the
names of some of the acts. Other possible errors have been left as printed
in the original sources. When information about the performers could be
located, it is provided; however, many of the performers and the acts they
performed are unknown today. An * denotes acts in this appendix which
also had performed at the Dixie and are described in Appendix 3. Thorp
sold the Hippodrome to Charles Somma on May 15, 1916. See bibliography
for other abbreviations used.

DATE OF NEWSPAPER	ACTS
1913: 03–15	Minstrels, the Griffin Sisters* Source: *IF.*
1913: 04–05	"Four big acts," the Griffin Sisters Source: *IF.*
1913: 04–05	Annual spring festival of the Society Minstrels. Appearing: Lemuel Eggleston, George Johnson, Andrew Bowler, Ben Deane, Arthur Dyson, Chit White, Dave Alexander, the Acca Four, and Harmony Quartet. Charles T. (Gippy) Smith was to perform the ragtime hit, "Will Hard Luck Follow Me all my Days?" which was to be sung by George Johnson. Ben Deane was to sing "I Wonder if She Thinks of Me?" Source: *RP.*

DATE OF NEWSPAPER	ACTS
1913: 04–05	An ad for "Minstrels." The ad noted there would be "40 natural black faces"—in other words, the Black performers would not be applying blackface. Tickets for the show were twenty-five cents to $1. Source: *RNL*.
1913: 04–19	Griffin Sisters, Pewees,* Morton and Allen Source: IF.
1913: 04–26	Griffin Sisters, Claybrooks, and Howard and Mason Claybrooks (Alfonso and Jennie)—novel musical act Howard and Mason—dancing Source of acts playing: *IF*; about the acts: *BiB*.
1913: 05–03	Easton and Easton,* The [illegible] Source of acts playing: *IF*; about the acts: *BiB*.
1913: 05–10	The Russells, Porter and Dewey, Original Rags, Means and Means The Russells (Joseph and Amanda)—singing, talking, dancing Porter and Dewey (Dewey's first name was Billy)—comedy, songs Original Rags (Arthur Wollings)—songs, monologue Means and Means—chair balancers and magic Source of acts playing: *IF*; about the acts: *BiB*.
1913: 05–10	Special benefit performance for the Knights of Pythias to benefit Eureka Company No. 1, Planet Company No. 8, and the Municipal Band. Source: *RP*.
1913: 05–17	The Russells, Haynes Dog and Pony Show Source: *IF*.
1913: 05–31	Boss and Radcliffe, the Andersons, Hackless and Christian Source: *IF*.
1913: 06–14	The Brinkleys, Alberta Whitman and Picks, The Three Sunbeams, Herbert Chadwick The Brinkleys (David and Daisy)—dancing, singing Alberta Whitman and Picks—singing, possibly male impersonation Source of acts playing: *IF*; about the acts: *BiB*.
1913: 06–21	The Marshalls, Spencer Finley, Blanche Thompson (There were two groups known as the Marshalls; it is not known which is intended here.) Source of acts playing: *IF*.

DATE OF NEWSPAPER	ACTS
1913: 06–28	The Miller Family, Madame Pam Wells, "Chicken Reel" Beaman Miller Family—singing, dancing "Chicken Reel" Beaman—singing, dancing Source of acts playing: *IF*; about the acts: *BiB*.
1913: 07–05	Criswell* and Bailey, William Willis, Bougia and Livingston Source: *IF*.
1913: 07–12	Watts and Turner, Bougia and Livingston, Lillian Brown Source: *IF*.
1913: 07–26	Martin and Chenault, Michaels and Michaels, Anita Gonzoley Michaels and Michaels (Dan and Emma)—singing, dancing Source of acts playing: *IF*; about the acts: *BiB*.
1913: 07–26	Miller and Bigeou, Sellman and Jones, Sam Davis Miller and Biegou (Irvine Miller and Esther Bigeou)—singing, comedy Sellman and Jones—comedy sketches Sam Davis—monologues, singing Source of acts playing: *IF*; about the acts: *BiB*.
1913: 08–09	Henderson and Henderson, John Cooper, Stewart Brothers John Cooper—ventriloquist Stewart Brothers—singing, comedy, dancing Source of acts playing: *IF*; about the acts: *BiB*.
1913: 08–11	Three Dancing Imps, Lillard and Lillard,* Alice Ramsey The Three Dancing Imps was a girls act. Source of acts playing: *IF*; about the acts: *BiB*.
1913: 08–23	The Stewart Brothers, Seminole Quartet,* Smith and Baker Source: *IF*.
1913: 09–06	John Wolds, Russell and Russell, Brown and Harris Brown and Harris (Bessie Brown and Estelle Harris)—singing, dancing Source of acts playing: *IF*; about the acts: *BiB*.
1913: 09–06	Allen and Morton, Elnora Wilson, Taylor and Taylor Allen and Morton—singing, comedy [There were two groups known as Taylor and Taylor; it is not known which is intended here.] Source of acts playing: *IF*; about the acts: *BiB*.

DATE OF NEWSPAPER	ACTS
1913: 09–13	Nicholas and Logan, Thomas and Ward, Neil Matthews Thomas and Ward ("Kid H." Thomas and Marguerite Ward)—dancing Neil Matthews (the "Whistling Rube")— whistling, old man specialty Source of acts playing: *IF*; about the acts: *BiB*.
1913: 09–20	The Clippers, Dancing Darrell,* King and Gee* The Clippers (Jesse and Della)—singing Source of acts playing: *IF*; about the acts: *BiB*.
1913–09–27	Allen and Morton, Elnora Wilson, Stewart and Brown Source: *IF*.
1913: 09–27	Dr. F. T. McFaden speaking at the Hippodrome under the auspices of the Young Men's League of the Third Street A.M.E. Church. Source: *RP*.
1913: 10–04	Deloyes and Jeffries, Tyler and Girwood, Robinson and Robinson Deloyes and Jeffries are also spelled Delyons and Jeffrey Source: *IF*.
1913: 10–11	Brown Girls, A. W. Williams, Brooks and Bowen A. W. Williams—singing, talking, comedy Source of acts playing: *IF*; about the acts: *BiB*.
1913: 10–18	Edgington and Butler, Buster and Rockpile,* Baby Mack Baby Mack—singing Source of acts playing: *IF*; about the acts: *BiB*.
1913: 10–25	Majestic Trio, Billy Cumby,* Bessie Edgington Majestic Trio—singing, dancing Bessie Edgington—singing, dancing, comedy Source of acts playing: *IF*; about the acts: *BiB*.
1913: 11–01	Buster and Rockpile, Johnson and Baylor, Seals and Fisher,* Mack Allen Johnson and Baylor—comedy Mack Allen—tightwire and slack-wire artist Source of acts playing: *IF*; about the acts: *BiB*.
1913: 11–08	Washburn and Piper, Martin and Motley, Seals and Fisher Washburn and Piper—singing, comedy Martin and Motley—follies, comedy Source of acts playing: *IF*; about the acts: *BiB*.
1913: 11–15	Burton and Robinson, Huggins and Cox, Lester McDaniels Burton and Robinson—singing, comedy Source of acts playing: *IF*; about the acts: *BiB*.

DATE OF NEWSPAPER	ACTS
1913: 11–22	Stovall and Stovall, Murphy and Walker, J. C. Priedgeon Stovall and Stovall (Martin and Motley)—singing, comedy Source of acts playing: *IF*; about the acts: *BiB*.
1913: 11–29	The Woodens, The Burtons, H. H. Puggsley The Woodens—bicycle and unicycle artists The Burtons ("Buzzin'" Wayne and Ebbie)—comedy Source of acts playing: *IF*; about the acts: *BiB*.
1913: 12–06	Abyssinian Trio, Brooks and Robinson, Senator Campbell Abyssinian Trio (Gertrude Jones Maude Brown, Olive Ellison)—singing, comedy Brooks and Robinson—singing, dancing Source of acts playing: *IF*; about the acts: *BiB*.
1913: 12–13	Gilliam and Cooke, H. H. Puggsley, Perrin and Blank, Edna Barrett Source: *IF*.
1913: 12–13	Rev. James E. Churchman on his way to Richmond to preach at the Hippodrome, was removed from the train for refusing to comply with orders from officials to move from his paid first-class accommodations to a separate train car reserved for "colored people." Source: *RP*.
1913: 12–20	S. H. Dudley and Company, Cecil Watts, The Butlers The Butlers (Gus E. and Trixie)—singing, dancing Source of acts playing: *IF*; about the acts: *BiB*.
1913: 12–27	Jones and Gray, Brown and Brown,* Lewis and Jones Jones and Gray—singing, talking, dancing Lewis and Jones—singing Source of acts playing: *IF*; about the acts: *BiB*.
1914: 01–08	Murphy and Walker, Lillard and Lillard,* Carrie Anderson Source: *IF*.
1914: 01–17	The Colemans,* Murphy and Walker, Burt Kenneth Source: *IF*.
1914: 01–24	Perrin and Crosby, Hendricks and Lee Perrin and Crosby—comedy sketches, singing Source of acts playing: *IF*; about the acts: *BiB*.
1914: 02–07	Chadwick and Crippen, King Williams, Spencer Finley Source: *IF*.
1914: 02–14	Criswell and Bailey, Filey and Philipp, Frank Dike Source: *IF*.

DATE OF NEWSPAPER	ACTS
1914: 02–24	Biblical Story of Satan [apparent local production] being staged for the benefit of the Home School for Delinquent Colored Girls Source: *RTD.*
1914: 02–28	Maude Jones, Taylor Due, Baker and Brown Source: *IF.*
1914: 03–07	Walker and Green, Francis Burton, Picks Source: *IF.*
1914: 03–21	Delyons and Jeffrey, Alberta Whitman, and Picks Source: *IF.*
1914: 03–23	Film screening for the benefit of the Friends' Orphan Asylum and the Missionary Society of the First Presbyterian Church. Source: *SLH*
1914: 03–21	Dora Patterson Trio, Ricks and Talbert Dora Patterson—music Ricks and Talbert—male impersonation, talking, singing, dancing Source: *IF.*
1914: 04–04	Muriel Ringgold, Original Rags, The Hillmans Muriel Ringgold—character comedienne, dancing (Muriel in photo) The Hillmans—singing, dancing, talking Source of acts playing: *IF*; about the acts: *BiB.*
1914: 04–11	Frank Williams, Johnson and Britton, Butler and Johnson Johnson and Britton (Sadie Britton)—singing, comedy Butler and Johnson—character singing Source of acts playing: *IF*; about the acts: *BiB.*
1914: 04–18	Allen and Marshall, Hester Kenton, Odum and Williams Hester Kenton—comedy, dancing, singing Source: *IF.*
1914: 04–25	Allen and Marshall, Little Trio Source: *IF.*
1914: 05–02	Sanders and Sanders, Jones and Jones, Leona Marshall* Jones and Jones—singing and dancing Source of acts playing: *IF*; about the acts: *BiB.*
1914: 05–09	Minstrel Morris, Too Sweets, Hugh Turner Minstrel Morris—eccentric juggler Too Sweets (Lulu and Long Willie)—singing, comedy Source of acts playing: *IF*; about the acts: *BiB.*

DATE OF NEWSPAPER	ACTS
1914: 05–16	Butler and Johnson, Gonzell White, Too Sweets Gonzell White—dancing, singing Source of acts playing: *IF*; about the acts: *BiB*.
1914: 05–16	Knights of Pythias leases Hippodrome for two nights for regional Pythian meetings. Source: *RP*.
1914: 05–23	Benefit for the Orphan Asylum and the Missionary Society of the First Presbyterian Church, special vaudeville features were to have included singing by the Abyssinian Trio. Source: *RP*.
1914: 05–30	Blanks Sisters, Johnnie Woods* Blanks Sisters (Berlena and Arceloa)—singing Source of acts playing: *IF*; about the acts: *BiB*.
1914: 06–06	Alonzo Moore, Lucas and Rose Alonzo Moore—Hindoo [*sic*] wonders, magic Source of acts playing: *IF*; about the acts: *BiB*.
1914: 06–13	Williams and Stevens, Scott and Simmons Williams and Stevens—variety Scott and Simmons—comedy, singing Source of acts playing: *IF*; about the acts: *BiB*.
1914: 06–20	Odum and Williams, The Arrants The Arrants—comedy, trombone solo Source of acts playing: *IF*; about the acts: *BiB*.
1914: 06–20	Robinson and White, music comedy and dancing. "Direct from Broadway": Goodbar and Lewis, singing. "Direct from Chicago": John Pamplin, heavy juggler Source: *RP*.
1914: 06–27	Russell and Owens All-Star Stock Company, headed by Bob Russell. Performers: Billie Owens, comedian; Anna Cook Pankey, "most recently prima donna of Cole and Johnson's Red Moon Co."; King Rastus and Cleo Mitchell, dancers; Chinese Walker and Grace Walker as the Chinaman and the Dancing Girl; Tillie Johnson and Jonell Perri, singers. Also: the two-act musical comedy, The Husband. Source: *RP*.
1914: 07–04	Sellmon and Jackson, Queen Dora, Howard and Day Sellmon and Jackson—comedy, singing Queen Dora ("The Marvelous")—mysterious dances Howard and Day (Irene Howard and George Day)—singing, dancing Source of acts playing: *IF*; about the acts: *BiB*.

DATE OF NEWSPAPER	ACTS
1914: 07–11	Massengale and Crosby, Russell and Russell Massengale and Crosby—singing, dancing Source of acts playing: *IF*; about the acts: *BiB*.
1914: 07–18	Tolliver and Chappelle, Glenn and Brogsdale, Bessie Oliver Tolliver and Chappelle—singing Source of acts playing: *IF*; about the acts: *BiB*.
1914: 07–24	King Rex, Two Johns,* Eva LaRhue Source: *IF*. The "Two Johns" were reported by *RP* on July 18, 1914, as being The Two Johnsons, Leona L. and Billy B., who sang, danced, and performed comedy. King Rex was described as a novelty roller-skate dancer. *RP* added that these performers would be performing a week of Broadway vaudeville.
1914: 08–01	Gordon and Glenn, King and Gee Source: *IF*.
1914: 08–08	Wells and Wells, Blackberry Comedy Four Wells and Wells—singing, comic acrobats Source of acts playing: *IF*; about the acts: *BiB*.
1914: 08–15	Patterson Jubilee Singers Source: *IF*.
1914: 08–22	Hendricks and Lee, Johnson and Baylor, Alice Ramsey Johnson and Baylor—comedy Source of acts playing: *IF*; about the acts: *BiB*.
1914: 08–29	Eva La Rhue, Pamplin Trio Source: *IF*.
1914: 09–05	Pete and Hayes Source: *IF*.
1914: 09–12	Drake, Walker Trio Source: *IF*.
1914: 09–19	Murphy and Walker, Laura Bailey, Bailey and Green Laura Bailey—tango dancer Source of acts playing: *IF*; about the acts: *BiB*.
1914: 09–26	Davis and Walton, Taylor and Taylor Davis and Walton—music Source of acts playing: *IF*; about the acts: *BiB*.
1914: 10–03	Tom Brown, Robinson and Russell Source: *IF*.

DATE OF NEWSPAPER	ACTS
1914: 10–10	Abyssinian Trio, The Barriers Source: *IF.*
1914: 10–24	Perrin and Crosby, White and Jordan Source: *IF.*
1914: 11–05	Wrestling match between Akri Sikaso, also known as the "Liberian Cyclone," and Billy Brandon, also known as the "Monarch Demon." A section of the theater was set aside for White people. Source: *RTD.*
1914: 11–07	Masengale and Crosby, Stewart Brothers Source: *IF.*
1914: 11–14	Noisy Four, Spencer Finley Source: *IF.*
1914: 11–21	Dare Devil Reynolds, Langster Brothers, Bonnie and Semoura Langster Brothers ("Saxophone Kids")—music Bonnie and Semoura—female impersonator, dancing, singing Source of acts playing: *IF*; about the acts: *BiB.*
1914: 11–28	Crosby and Neeley, Brown and Pinkey Brown and Pinkey—dancing, singing Source of acts playing: *IF*; about the acts: *BiB.*
1914: 11–28	Memorial exercises of Capital City Lodge No. 11 of the Improved Benevolent and Protective Order Elks of the World (IBPOEW), along with a musical program. Source: *RP.*
1914: 11–28	Film to benefit the Building Fund of the First Presbyterian Church. Source: *SLH.*
1914: 12–05	Davis and Greer, Brown and Pinkey Source: *IF.*
1914: 12–05	Performers were at a Thanksgiving benefit outside the theater given by the Mecca Temple of the Improved Dramatic Order of the Knights of Khorassan. They were Harry L. Thomas, a singer, and Crosby and Neely (James and Walter, respectively), also singers. They were accompanied by Curtis Jordan at the piano. Jordan was possibly from Richmond. Source: *RP.*
1914: 12–12	Tim and Hester Moore, Howard and Mason Tim and Hester Moore—singing, comedy Source of acts playing: *IF*; about the acts: *BiB.*

DATE OF NEWSPAPER	ACTS
1914: 12–19	Demos Jones Trio, Howard and Mason Demos Jones Trio—singing, dancing Source of acts playing: *IF*; about the acts: *BiB*.
1914: 12–26	Dorsey, Lazzo Trio, Miller Family Source: *IF*.
1914: 12–26	Johnny Miller, "premier" drummer Source: *IF*.
1915: 01–02	Martin and Ramsey, The Goodlettes Source: *IF*.
1915: 01–09	Three Cuban Nightingales, Tim and Hester Moore Three Cuban Nightingales (Effie King, Nina Marshall, Violet Van Vierah) Source of acts playing: *IF*; about the acts: *BiB*.
1915: 01–16	Tim and Hester Moore, Clement Sisters Clement Sisters (Carrie and Mamie)—singing Source of acts playing: *IF*; about the acts: *BiB*.
1915: 01–16	Granstaff and Davis, comedy musicians; and Logan and Keys, sister act Source: *RP*.
1915: 01–23	Granstaff and Davis, Tom Melton, Forsyne and Hill Granstaff and Davis—trombone, trumpet solos Source of acts playing: *IF*; about the acts: *BiB*.
1915: 01–30	Gant and Perkins, Neeley and Owens Gant and Perkins—singing Source of acts playing: *IF*; about the acts: *BiB*.
1915: 02–06	Ramsey and Nickerson, Braxton and Nugent Braxton and Nugent—comedy Source of acts playing: *IF*; about the acts: *BiB*.
1915: 02–06	Richardson and Towel, singing fools; Charlie Anderson, character singing comedian Source: *RP*.
1915: 02–13	Richardson and Towel, Charles Anderson (There were two acts known as Charles Anderson; it is not known which is intended here.) Source of acts playing: *IF*; about the acts: *BiB*.
1915: 02–20	Nichols and Jones, Hellens and Austin Hellens and Austin—comedy, singing Source of acts playing: *IF*; about the acts: *BiB*.

DATE OF NEWSPAPER	ACTS
1915: 02–27	Allen and Wiggins, Van and Clovette Allen and Wiggins—talking, dancing, singing Source of acts playing: *IF*; about the acts: *BiB*.
1915: 03–06	The Vervalin Trio, Wilkinson and Phillips The Vervalin Trio ("The Great Clemo")—variety Source of acts playing: *IF*; about the acts: *BiB*.
1915: 03–13	Bowman and Burnette, Moore and Hudgins Source: *IF*.
1915: 02–13	Allen and Wiggins in a new act: "Two Fools and a Fiddle"; Edwards and Hardee, singing and dancing musical sketch artists Source: *RP*.
1915: 03–20	Public meeting to hear the attorneys who argued recent test cases at the Supreme Court [the cases were legal challenges to Richmond's 1911 segregation ordinance]. Source: *RP*, also *SLH*.
1915: 03–20	Film screening to benefit the Missionary Society of the First Presbyterian Church Source: *SLH*.
1915: 03–27	Hoyt and Starks, Ethlyne and Lake Hoyt and Starks (two women)—singing, dancing Source of acts playing: *IF*; about the acts: *BiB*.
1915: 03–29	Edwards and Hardee, Allen and Wiggins Edwards and Hardee—singing, dancing, comedy Source of acts playing: *IF*; about the acts: *BiB*.
1915: 04–03	Three Cuban Nightingales, Washburn and Piper Washburn and Piper—singing, comedy Source of acts playing: *IF*; about the acts: *BiB*.
1915: 04–10	Floyd and Jackson, Johnson and Morgan Source: *IF*.
1915: 04–17	Dick and Struffin, Yager De Lor and Dandy Source: *IF*.
1915: 04–24	Henderson and Wise, Richardson and Towel Source: *IF*.
1915: 05–01	Stock company Source: *IF*.
1915: 05–08	Johnson and Johnson [also known as The Two Johnsons) Source: *IF*.

DATE OF NEWSPAPER	ACTS
1915: 05–15	The Ferroars, Burris, Stewart and Dease Source: *IF.*
1915: 05–15	Benefit performance for the First Battalion of the Uniform Rank, Knights of Pythias Source: *RP.*
1915: 05–22	The McCarvers, Gaston and Brown The McCarvers (Billie and Sadie)—singing Source of acts playing: *IF*; about the acts: *BiB.*
1915: 05–29	Rollison and Douglas, The McCarvers Source: *IF.*
1915: 06–05	The Freemans, and Thompson, Cooper, and Thompson The Freemans—singing, dancing Thompson, Cooper, and Thompson—singing Source of acts playing: *IF*; about the acts: *BiB.*
1915–06–12	Susie Sutton,* Johnson and Johnson Source: *IF.*
1915: 06–26	Susie Sutton, Bradford and Janette, Charles Melton Source: *IF.*
1915: 07–17	Kenner and Williams, Burt Murphy Kenner and Williams (a stock company)—variety Source of acts playing: *IF*; about the acts: *BiB.*
1915: 08–04	Johnnie Woods and Little Henry* Source: *IF.*
1915: 08–07	S. H. Dudley and his mule, accompanied by William Hodgkins; and Hattie Akers and Emma Jackson Source: *IF.*
1915: 09–01	Benefit for National Colored Old Folks Home Source: *RP.*
1915: 09–04	The Watts Brothers, Riley and Hudgins, Heater Kenton The Watts Brothers—music Johnny Hudgins—impersonator (impersonates Charlie Chaplin) Source of acts playing: *IF*; about the acts: *BiB.*
1915: 09–04	Melton's Violin Club, Invincible Chorus, Hippodrome Orchestra, Sabbath Glee Club (20 musicians and 50 singers); benefit of Richmond Hospital Source: *RP.*
1915: 09–18	Ed Tolliver and Miss Chappell Source: *IF.*

DATE OF NEWSPAPER	ACTS
1915: 09–18	Benefit for Ray family of Henrico County, whose home was destroyed by a storm Source: *RP.*
1915: 09–25	Thornton, Greer, and Hardaway Source: *IF.*
1915: 09–25	Helen Bumbray and Rena Wills, Riley Hudgins Source: *IF.*
1915: 10–02	Walker Stratton Comedy/Variety Source of act playing: *IF*; about the acts: *BiB.*
1915: 10–09	Benefit for National Colored Old Folks Home Source: *RP.*
1915: 12–25	Louise Cook singing (soprano) Source of act playing: *IF*; about the acts: *BiB.*
1916: 04–15	Russell and Gadson, Sam and Happy Source: *IF.*
1916: 01–08	The Black Cat Source: *IF.*
1916: 01–15	Vaudeville de Luxe, the Singing and Dancing Girls direct from Broadway Source: *RP.*
1916: 01–29	Susie Sutton and T. Spencer Finley Source: *IF.*
1916: 01–29	Burns and Burns Source: *IF.*
1916: 02–02	Akers and Jackson Source: *IF.*
1916: 03–11	Invincible Four Blind musicians Source: *RP.*
1916: 03–11	Hippodrome Orchestra plays a benefit at the True Reformers' Auditorium Source: *RP.*
1916: 04–15	Film and sacred music benefit for the Friends Orphan Asylum and the Missionary Society of the First Presbyterian Church Source: *RP.*

DATE OF NEWSPAPER	ACTS
1916: 04–29	Hippodrome Orchestra plays a benefit at Richmond Beneficial Insurance Company. Source: *RP*.
1916: 05–06	*Damon and Pythias* film benefit for First Battalion of the Uniform Rank, Knights of Pythias, and the Pythian Cadet Battalion. The Drill Team of the Pythian Cadets performs. Source: *RP*.
1916: 05–06	Hippodrome Orchestra plays a benefit at Richmond Beneficial Insurance Company. Source: *RP*.

APPENDIX 6

Theaters in Richmond, circa 1917

Information is taken from the 1918 Richmond City Directory (page 138) except as indicated here. Information from a city directory in a given year likely reflects information that was gathered the year before (in this case, 1917). The information under the column heading "General Type of Theater" is extrapolated from the kinds of ads the theaters were running in local newspapers in 1917 or from publications or websites that deal with the history of Richmond theater. The Dixie, Globe, and Hippodrome were marked in the city directory with asterisks, meaning they were theaters for Black patrons only. In the case of the Hippodrome, at least, an occasional event would be opened also to White patrons. The largest Richmond theaters were opened before the advent of moving pictures and sometimes had segregated seating available, usually in balconies (called "gallery" seating), for Black patrons. The Strand, for example, advertised in the October 4, 1917, *Richmond Times Dispatch* for "colored" employees to work in the "colored" gallery. Seating capacity for the Bluebird was not listed in the directory; this number is taken from the *Richmond Times-Dispatch* article announcing its opening in March 1917. Wilmer, Vincent, and Wells was a Jake Wells' group. At this point in his career, Wells was living in North Carolina and running theaters with various groups across the South.

THEATER NAME OWNER/MANAGEMENT INFORMATION	LOCATION	GENERAL TYPE OF THEATER (IN 1917)	SEATING CAPACITY
Academy of Music Leath Theatrical Co., Inc; Leo Wise, local manager	105 North Eighth	Live theater	1,600

THEATER NAME OWNER/MANAGEMENT INFORMATION	LOCATION	GENERAL TYPE OF THEATER (IN 1917)	SEATING CAPACITY
Albion n/a	211 North Third	Films	372
City Auditorium City of Richmond	909 West Cary	Large events	3,698
Bijou Chesapeake Amusement Corp.; H. B. McNiven, local manager	812 East Broad	Vaudeville	1,488
Bluebird Bluebird Theatre Co.; Walter J. Coulter, manager	620 East Broad	Films	700
(old) **Colonial** Wilmer, Vincent and Wells; Harry Bernstein, local manager	716 East Broad	Vaudeville and films	1,200
Dixie Charles Somma; Raymond M. Hollinger, manager	18 West Broad	Films and Vaudeville	300
Globe Chesley Toney	510 North Second	Films	unknown
Hippodrome Charles Somma	530 North Second	Vaudeville and films	700
Isis Chesapeake Amusement Corp.; H. B McNiven, local manager	808 East Broad	Films	750
Little Theatre n/a	112 West Broad	Films	unknown
Lyric W.A.M.A. Co.; Charles W. Rex, local manager	901 East Broad	Vaudeville and films	1,576
New Theatre Willard H. Richardson; Robert H. Richardson, manager	206 East Broad	Films	440

THEATER NAME OWNER/MANAGEMENT INFORMATION	LOCATION	GENERAL TYPE OF THEATER (IN 1917)	SEATING CAPACITY
Odeon (Miss) Janette Allen, manager	211 North Sixth	Films	496
Rex W. H. Hoover; T. J. Gaddy, manager	700 East Broad	Films	325
Strand n/a	118 West Broad	Vaudeville and films	1,025
Theato Chesley Toney	500 East Broad	Films	350
Toney Chesley Toney	512 ½ Louisiana	Films	225
Victor Martin Theatrical Co.; John F. Lay, manager	800 East Broad	Films	350

APPENDIX 7

Inventory of the Victor Theater, July 1926

The inventory is the one attached to court documents dealing with Thorp's failure to make a Victor Theater payment and which resulted in the allegations from her that she was pressured into the purchase at an unfair price. Some prices of the listed tangible assets were provided in the document and appear below. The list is of interest to the student of theater histories for the detail it provides of the physical property of a typical, if medium-sized, theater from the mid-1920s. Errors were left as they were in the original document. (Document source: Richard Watkins Carrington Papers, 1880–1933, folder entitled "1925–1929," Box 38, Albert and Shirley Small Special Collections Library, University of Virginia, Charlottesville, Virginia.)

17	electric beam fixtures
1	2-unit automatic ticket machine
1	9" buzz fan
3	2-light ceiling fixtures
2	type E Power's projecting machines
1	75-amp Westinghouse generator with 2 ballast rheostats, 2 circuiting switches, vole, and armature
1	30- to 60-amp compensator
1	16" buzz fan
1	16" exhaust fan
6	66" ceiling fans
3	indirect panel glass fixtures
6	ornamental exit boxes ($400)
1	2-Hp 3-phase organ motor
1	10-amp 10-volt organ generator
1	16" buzz fan ascelator [*sic*]

1	flexible arm piano lamp
1	5-Hp 3-phase motor
1	22' footlight 200 feet [sic]
2	22' border lights 30 ft [sic]
5	ornamental electric brackets complete with holders and glass
1	30" by 14' porcelain electric sign VICTOR
1	5' by 15" chasing border around sign VICTOR
1	8-point sign flasher
2	500-watt flood lights
3	ceiling effects fancy glass
1	5-HP motor starter
25	4-watt G25 frosted lamps
56	75-watt PS22 clear
192	10-watt S14 amber orange, 37 cents
118	10-watt S14 frosted, 37 cents
7	500-watt PS40 clear, $2.00
6	25-watt S17 amber orange, 37 cents
	(List Price of Lamps Given)
1	Keneticut [sic] combination blower
1	red, black, and gold satin stage setting consisting of 4 borders
2	leg drops
1	close in drop on traveler
1	[illegible] by 18' gold fiber screen
8	sets of lines, consisting of 300' [of] ½-inch grass rope
16	3-pulley blocks
8	2-pulley blocks
8	1-pulley blocks
1	4' by 4' 12" rewinding bench galvanized iron
1	6-department 200' reel safety cabinet
1	ticket chopper
1	6' monsoon fan
2	3-sheet frames galvanized iron
3	6-sheet frames galvanized iron
4	1-sheet frames galvanized iron
1	Brandt automatic change maker
1	revolving office chair
3	oak kitchen chairs

1	2'x 3' foot oak table
4	photographic frames stills
1	14"x 24" Polychrome mirrors
6	14"x 24" Polychrome mirrors
2	5-foot burlap screens
504	theatre chairs
1	Kingsbury upright piano [Author's note: This was crossed out in the original document.]
1	Smith unit organ
	15' 4" leather belt
1	Pyrene fire extinguisher
2	Jubilee fire extinguishers
1	rewinder
	1200-amp 3-poll Bull Dog safety switch
1	30-amp 2-poll S.D. meter cabinet
1	100-amp 3-poll S.D. safety switch
1	60-amp 3-poll S.D. safety switch
5	80-amp 2-poll S.D. safety switch
1	30x36 cabinet
1	18x36 cabinet
1	5 KVA balance coils
8	30-amp 3-wire DB panel switches
8	10" snap switches
1	60" cutout
1	30" cutout
3	60" D.P. knife switches
1	100 A.D.P.D.T. switches
2	100 A cutouts
1	6-section low pressure boiler
8	8 sections wall radiators
6	8 sections radiators
244	[ditto marks here, unclear as to what they refer] radiators
1	iron enamel lavatory
2	iron enamel closets
1	2" [sic] urinal trough
2	18" pipe rails
1	6" pipe rail

NOTES

PREFACE

1. This discussion of capitalization is based on thought expressed by the Center for the Study of Social Policy which can be accessed online at: www.cssp.org. In the interest of full disclosure, the author identifies as White; at her marriage she took on the surname of her husband who is ethnically Asian.

INTRODUCTION

1. This version of the story of Thorp's dealings with Jacobson, which is likely mostly true, is based on the following accounts which tell it with slightly differing details: Virginia Lee Cox, "Woman was Pioneer 'Movie' Owner in Richmond," *Richmond Times-Dispatch* (Richmond, Virginia) *(RTD)*, Jan. 10, 1926; Harry Tucker, "Harry Tucker Recalls First Movies Here—Gone Are Ye Old Theatres of Other Days!", *RTD*, Nov. 15, 1931; Robert Golden, "Early Movies Here Too Poor To Advertise, O. M-A-T Finds," *RTD*, Apr. 3, 1939; and Edith Lindeman, "Early Days of Movies Here are Recalled," *RTD*, Apr. 23, 1944. Date of the opening of the storefront Dixie: "New Theatre Opens Today," *Richmond Evening Journal (Richmond, Virginia) (REJ)*, May 4, 1907.

2. As if competing with televised streaming services isn't enough, at the time of publication, the effects of the COVID-19 pandemic are still being sorted out.

3. Richard Butsch, "The Making of American Audiences: From Stage to Television, 1750–1990," *Cambridge Studies in the History of Mass Communication* (Cambridge University Press, 2000), 14. Butsch provides an excellent overview of the cultural phenomena of cinema in the United States.

4. R. T. Watson, "World-Wide Streaming Subscriptions Pass One Billion During Pandemic," *Wall Street Journal*, Mar. 18, 2021, https://www.wsj.com.

5. See Kathryn Fuller-Seeley and Karen Ward Mahar, "Exhibiting Women: Gender, Showmanship, and the Professionalization of Film Exhibition in the United States, 1900–1930," in the *Women Film Pioneers Project*, Jane Gaines, ed., Columbia University Libraries, 2012, accessed Jul. 10, 2021, https://wfpp.columbia.edu.

CHAPTER 1

1. Capitol Theater, advertisement, *RTD*, Jan. 28, 1928. *The Jazz Singer*, staring Al Jolson, had its world premiere in New York City on Oct. 7, 1927. The *RTD* ad noted that Richmond was one of only three U.S. cities chosen to show the film in "pre-release." The Capitol was not a Thorp theater.

2. Cox, "Woman," *RTD*, Jan. 10, 1926.

3. "Virginia, Death Records, 1912–2014" (digital image s.v. "Mrs. Amanda E. Thorp"), Ancestry.com. A birth certificate for Amanda Thorp could not be located. Thorp consistently used the "E" middle initial of her name throughout her lifetime; however, its expansion cannot be found in any official documentation. Frances Watson, writing in an unsourced article in the Fall 1978 non-peer reviewed *Richmond Quarterly*, gave "Ellen" as the expansion (Frances Watson, "Amanda Ellen Thorp: Richmond Motion Picture Pioneer," *Richmond Quarterly*, Fall 1978, 39–41). Watson's article is unsourced, however, and there are several errors in it; the *Richmond Quarterly* itself was an independent, informal journal published for a short time in the 1970s and 1980s. More on the middle initial "E" mystery will be developed herein.

4. 1870 details are from the 1870 U.S. Census, Granville, Licking County, Ohio (digital image s.v. "Amanda E. Thorp"), Ancestry.com.

5. The Granville Female Seminary evolved into today's Denison University, a well-regarded private liberal arts college.

6. 1880 details are from the 1880 U.S. Census, Pataskala, Licking County, Ohio (digital image s.v. "Amanda E. Thorp"), Ancestry.com. No relatives of the elder Isaac or Catherine of their generation or older are known to any degree of certainty.

7. "Ohio, County Marriage Records, 1774–1993" (digital image s.v. "Amanda E. Baughman"), Ancestry.com.

8. "Virginia, Death Records, 1912–2014" (digital image s.v. "Waldo Franklin Thorp"), Ancestry.com. A birth certificate for Waldo Thorp could not be located.

9. "U.S., Headstone Applications for Military Veterans, 1925–1970" (digital image s.v. "Franklin T. Thorp"), Ancestry.com.

10. 1870 U.S. Census, Newark, Licking County, Ohio (digital image s.v. "Sarah Thorp"), Ancestry.com.

11. 1850 U.S. Census, Jersey Township, Licking County, Ohio (digital image s.v. "Franklin Thorp"), Ancestry.com.

12. "U.S., Civil War Soldier Records and Profiles, 1861–1865" (digital image "Franklin Thorp"), Ancestry.com.

13. "Civil War Draft Registrations Records, 1863–1865," National Archives and Records Administration (NARA) (digital image s.v. "Frank T. Thorp"), Ancestry.com. Also, "Official Roster of the Soldiers of the State of Ohio in the War of the Rebellion, 1861–1866," Vol. III: 276, *FamilySearch.org*. The information about Frank's discharge: "Registers of Deaths of Volunteers, 1861–1865," NARA (digital image s.v. "Franklin T. Thorp"), Ancestry.com (despite the fact that he was only injured and did not die as the title of the register implies). Since one of the jobs of battlefield medical personnel was to keep soldiers in the fight as much as possible, Frank's injury must have either been serious or there were extenuating circumstances. For a more detailed account of the actions of the Ohio 27th Regiment, see Mike Mangus, "27th Regiment Ohio Volunteer Infantry (1861–1865)," Feb. 7, 2014, https://www.ohiocivilwarcentral.com.

14. "U.S. Civil War Pension Index" (digital image s.v. "Thorp, Franklin T."), Fold3.com.

15. "From Licking Country," *Daily Ohio Statesman* (Columbus, Ohio), Oct. 4, 1865.

16. "Newark, Ohio," Ohio History Central, accessed Mar. 1, 2021, https://ohiohistorycentral.org.

17. "Westward the Star of Empire Takes its Flight," *Newark Advocate* (Newark, Ohio) (*NA*), Apr. 14, 1881.

18. "Baby Show," *NA,* Sept. 10, 1887.

19. "Local Legislation," *NA,* Aug. 8, 1882, mentions Frank's law enforcement work, though there are several others mentioning his election or appointment as the case may be. "Burke," *NA,* Apr. 2, 1888, describes the arrest of "one of the toughest characters in Ohio" in the course of which Frank and other officers were beaten up pretty badly; this is one of a handful of articles over the course of Frank's law enforcement career which describes him as being assaulted while on the job. Frank's occupation was listed as baker in "Civil War Draft Registrations Records, 1863–1865," NARA (digital image s.v. "Frank T. Thorp"), Ancestry .com. Also, "25 Years Ago," *NA,* May 22, 1917 (actually first published in a May 22, 1882, article which could not be located) mentions he had accepted a position as a baker in Charlie Huber's bakery in Newark; and "Personal Points," *NA,* Dec. 12, 1904, mentions he had spent the summer working "at his trade" as a baker. The 1905 Newark City Directory lists him as a baker living at No. 11½ West Main (Newark [Ohio] City Directory, 1905 [332, digital image s.v. "Thorp Frank T"], Ancestry.com.) "Photographs," *NA,* June 27, 1904, mentions Frank's dalliance in the cornet band. Neither Frank nor Amanda can be located in the 1890 or 1900 regular censuses, although he is located in Newark without an address given in 1890 (1890 Special Veterans Schedule of the U.S. Census, Newark, Licking County, Ohio [digital image s.v. "Franklin T. Thorp"], Ancestry. com*).* "Newark News," *Cleveland Plain Dealer (Cleveland, Ohio) (CPD),* Dec. 14, 1896, mentions Frank working as a mail courier in Newark. "Police Court," *NA,* Apr. 22, 1886, reports Frank had arrested a "colored" couple on charges of resisting and insulting an officer, but he, instead, was temporarily suspended from the force after the charges were dropped. The race of the alleged perpetrators was noted in the article and is provided here because of the possible implications of at least a somewhat liberal attitude present in Newark that a Black couple could be charged with a crime and instead the White officer could be suspended.

20. "List of Pensioners in Licking County," *NA,* Nov. 20, 1883. The reason for Frank's pension is listed as "iritus," a swelling and irritation in the colored ring around the eye's pupil. The value of his salary today was obtained from "Prices for 1860, 1872, 1878 and 1882—Groceries, Provisions, Dry Goods and More," Choosing Voluntary Simplicity, accessed Aug. 1, 2021, http://www .choosingvoluntarysimplicity.com.

21. "Birthday Surprise and Presentation," *NA,* Jul. 29, 1889.

22. "Application for Admission, Ohio Soldiers' and Sailors' Orphans' Home,"

Greene County (Ohio) Public Library Online Resources, n.v. "Waldo F. Thorp," accessed May 19, 2021, https://greenelibraryresource.info.

23. W. L. Douglas, advertisement, *NA*, Jan. 3, 1894.

24. "Ohio Soldiers' and Sailors' Orphans' Home," Ohio History Central, accessed Jul. 12, 2021, https://ohiohistorycentral.org.

25. Untitled brief, *NA*, Dec. 30, 1897.

26. E.g., untitled briefs, *NA*, Dec. 30, 1897, Dec. 21, 1898, and Mar. 21, 1900.

27. "Police Court," *NA,* Nov. 5, 1898.

28. "Police Court," *NA*, Oct. 23, 1899.

29. "Six Bound Over," *NA*, Jan. 26, 1900.

30. "The Trial," *NA*, Jan. 25, 1900.

31. 1900 U.S. Census, Fourth Ward, Licking County, Ohio (digital image s.v. "Waldo Thorp"), Ancestry.com. A notation indicates that Licking County Jail entries are on lines 86–100. Waldo appears on line 88.

32. "Personal Points," *NA*, Feb. 26, 1900.

33. "Court," *NA*, Jan. 30, 1899.

34. Amanda Thorp cannot be located in the 1900 census.

35. "Personal Points," *NA*, June 27, 1900.

36. "Ohio, County Marriage Records, 1774–1993" (digital image s.v. "Walter F. Thorp"), Ancestry.com.

37. "Thorp-Baker Wedding," *NA*, Feb. 15, 1901.

38. Cox, "Woman," *RTD*, Jan. 10, 1926. As always in retrospective pieces like this one, despite being based on an actual interview with Thorp, there are errors either on the part of the reporter or by Thorp herself who misremembered or deliberately massaged the record. Although some of the minute details of the article are incorrect, the generality that she was in the service industry before moving into showing moving pictures is supported by primary newspaper sources.

39. "The Commercial Hotel," *NA,* May 25, 1901 (the establishment was variously referred to as "hotel" or "house" in the local press). The short article is puzzling in one notable aspect: in the way it lists her name. It notes, "The Commercial Hotel on South Fifth Street has this spring passed into the hands of Mrs. Nellie Thorpe [*sic*] who formerly conducted a boarding house on West Main Street. Mrs. Thorpe has repapered, renovated, and improved the house until it presents a homelike and comfortable appearance. Mrs. Thorpe will no doubt conduct the hotel as successfully as she did her former establishment on West Main Street." A untitled brief in the same paper published two months before, on March 14, noted that "Mrs. Carrie Mayer of Chicago Junction was the guest of Mrs. Nellie Thorpe on West Main Street." One other article, "Personal Points," *NA*, Apr. 27, 1900, noted that Mrs. Nellie Thorp had visited friends in Utica, Ohio. Though no other newspaper articles can be found that ties Amanda to the name "Nellie," this must be her. As noted earlier, the expansion of the "E" as a middle initial in Amanda's name is a mystery. If the Nellie of these articles

is Amanda, it could be a diminutive for Ellen, lending credence to that detail, at
least, of the *Richmond Quarterly* mentioned previously (Watson, "Amanda Ellen
Thorp," *Richmond Quarterly*).

40. "The Commercial Hotel," *NA*, May 25, 1901.

41. Newark City Directory, 1902 (286, digital image s.v. "Thorp Amanda E"
and s.v. "Thorp Waldo F"), Ancestry.com. City directories often reflect information that was gathered the year before due to the time it took to obtain the data
and then to print it.

42. "Personal Points," *NA*, Apr. 27, 1900, Mar. 14, 1901, and Sept. 4, 1901.

43. "Pretty," *NA*, Mar. 11, 1902, and "Police Court," Jul. 7, 1902.

44. Paid advertising brief, *NA*, Feb. 18, 1903.

45. "The Courts," *NA*, May 21, 1902.

46. "The Courts," *NA*, May 31, 1902.

47. "Knocked Down," *NA*, June 18, 1902.

48. "Clothes Came Back," *Democrat and Standard* (Coshocton, Ohio), Feb.
10, 1903. Stealing clothing wasn't necessarily a perverse obsession that Waldo
had: the papers of this era are full of stories of people stealing clothing items from
each other.

49. "The Courts," *NA*, May 9, 1903.

50. "The Courts," *NA*, Feb. 23, 1903.

51. "Newark News," *Columbus Dispatch* (Columbus, Ohio) (*CD*), May 10,
1903.

52. "Three Newark Prisoners Attempted Jail Delivery," *CD*, May 19, 1903,
and "Thorp and Thrapp," *NA*, June 20, 1903. Joseph Thrapp, one of the three
involved, was alleged to have had several saws hidden in his cell. For that and
for cutting the face of the officer who confronted him, he was sentenced to an
additional eight years of prison. The other two men, a James Costley and Waldo,
seemed to merely be willing to escape if the situation presented itself. For that
reason, they received no additional punishment.

53. "Gasoline," *NA*, Sept. 1, 1904.

54. "Waldo Thorp is Again in Trouble," *NA*, Aug. 22, 1905, and "Guilty,"
NA, Nov. 23, 1904.

55. Newark City Directory, 1905 (332, digital image s.v. "Thorpe Mrs A E"),
Ancestry.com.

56. Newark City Directory, 1905 (332), Ancestry.com.

57. "New 'Phones," *NA*, Apr. 5, 1904.

58. "News in Brief," *NA*, Oct. 18, 1904.

59. "Waldo Thorp is Again in Trouble," *Cincinnati Enquirer* (Cincinnati,
Ohio) (*CE*), Aug. 22, 1905. Ethel's patronymic suffered various misspellings in
the press.

60. Licking County, Ohio, Marriage Certificate (digital image s.v. "Waldo F.
Thorp," and s.v. "Ethelda Mae Schmutzle"), Ancestry.com.

61. "With a Rope," *NA*, Aug. 22, 1905. Though to be fair, Della's name had

also been mentioned by the local paper a couple of times in the past when her behavior wasn't particularly exemplary either.

62. E.g., "The Police Court," *NA*, Jul. 7, 1902.

63. "Court Notes," *NA*, Mar. 21, 1906. Thorp's mother had suffered a stroke.

64. "Personal Points," *NA*, Dec. 12, 1904.

65. "Court Notes," *NA*, Sept. 27, 1905.

66. "Picture Show," *Bucyrus Evening Telegraph* (Bucyrus, Ohio) (*BET*), Jul. 27, 1906. Cox, "Woman," *RTD*, Jan. 10, 1926, reported that Thorp said she had paid "exactly $350" for her first theater in Ohio "in a dwelling house on a prominent corner in a little town," to Thorp, an exorbitant price. Those details don't completely match other documentation. In particular, the "dwelling house" was probably only meant to be "house," a term often used in the entertainment business to describe the physical surroundings of a theater. Wonderland was in a commercial building, not a dwelling house. Thorp did not purchase the building Wonderland occupied; the $350 likely was the annual lease cost.

CHAPTER 2

1. Roger Manvell, "Film," *Britannica*, Apr. 25, 2022, https://www.britannica.com. The quoted material here is a summary and condensation of the online post.

2. "Comprehensive List of Electric Theaters and Nickelodeons; Ohio," *Billboard*, Dec. 15, 1906, 32. The first nickelodeon is thought to have been established in western Pennsylvania in 1905. In the early years, they spread in an ever-widening circle from there, meaning Ohio was an early adopter. Both Pennsylvania and Ohio in these early lists of nickelodeons are shown to be well represented. Eileen Bowser, in *The Transformation of Cinema, 1907–1915,* says the number of nickelodeons in the United States doubled between 1907 and 1908 to around 8,000 (University of California Press, Berkeley, 1994, 4–6).

3. Population numbers for Bucyrus extrapolated from the U.S. Census, 1900 and 1910.

4. Cox, "Woman," *RTD*, Jan. 10, 1926.

5. "Wonderland Theatre," *BET*, Aug. 11, 1906.

6. Earl P. Hart, "Hart Writes of the Movie Business," *BET*, Mar. 14, 1914.

7. "Wonderland" and "Wonderland Theatre," *BET*, Aug. 11, 1906 (two articles).

8. Russell Merritt, "Nickelodeon Theaters, 1905–1914," *in* Tino Balio, *The American Film Industry*, Project Muse, (University of Wisconsin Press, 1985), 86. Notice that even in 1985, the presumption was that the theater manager was male. A modern reproduction of a typical illustrated song, "Take Me Out to the Ballgame" (which was recorded from the original wax cylinder recorded by Edward Meeker) can be seen and heard at: https://www.youtube.com/watch?v=ToytGaO2uXU.

9. Merritt, "Nickelodeon Theaters," 88.

10. Cox, "Woman," *RTD*, Jan. 10, 1926.

11. Cox, "Woman," *RTD*, Jan. 10, 1926.

12. Readers may note the similarity between this business model and the one which Netflix used in the early days of its business when it mailed DVDs to customers who would then return them in order to get another.

13. "Exhibitors Form National League," *Moving Picture World (MPW)*, Aug. 19, 1911, 441–442.

14. This equation is based on data provided in "Comprehensive List," *Billboard*, Dec. 15, 1906, 32. The magazine provided admission costs, number of daily shows, and seating capacity for Wonderland as well as the other several hundred nickelodeons in their list of these theaters that existed at the time. "Wonderland," *BET*, Aug. 11, 1906, however, indicated theater hours at Wonderland were from 1–5 and 7–10 pm, meaning there likely were 14 showings if, as is probable, they were 30 minutes apart without breaks. M. C. Coulter, father of Walter and Robert Coulter, men that Thorp would mentor over the years, recalled the Wonderland Theater originally could seat 100 ("Buys Picture Show in Virginia City," *BET*, Sept. 22, 1919).

15. The titles as listed in the early ads were sometimes an approximation of the "official" titles, especially as regards punctuation. This first film mentioned can be found in movie databases as *Love vs. Title; or, An Up-to-Date Elopement*, Vitagraph Co. of America, 1906. No information can be located on *Angler's Dream*, which unfortunately is very common in regard to many of the early films since many are lost. Appendix 1 lists all titles of films known to have been shown at the Wonderland under Thorp's ownership, but the titles are provided as originally advertised; no effort has been made to correct any original errors. Further information on the films may or may not be located at the American Film Institute's online catalog at aficatalog.afi.com as well as other film databases.

16. Photograph from the collection of Doug Godwin, Bucyrus, Ohio.

17. "Mrs. Thorp Doesn't Hesitate About Dates; Showed Films Back in 1904," *MPW*, Feb. 21, 1920, 1234. The article says she was showing films in Bucyrus in 1904, but she did not open the Wonderland until 1906. She may have shown films at her Hotel Franklin in Newark as early as 1904, however.

18. Cox, "Woman," *RTD*, Jan. 10, 1926.

19. Craig Morrison, "From Nickelodeon to Picture Palace and Back," *Design Quarterly*, (1974), 9.

20. From James Agee's influential essay, "Comedy's Greatest Era," which originally appeared in *Life* magazine, Sept. 3, 1949. Reprinted in "Comedy's Greatest Era – by James Agee," *Scraps from the Loft*, Nov. 17, 2019, https://scrapsfromtheloft.com.

21. Wonderland Theater, advertisement, *BET*, Jan. 21, 1907.

22. Wonderland Theater, advertisement, BET, Mar. 5, 1907.

23. Wonderland Theater, advertisement, *BET*, Mar. 20, 1907.

24. Wonderland Theater, advertisement, *BET*, Oct. 9, 1906.

25. Wonderland Theater, advertisement, *BET*, Oct. 16, 1906.

26. Wonderland Theater, advertisement, *BET*, Nov. 2, 1906.

27. "New Machine," *BET*, Dec. 28, 1906.

28. "Man Blown to Pieces," *BET*, Nov. 26, 1906.

29. "Blown to Atoms by Nitro-Glycerine," *Brockway Record* (Brockway, Pennsylvania) (*BR*), Nov. 30, 1906.

30. "Mr. Morey to Quit Gas Well Shooting," *NA*, Aug. 21, 1906.

31. "Man Blown to Pieces," *BET*, Nov. 26, 1906.

32. "Settling Morey Estate," *Times Recorder* (Zanesville, Ohio), Dec. 12, 1906.

33. "Blown to Atoms," *BR*, Nov. 30, 1906.

34. "Obituary: Mrs. William Morey," *NA*, Mar. 7, 1904.

35. "Man Blown to Pieces," *BET*, Nov. 26, 1906.

36. Cox, "Woman," *RTD*, Jan. 10, 1926.

37. Electrical outages: "Lights Went Out," *BET*, Jan. 12, 1907. Films not arriving: e.g., "The Passion Play Pictures," *BET*, June 6, 1907. Films in poor condition: e.g., "Passion Play," *BET*, Apr. 24, 1907. Equipment breakdowns: e.g., "Machine Repaired," *BET*, Jan. 2, 1907. Upgrading the physical space: untitled brief, *BET*, Oct. 30, 1906 (in this case, constructing a ticket booth). Hiring employees: "Girl Wanted," classified advertisement, *BET*, Apr. 17, 1907.

38. "Man Blown to Pieces," *BET*, Nov. 26, 1906.

39. *BET*, multiple references, 1901–1906.

40. 1900 U.S. Census, Crawford Township, Wyandot County, Ohio (digital image s.v. "Thos. H. Hart"), Ancestry.com.

41. On the Hart Brothers: multiple references in *BET*, 1901–1906.

42. Hart Bros. Music Co., advertisement, *BET*, May 11, 1907.

43. The piano was there by May 13, 1907, (Wonderland, advertisement, *BET*, May 13, 1907) because Earl Hart was playing it to accompany Newman Browarsky who was singing the illustrated the song that night.

44. Wonderland, article-advertisement, *BET*, Jan. 17, 1907.

45. Wonderland, advertisement, *BET*, Jan. 31, 1907. No doubt the punch bowl was a pressed glass product manufactured by the famous (even at that time) Heisey Glass Company in Newark.

46. "Counted Beans," *BET*, Feb. 5, 1907.

47. "Bean Contest of Wonderland Theatre Won by Young Lady," *BET*, Mar. 1, 1907.

48. Wonderland, advertisement, *BET*, Feb. 11, 1907.

49. Wonderland, advertisement, *BET*, Feb. 21, 1907. Further information on the four listed films could not be located.

50. Wonderland, advertisement, *BET*, Feb. 22, 1907.

51. Wonderland, advertisement, *BET*, Mar. 5, 1907.

52. Wonderland, advertisement, *BET*, Mar. 15, 1907.

53. Theatorium, advertisements, *BET*, Mar. 5, 1907, Mar. 4, 1907, Mar. 18, 1907, and Apr. 4, 1907.

54. Wonderland, advertisement, *BET*, Apr. 15, 1907. No further informa-

tion could be learned about the slides, including whether or not they were slides shown through the medium of film. At least three films were made of the tragedy.

55. Theatorium, advertisement, *BET*, Apr. 12, 1907, and Apr. 15, 1907. Film: *The Unwritten Law*, S. Lubin, Mar. 2, 1907.

56. There were a number of versions of *Passion Play* pictures circulating at this time, and it is not possible to sort out from the information available which version is meant in the various references to films on this subject as they come up over the years as movies Thorp showed in her theaters. When speaking of a series, however, she may have been referring to a series of reels produced in January 1903, although there appear to be more than 20 reels of that series at that time (*Passion Play*, American Film Institute, accessed on August 1, 2022, catalog.afi.com.)

57. Wonderland, advertisements, *BET*, Apr. 22, 1907, Apr. 23, 1907, and Apr. 24, 1907.

58. There were a number of films produced in the era about this Easter subject, and it is not known which ones the two theaters screened.

59. Untitled brief, *Bucyrus Telegraph-Forum* (Bucyrus, Ohio) (*BTF*), Apr. 2, 1907.

60. Neither the "Comprehensive List," *Billboard*, Dec. 15, 1906, 32, nor "Combined List," Sept. 5, 1908, 33, listed a nickelodeon in Washington C.H. in lists purported to be "complete," however.

61. *Sanborn Fire Insurance Map from Washington Court House, Fayette County, Ohio*. Sanborn Map Company, August 1907, www.loc.gov.

62. Population numbers extrapolated from U.S. Census data, 1900 and 1910.

63. Untitled brief, *BTF*, Apr. 2, 1907, and others.

64. 1902 map of railroads in Central Ohio, author's collection.

65. Untitled brief, *BTF*, Feb. 11, 1908. It is not known when Walter started working at the theater at Washington Court House.

66. 1900 U.S. Census, Bucyrus Township, Crawford County, Ohio (digital image s.v. "Mathew C. Coulter"), Ancestry.com.

67. Untitled brief, *BTF*, June 14, 1907.

68. Edith Lindeman, "Unsung Heroes of Film World Rate Applause," *RTD*, May 23, 1951.

69. Location of the Coulter home: Bucyrus (Ohio) City Directory, 1909–1910 (59, digital image s.v. "Coulter Matthew C"), Ancestry.com.

CHAPTER 3

1. "Railroad," *BTF*, Apr. 19, 1907.

2. "The Railroads are Prepared," *Bucyrus Journal* (Bucyrus, Ohio) (*BJ*), Apr. 19, 1907.

3. E.g., "In Bucyrus [back-in-the-day type column]," *Telegraph-Forum* (Bucyrus, Ohio) (*BTF*), May 5, 1932, but regarding May 5, 1907.

4. E. T. B., "Jamestown Exposition as Seen with Dayton Eyes," *DH*, Aug. 29, 1907.

5. "The Negro Building at the Jamestown Ter-Centennial Exposition," Library of Virginia, accessed Mar. 18, 2021, https://encyclopediavirginia.org, quoting the *New York Times* (nfi). For more information about the portrayal of these three groups, much of which was controversial even at the time, see, for example, Brian de Ruiter, "Jamestown Ter-Centennial Exposition of 1907," Library of Virginia, accessed Mar. 18, 2021, https://encyclopediavirginia.org.

6. Reiko Hillyer, "On to Richmond: Richmond and the New Dominion," in *Designing Dixie: Tourism, Memory and Urban Space in the New South* (University of Virginia Press, 2015), 88–90.

7. Lindeman, "Early Days of Movies Here Are Recalled," *RTD*, Apr. 23, 1944.

8. "Richmond's Pioneer Movie Exhibitor Quits the Field," *RTD*, Dec. 7, 1923.

9. Cox, "Woman," *RTD*, Jan. 10, 1926.

10. "New Theatre Opens Today," *Richmond Evening Journal* (Richmond, Virginia) *(REJ)*, May 4, 1907. In interviews later in life, Thorp said her Dixie was first located in a room at the Colonial (at 718 E. Broad). Confusion arises because theater names in Richmond would sometimes move when owners moved to new buildings even though a theater might occupy the old one. In 1905, the Bijou moved to 816–818 E. Broad. The old Bijou, renovated, became the Colonial Theater. Both *REJ* and Thorp are referring to the same building but are using different names for it (she calls it the Colonial; the newspaper calls it the "old Bijou annex"). Richmond (Virginia) City Directory, 1908, has the Colonial at 718 East Broad ([1153, digital image s.v. "Colonial"], Ancestry.com); Richmond City Directory, 1909, has the (new) Bijou at 810–814 E. Broad ([1154, digital image s.v. "Bijou"], Ancestry.com). The Dixie, therefore, was located in a room in the building at 718 E. Broad. Both the Colonial and the (both old and new) Bijou were located on the other side of the street from the sprawling Murphy's Hotel also located at Eighth and Broad.

11. "Woman's Success an Object Lesson," *Richmond Virginian (RV)*, Sept. 15, 1912.

12. "Queries and Answers," *RTD*, Jul. 14, 1907. According to the article, Richmond was second only to Hoboken, New Jersey, with a population density in Richmond at 22½ persons per acre. The paper did not provide the sourcing of this data but did mention they were from information available before the 1906 Richmond City annexation.

13. "Mother Dead," *BJ*, May 10, 1907.

14. "Mother Dead," *BET*, May 4, 1907.

15. "At the Dixie," *REJ*, May 22, 1907.

16. Though it is not for certain, these were probably the 1903 multi-reel films. Information about what company produced the films could not be located.

17. Wonderland, advertisement, *BET*, June 14, 1907.

18. Theatorium, advertisement, *BET*, June 21, 1907.

19. "Passion Play Here All Week," *BET*, June 17, 1907.

20. "Preparing for Vaudeville," *BET*, Aug. 26, 1907.

21. "Get Left at Cedar Point," *BET*, Aug. 12, 1907.

22. "Take Vacation," *BET*, Aug. 12, 1907.

23. 1910 U.S. Census, Newark Township, Licking County, Ohio (digital image s.v. "Albert Schmutzler"), Ancestry.com.

24. "Take Vacation," *BET*, Aug. 12, 1907.

25. Wonderland, advertisement, *BET*, Aug. 13, 1907.

26. "Hart Brothers Still in Charge," *BET*, Sept. 11, 1907.

27. Untitled brief, *BTF*, Feb. 11, 1908.

28. Martin Staples Shockley, a noted Richmond theater historian, found the first documented theatrical production in the city was staged in 1784 in a space called the New Theater (Martin Staples Shockley, "A History of the Theatre in Richmond, Virginia, 1819–1838" [PhD diss, University of North Carolina, Chapel Hill, 1938], p. i [Preface]). Theaters in Richmond, by far and away, are thought to have served White patrons exclusively or nearly so until the end of Jim Crow in the mid 1960s, with Black patrons only occasionally accommodated in separate galleries in balcony spaces.

29. E.g., "Amusements," *RTD*, June 3, 1908.

30. "Moseley's European Hotel and Cafe," *Indianapolis Freeman* (Indianapolis, Indiana) (*IF*), Mar. 23, 1907, and Frank C. Bostick, advertisement, *Richmond Planet* (Richmond, Virginia) (*RP*), Mar. 30, 1907.

31. Contemporaneous newspaper reporting of the early 1900s is White-centric with a White default (persons mentioned are assumed to be White; African Americans were identified as to race). Black press existed along with its White counterpart, including in Richmond, but reporting even in these Black newspapers was not always Black-centric. It's complicated, but the following web article can serve as a beginning in understanding the contradictions: Carrie Teresa, "The Jim Crow-Era Black Press: of and for its Readership," The American Historian, (courtesy of the Library of Congress), https://www.oah.org. This present narrative itself, telling the story of Amanda Thorp, is written with a White default: where race is not identified, virtually every reader will correctly assume that the individual being described is White. Racial identity becomes relevant in many parts of this narrative and when it does, it is identified.

32. "Produce Market," *RTD*, Jul. 19, 1908.

33. Eric Jay Dewberry, "Jake Wells Enterprises and the Development of Urban Entertainments in the South, 1890–1925" (PhD diss, Georgia State University, Athens, 2010), 84.

34. Classified advertisement, *REJ*, Nov. 14, 1907. Again, it is not certain which passion play pictures were showing.

35. "Manchester," *REJ*, Nov. 22, 1907. This part of Manchester was annexed to Richmond in 1910 and after that was often called Southside.

36. Thorp held the theater for such a short time that the city directories did not record its existence. The 1907 Richmond city directory has the building vacant; the 1908 city directory has it as occupied by J. B. Wescott; the 1908 city directory has it as The Royal Moving Pictures associated with J. B. Wescott; the 1910 city directory has it as The Royal moving pictures, possibly associated

with C. G. Stadelmeyer. Thorp would have owned the theater sometime between Wescott and Stadelmeyer. When Thorp took it over, she likely gussied
it up somewhat, but it likely still featured benches or wooden chairs as seating
as her own original Dixie across the river would have had. Today the brick
building on Hull Street which housed her New Wonderland is vacant. A rusty
"Southside Hardware" marquee sign points to its life for several former decades
as an independent, Black-owned hardware store which today is considered its
historic use.

37. "Mrs. Thorp Doesn't Hesitate About Dates," *MPW*, Feb. 21, 1920, 1234.

38. Wonderland advertisement, *Daily Press* (Newport News, Virginia) (*DP*),
June 17, 1908. On Oct. 6, 1908, the paper reported that new managers, last name
"Crall," had taken over the Wonderland there, but there was no information as to
whom had previously managed the theater ("Vaudeville and Pictures," *DP*, Oct.
6, 1908).

39. Norfolk (Virginia) City Directory, 1907 (794, digital image s.v. "Wonderland"), Ancestry.com.

40. Cox, "Woman," *RTD*, Jan. 10, 1926. Thorp may have learned in Norfolk
that a segregated theater which perhaps accommodated Whites on one side of
a central aisle and Blacks on the other (instead of one patronized either wholly
by Whites or wholly by Blacks) did not maximize profits. In the racial norms of
the time, Whites likely would not be as willing to patronize a theater which also
catered to Blacks—so half of it conceivably could have been filled with African
American patrons while the other half was virtually empty, not the best for the
bottom line. It is even easy to imagine Black patrons being turned away for lack
of space while the White side was only partially filled.

41. Classified advertisement, *REJ*, Dec. 31, 1907.

42. Classified advertisement, *REJ*, Jan. 23, 1908.

43. "Cheap Theatres Must be Safer," *RTD*, Mar. 13, 1908.

44. "Fire in Negro Theatre," *RTD*, Sept. 6, 1907.

45. "The Alarm," *BTF*, Dec. 31, 1907.

46. "Cheap Theatres Must be Safer," *RTD*, Mar. 13, 1908.

47. Cox, "Woman," *RTD*, Jan. 10, 1926.

48. The building today is an art gallery and part of Richmond's Downtown
Historic District. It is architecturally distinctive because part of the façade is cut
at an angle, reflecting the triangular relationship of Brook Road to Broad Street.

49. The February date comes from a Bucyrus newspaper and is the last information placing Coulter as being in Ohio before showing up in Virginia (Personals, *BET*, Feb. 18, 1908). In 1929, Coulter told the *Richmond Times-Dispatch* in
a retrospective article that he was in Norfolk in 1908 managing a theater—which
had to have been Thorp's despite many errors in the article (Horace Melvin,
"Coulter Knew 4 Warners in Pioneer Days," *RTD*, Jul. 14, 1929).

50. Max Alvarez, "The Origins of the Film Exchange." *Film History*, vol. 17,
no. 4, 2005, 438.

51. Merritt, "Nickelodeon Theaters," 91.

52. Cox, "Woman," *RTD*, Jan. 10, 1926.

53. Untitled brief, *RTD*, Apr. 27, 1908.

54. Cox, "Woman," *RTD*, Jan. 10, 1926.

55. "Moving Picture Shows," *RTD*, Mar. 29, 1908.

56. Dixie, advertisement, *REJ*, May 16, 1908. A film of "the great Paris fire scene" cannot be located.

57. "The Dixie Theatre Today Opened in New Location," *REJ*, May 16, 1908, and classified advertisement, *REJ*, May 20, 1908. In Richmond, in the days before refrigeration, ice collected over the winter from local ponds and rivers if the weather had been cold enough or from those further north if not, was stored in straw-insulated cellars of ice houses, and sold to consumers through spring and summer as long as it was available. A classified ad in the *Richmond News Leader* advertised deliveries of ice (the quantity was provided as "per 100" [nfi, but perhaps refers to 100 pounds] for 40 cents on May 6, 1908.

58. "Dixie Says This," *REJ*, June 4, 1908. Though this appears as a small "article" in the paper, it was likely a paid advertisement.

59. Advertisement, Gem Theater, *REJ*, June 4, 1908.

60. Advertisement, Colonial, *REJ*, May 25, 1908. The Colonial was a much larger building with correspondingly higher overhead costs and more luxurious surroundings than the Dixie or the other new movie theaters, hence the higher admission cost. It was much more refined at that point in time to attend a movie, as scandalous as that act in itself might be, at the Colonial than it would be at one of the nickelodeons, even one such as the Dixie which was making as much effort as possible to be "high class."

61. "Theatre to Open in Schmidt's Old Store," *Richmond News Leader* (Richmond, Virginia) (*RNL)*, Apr. 12, 1907.

62. "To Rebuild Theato," *RTD*, Sept. 26, 1908.

63. "Colored Folk to Have a Theatre." *REJ*, June 11, 1908. The theater had a successful run for about a year. In addition to screening films, a number of well-known early Black vaudeville acts performed there, bringing in White patrons as well as Black. The building it was in was sold in June 1909, but the theater may have stopped operating a couple of months before that. Owners of the theater were the Rainey brothers, but little is known about them, including whether they were Black or White. Sources: "Are Accused of Robbing Theato," *REJ*, Aug. 1, 1908; "Alderman Complains of Noisy Negro Theatre," Aug. 28, 1908, and "Real Estate and Business News," *RTD*, June 29, 1909. 700 West Broad is located at the corner of today's Belvidere and Broad streets, across from today's Institute for Contemporary Art at Virginia Commonwealth University.

64. "Moving Picture Mad in Richmond," *REJ*, Jul. 28, 1908.

65. Fuller-Seeley, *Celebrate Richmond Theater* (The Dietz Press, 2002), 27.

66. "Amusements," *REJ*, June 16, 1908. There are several versions of this film; it is not known which one she screened on this date.

67. Curtis Bernhardt, director, *Damon and Pythias*, International Motion Picture Enterprises and Metro-Goldwyn Mayer, Sept. 1962.

68. Untitled brief, *REJ*, Aug. 4, 1908. As discussed more fully later, the popularity of the Pythian film arguably would have been more marketable in Richmond to Black audiences than White at the time. For more information on the Pythian organization's unique connection to Richmond, especially to Black Richmonders, see, for example, Sarah Nerney, "A Knight Unlike Any Other: John Mitchell Jr. and The Knights of Pythias," Uncommonwealth (blog), Library of Virginia, December 16, 2015, https://uncommonwealth.virginiamemory.com.

69. *Gans-Nelson Fight*, Miles Bros., Dec. 1906.

70. Quotes regarding the success of the showing of the Dixie's showing of the fight: "Moving Picture Mad in Richmond, *RNL*, Jul. 28, 1908. Regarding the fight itself (as well background on the racist challenges Gans faced as a professional athlete), see: Michael Carbert, "Fight City Legends," The Fight City, Jul. 25, 2022, https://www.thefightcity.com.The Gans-Nelson fight also, of course, would have been of keen interest to a Black audience. Since it is does not seem likely that the Dixie admitted Black Richmonders to the showings of the fight, the Ideal Theater might have filled the void as it was scheduled to show the film of the fight the week of August 1, the week following Dixie's initial showings (untitled brief, *RP*, Aug. 1, 1908).

71. "Mrs. Thorp Doesn't Hesitate," *MPW*, Feb. 21, 1920.

72. "Picture Theatre on Doyle's Corner," *REJ*, Jul. 29, 1908, and Richmond City Directory, 1908 (1153, digital image s.v. "Rex"), Ancestry.com.

73. "In Dixie Land for Hart Brothers," *RTD*, Nov. 20, 1908, and Cox, "Woman," *RTD*, Jan. 10, 1926. An "orchestra" in those days, playing in the nickelodeons, were often small groups of three-four players. Thorp remained owner or part owner with the Hart brothers of the Bucyrus Wonderland until at least late 1907, but the *Bucyrus Evening Telegraph* reported that in January 1909, Wonderland had been sold to a Mr. Elberson of Bucyrus ("Will Close Wonderland: Theatre Temporarily Out of Business," BET, Jan. 16, 1909). The Hart Brothers, who had taken over Wonderland at some point, went on to open theaters in other cities in Ohio and possibly other midwestern states as well as in Arizona, ending up in Long Beach, California, by 1911, according to several news articles in the *Bucyrus Evening Telegraph* and other newspapers over the years. The Wonderland Theater in Bucyrus went permanently out of business in April 1911 ("Turning Back" [a retrospective column], *BET*, Apr. 16, 1936).

74. The 1909 Richmond City Directory shows both of them as proprietors for the Dixie at Brook and Broad, but only Amanda as proprietor of the Rex (Richmond City Directory, 1909 [1947, digital image s.v. "Thorp Mrs A E & Son" and s.v. "Thorp Amanda E"], Ancestry.com).

75. "At the Airdome." *REJ*, June 12, 1909, For more information about Idlewood, see, for example, Dale M. Brumfield, "Live Fast, Dies Hard—Richmond's

Idlewood Amusement Park," Theme Park Babylon, accessed June 22, 2022, https://www.dalebrumfield.net.

76. David S. Hulfish, *Motion-Picture Work: A General Treatise on Picture Taking, Picture Making, Photo-Plays, and Theatre Management and Operation* (American School of Correspondence, 1913), 195.

77. Opening of Airdome: Airdome Theater, advertisement, *RJ*, May 22, 1909. Closing: Airdome at Idlewood, advertisement, *REJ*, Sept. 13, 1909. "Polite vaudeville": Airdome Idlewood Park, advertisement, *RNL*, Jul. 29, 1909. "Cakewalking and minstrels": Airdome at Idlewood, advertisement, *REJ*, Sept. 13, 1909.

78. The many Airdome ads mentioned a great variety of vaudeville acts, among these, as mentioned: "equilibrist unicyclists," *REJ*, May 22, 1909, and "eccentric monologists," *REJ*, Aug. 14, 1909. Amateur night: e.g., "Amateur Night at the Airdome," *REJ*, June 18, 1909. Admission price and showing times: e.g., Airdome Theater, advertisement, *REJ*, May 22, 1909.

79. Cox, "Woman," *RTD*, Jan. 10, 1926.

80. "Trade Notes," *MPW*, June 1, 1907, 216.

81. Much has been written about the historical experience with leisure among African Americans. For more information, for example, see Vernon Lee Andres, "African American Leisure Lifestyles," Encylopedia.com, Cengage, accessed Aug. 2, 2022, https://www.encyclopedia.com.

82. In 1911, the Richmond City Council passed a segregation ordinance that restricted African American occupancy to those blocks in which Blacks already made up a majority of the residents. Source: Hillyer, "On to Richmond": 113.

83. 1900 U.S. Census, demographic summary information.

84. Cox, "Woman," *RTD*, Jan. 10, 1926.

85. Gregory A. Waller, "Another Audience: Black Moviegoing, 1907–16," *Cinema Journal*, vol. 31, no. 2, 1992, 4, quoting the *Indianapolis Freeman*, Aug. 1, 1908 (the original *Freeman* reference could not be located).

86. Waller, "Another Audience," 17.

87. Williams Clifford, "A Ringing Appeal to the Negro Race" (guest editorial), *RP*, Mar. 6, 1920. Clifford also noted that all-Black patron theaters were still scarce across the county at this point, which was a decade after Thorp had opened theaters in Richmond for African Americans only.

88. "The Pekin and Ollie Demsey Always Make Good," *IF*, Aug. 21, 1909.

89. "The Clarks Making Good," *IF*, Feb. 12, 1910. The announcement only noted that the Clarks were performing in Richmond, and it is possible that they were located at one of the other all-Black venues such as one of Charles Moseley's establishments.

90. Henry T. Sampson, *Blacks in Blackface: A Sourcebook on Early Black Musical Shows* (Lanham, Maryland, The Scarecrow Press, Inc., 2014), 2nd ed., vol. 1, 159. *Blacks in Blackface* is an essential, though misleadingly named reference since it covers Black vaudeville in general, not just Blacks in blackface. No additional information on the songs the Bradfords sang could be located.

91. Geoffrey C. Ward, writer, and Ken Burns, director, *Unforgivable Blackness: The Rise and Fall of Jack Johnson*. Public Broadcasting System (PBS), 2004. The quote from Burns: "About the Film," Unforgivable Blackness, PBS, accessed August 3, 2022, https://www.pbs.org. The Burns-Johnson fight was filmed, but no evidence can be located that the picture was shown in Richmond— it likely was too expensive for the nickel theaters and was probably deemed inappropriate, for racial reasons, for the larger theaters that could show higher-priced films. Johnson defended his title again on July 4, 1910, in Reno, Nevada, against fellow (White) American James J. Jeffries. The result of that fight sparked significant racial riots in many parts of the country—though apparently not in Richmond. Blacks were the primary victims of the violence. That match was also filmed but was banned in many cities. No evidence that it was shown in Richmond can be located. The front-page article, "Police May Bar Fight Pictures," *RTD*, Jul. 6, 1910, reported that the film was likely to be banned, and noted that the "mayor was ready to act on [any] complaint if citizens show reason" (i.e., fear for ostensible violence).

92. Dixie Theater, advertisement, *RP*, Mar. 28, 1910.

93. "Echoes from the Grand Lodge," *RP*, June 26, 1909. For more information about Black Pythians in Richmond, see "Artifact Spotlight," *RTD*, Aug. 12, 2018, https://richmond.com. No further information about a Pythian parade film could be located.

94. "Presidential Reception in Richmond," *RTD*, Mar. 5, 1910.

95. "Dudley Adds Other Links to His Chain," *IF*, Jul. 6, 1912 (as quoted in Athelia White, "He Paved the Way for T.O.B.A.," *The Place Perspective in Music*, Autumn 1982: 173; the original article could not be located). The Moseley theaters were not part of the Dudley Circuit but rather brought in Black vaudeville performers as independent acts.

96. "What's What on the Dudley Circuit," *IF*, Mar. 1, 1913, notes that "special pictures" would be shown with the Molloy and Molloy singing act, indicating the films may have been shown as filler.

97. Classified advertisement, *RTD*, Aug. 3, 1913, and Cox, "Woman," *RTD*, Jan. 10, 1926. The photograph of the interior of the Dixie in the 1926 article, taken shortly after theater first opened, shows it only took up the front third or so of the first floor of 18 West Broad, meaning there was plenty of room to extend the theater toward the back of the building.

98. "Dixie Theatre Closes its Doors," *RV*, May 9, 1913.

99. A "Dunlap pony" may have been what is today called a Shetland pony.

100. "Dunlap Pony, Buggy, and Harness Contest," *RP*, May 9, 1914; "Boys' and Girls' Contest," Aug. 15, 1914; Boys' and Girls' Contest, advertisement, Sept. 5, 1914; and "Boys'-Girls' Contest," Dec. 5, 1914. No explanation was given as to what had happened to make the pony and cart unavailable.

101. The phrase "year of racial reckoning," used often in contemporary media descriptions of what happened that summer not only in Richmond but in many

cities across the country, is used for lack of a better term. It is imperfect for many reasons, but the issues are too complex and too well-reported in other publications to go into here.

102. Thessaly La Force, Zoe Lescaze, Nancy Hass, and M. H. Miller, "The 25 Most Influential Works of American Protest Arts Since World War II," *The New York Times Style Magazine*, Oct. 15, 2020, https://www.nytimes.com.

103. "Richmond's Pioneer Movie Exhibitor Quits the Field," *RTD*, Dec. 7, 1923.

104. "Calve Terrified by Applause over 'Dixie'," *RTD*, Feb. 27, 1908.

CHAPTER 4

1. "Picture Shows Become a Problem," *RTD*, Jan. 9, 1909.

2. "Prohibit Jams in Theatre Lobbies," *RTD*, Aug. 14, 1909.

3. "Police Must Keep Crowds on Move," *RTD*, Sept. 29, 1909.

4. There are dozens of such newspaper articles; see, for example, "Fighters Fined," *REJ*, May 17, 1909, and "Police Court Cases," *RTD*, Aug. 25, 1909.

5. "Moving Picture Shows Must Remove Obstacles," *RNL*, Jan. 15, 1910.

6. "Capital City is Vaudeville Crazy," *Mathews Journal*, May 19, 1910.

7. "Only Syndicate Shows Coming," *RTD*, Aug. 21, 1909.

8. "Thorp Case to be Filed This Month," *REJ*, Jan. 14, 1909.

9. "Says Skeggs was Lured Away," *Baltimore Sun* (Baltimore, Maryland) (*BSun*), Jan. 14, 1909. Details of the affair were also published in "Woman Sues for $10,000," *Washington Post* (Washington, D.C.) (*WP*), Jan. 14, 1909; "Wife Sues for $10,000," *Western Sentinel* (Winston-Salem, North Carolina), Jan. 19, 1909, and probably others.

10. "Wants Pay for Husband's Love," *RTD*, Jan. 14, 1909, and "Sues the Picture Queen for $10,000," *RTD*, Jan. 13, 1909.

11. "Asks Release," *RTD*, Jan. 24, 1909.

12. The 1940 census shows John Franklin Skeggs, 85, and his wife Sadie, 71, living together as husband and wife at 201 Jeter Street in Richmond (1940 U.S. Census, Lee Ward, Richmond, Virginia [digital image s.v. "John Franklin Skeggs"], Ancestry.com).

13. Earl P. Hart of the Hart brothers referred to her as the "movie queen" in 1914 (Hart, "Hart Writes," *BET*, Mar. 14, 1914), Lindeman refers to her as the "Dixie Movie Queen" and referenced a *New York Telegram* "of those days" (NFI) which referred to her as "Dixie's Queen of the Movies" (Lindeman, "Early Days," *RTD*, Apr. 23, 1944). There are some others.

14. "Police Court Cases," *RNL*, Jul. 14, 1909.

15. This paragraph combines elements of the reporting and misreporting in articles which appeared in: "Mother Faints at End of Search for Daughter," *Washington Herald*, (Washington, D.C.), Apr. 11, 1911; "Elopers Caught Barely in Time to Prevent Wedding," *Washington Times* (Washington, D.C.), Apr. 11, 1911;

"Richmond Elopers Foiled," *WP*, Apr. 11, 1911; "Elopers Foiled," *Free Lance* (Fredericksburg, Virginia), Apr. 15, 1911; "Licenses Issued in Washington," *BSun*, Apr. 11, 1911; and "Detective Foils Eloper's Plans," *RV*, Apr. 11, 1911.

16. Called the "crime of the century" at the time, the murder has been the subject of several books, many articles, and even a true crime podcast or two.

17. "Newark Man Was Acquainted with H. Clay Beattie," *NA*, Nov. 27, 1911.

18. "Real Estate Transfers," *Evening Herald* (Norwalk, Ohio), Dec. 8, 1911. Amanda would not have been thinking about putting a theater in Chicago Junction; there were few potential patrons around for miles in that part of very rural Ohio.

19. "Joyful Reunion," *CD*, Oct. 8, 1911.

20. Jennifer Fronc, "Local Public Opinion: The National Board of Review of Motion Pictures and the Fight against Film Censorship in Virginia, 1916–1922," *Journal of American Studies*, 47, no. 3 (2013): 726.

21. "Uncle Tom Scene Halted by Police," *RTD*, Aug. 27, 1910. Two film versions of *Uncle Tom's Cabin* were released in 1910; it is not known for certain which one was screened at the Rex. A shorter, one-reel version was that of Barry O'Neil, director, *Uncle Tom's Cabin*, Famous Players-Lasky Corp., Jul. 26, 1910. A three-reel version was that of Frederick A. Thomson, director, *Uncle Tom's Cabin*, Vitagraph Co. of American, Jul. 26, 1910. The *Times-Dispatch* description of the film seems to imply that it was the longer version that appeared at the Rex.

22. "Chaloner to be Newspaper Man," *RTD*, Nov. 18, 1912, and many others. For more information on Chaloner, see Carole Haber, "John Armstrong Chaloner (1862–1935)," Encyclopedia Virginia, Virginia Humanities, accessed Mar. 9, 2021, https://encyclopediavirginia.org.

23. "Ablaze" quote: "Fire is Started in Two Buildings," *RTD*, Mar. 18, 1911. Thorp's comments: "Reopening of Rex," *RTD*, Apr. 5, 1911.

24. "Theatre is Closed," *RTD*, Mar. 28, 1911.

25. "Reopening of Rex," *RTD*, Apr. 5, 1911. In an article the *News Leader* published on March 27, the paper reported the original alarming language which the *RTD* subsequently used to describe the alleged fire risk at the Rex. An inspector, according to the *News Leader*, had gone to the Rex on March 27 to inspect it after the fire. He had discovered there "a large quantity of high combustibles in the form of motion picture films stored in a compartment in the basement enclosed by wooden partitions, a veritable mine of deadly explosives likely to blow up the building at any hour." He added, "The picture films are as dangerous as guncotton and nitroglycerine and the least spark would suffice to cause an explosion that would blow up the theatre." (*RNL*, "Mine of Explosives Under Rex Theatre," Mar. 27, 1911.) The *RTD* comments may have been trolling inaccuracies originally reported in the *News Leader*.

26. "Woman Fined for Abusing Officer," *RNL*, June 25, 1913.

27. "Car and Highway," *RV*, Feb. 1, 1913.

28. "1914 Detroit Electric Model 47 Brougham, Personal Car of Clara Ford," The Henry Ford Museum, accessed Jan. 3, 2022, https://www.thehenryford.org.

29. "All Right to Kiss in Picture Shows," *RTD*, May 24, 1913. The Exhibitors' League was the first attempt by movie theater owners in the Commonwealth to organize to respond to issues they all faced, such as censorship and Sunday closings (blue laws).

30. Though some African Americans were running movie theaters in Virginia (including in Richmond) at the time, there is no indication that any African American was a member of the Moving Picture Exhibitors' League.

31. "Girl Wanted," *BET*, Apr. 17, 1907.

32. Golden, "Early Movies," *RTD*, Apr. 3, 1939.

33. E.g., "Society Folk in Play for Charity," *RTD*, Feb. 27, 1908.

34. "Brick vs. Chair," *RTD*, Jul. 11, 1907.

35. Untitled brief, *RTD*, Feb. 26, 1908.

36. "To Rebuild Theatre," *RTD*, Sept. 26, 1908.

37. Richmond City Directory, 1911 (130, digital image s.v. "Theato"), Ancestry.com.

38. "Fire in Negro Theatre," *RTD*, Sept. 6, 1907.

39. "Says Skeggs was Lured Away," *BSun*, Jan. 14, 1909.

40. Hart, "Hart Writes," *BET*, Mar. 14, 1914.

41. Untitled brief, *RTD*, Jul. 2, 1909.

42. "Southside," *RNL*, June 10, 1911.

CHAPTER 5

1. Photograph caption, *RTD*, Sept. 1, 1912.

2. Photograph caption, *RV*, Sept. 15, 1912.

3. "Mrs. A. E. Thorp Will Build," *BET*, Jan. 31, 1913.

4. Ken Roe, "Hippodrome Theatre," Cinema Treasures, accessed June 15, 2021, http://cinematreasures.org. The comment is curious in that it sources the information to a Richmond City building permit, but no permit could be located.

5. "Woman's Success," *RV*, Sept. 15, 1912. It is duly noted that the *Virginian* reporter could not resist the occasional sexist comment.

6. For more about Maggie L. Walker, see, for example, "Maggie Lena Walker," National Historic Site, Virginia, National Park Service, June 18, 2021, https://www.nps.gov.

7. "Woman's Success," *RV*, Sept. 15, 1912.

8. "Woman's Success," *RV*, Sept. 15, 1912.

9. Waller, "Another Audience": 10. Waller's analysis of Black moviegoing (and vaudeville attendance) in the early twentieth century is very helpful in understanding the complexities of the reception by both Blacks and Whites of the Black entertainment venues which were arising in Richmond and the Black entertainers who were performing in them.

10. "Woman's Success," *RV*, Sept. 15, 1912.

11. "The Hippodrome," *RP*, May 3, 1913.

12. Hillyer, "On to Richmond": 113, discusses the increasing segregation of Richmond in the early 1900s.

13. R. W. T., "The Passing Show in Washington," *IF*, Jul. 24, 1915.

14. Richmond City Directory, 1915 (169, digital image s.v. "Hippodrome"), Ancestry.com.

15. Hippodrome, advertisement, *RP*, May 5, 1913; Hippodrome, advertisement, *RP*, Mar. 28, 1914; "That Anti-Segregation Meeting," *RP*, Mar. 27, 1915; and other ads and articles about shows and other events at the Hippodrome.

16. "The Frogs Club (Artists Organization) is Formed," African American Registry, accessed Aug. 12, 2021, https://aaregistry.org. The other cities which presented the show were Philadelphia, Baltimore, and Washington, D.C.

17. Hippodrome, advertisement, *RTD*, Aug. 13, 1913.

18. "What's What," *IF*, Dec. 20, 1913, and "News of the Nation's Capital," Aug. 7, 1915.

19. "Cyclone and Demon to Meet," *RTD*, Nov. 5, 1914.

20. E.g., Hippodrome, advertisement, *IF*, Apr. 24, 1915.

21. "Colored Pythians Meet Here This Week," *RTD*, June 15, 1914, and "That Anti-Segregation Meeting," *RP*, Mar. 27, 1915.

22. "Virginia," *Motion Picture News (MPN)*, Jul. 25, 1914, 59. This news snippet illustrates the minutiae that the myriad cinema trade publications printed within their pages.

23. Hippodrome, advertisement, *RP*, June 20, 1914. Movie: *The Fall of the Mighty,* Al Bartlett Film Manufacturing Company, 1913.

24. "Broadway Vaudeville at Hippodrome," *RP*, Jul. 18, 1914. Movie: *Dandy Jim's Dream*, Afro-American Film Company, 1914.

25. Ad: Hippodrome, advertisement, *RP*, Sept. 5, 1914. Film: William R. Daly, director, Carl Laemmle, Jr., producer, *Uncle Tom's Cabin*, World Film Company, 1914. The book, *Uncle Tom's Cabin*, was the best-selling novel and the second best-selling book of the 19th century, following only the Bible, and was the most-filmed book of the silent-film era. Charles Gilpin, an African American actor who was a Richmond native, was originally cast in the part of Uncle Tom role in a 1913 version but was released because his "portrayal was too aggressive" ("'An Epic of the Old South:' Universal Super Jewel Production [1927]," Uncle Tom's Cabin & American Culture: A Multi-Media Archive, Stephen Railton, director, University of Virginia, accessed Jan. 27, 2022, https://en.wikipedia.org.) Much scholarship is available about the book itself and the plays and films that origi-nated from it. Jason Richards, examined, for example, how four black characters, including Uncle Tom, "employ blackface and colonial mimicry simultaneously to resist and conform to various aspects of national identity, (all the while testing) racial barriers." (Jason Richards, "Imitation Nation: Blackface Minstrelsy and the Making of African American Selfhood in *Uncle Tom's Cabin*," in *NOVEL: A Forum on Fiction*, Spring 2006, 204.)

26. Untitled brief, *IF*, Mar. 21, 1914.

27. "A Card of Thanks," *IF*, Sept. 7, 1912.

28. "Benefit for Henry F. Watterson, *IF*, Dec. 26, 1914.

29. "Seen and Heard While Passing," *IF*, Nov. 13, 1915.

30. Classified advertisement, *RTD*, Aug. 3, 1913.

31. Dixie, advertisement, *IF*, Feb. 13, 1915.

CHAPTER 6

1. "Pulled Girl out of Bed for Morning Auto Ride," *RTD*, Aug. 22, 1915. The account is graphic in its description of violence during the act. The story attracted at least some out of town press coverage; "Virginia News," *Alexandria Gazette*, (Alexandria, Virginia), Nov. 10, 1915, for one, had a short summary of it in which it helpfully provided "Miss Baker's" first name as Faun. The relationship of Faun Baker to Waldo: "Apart 10 Years, Seeks Divorce," *Buffalo Courier* (Buffalo, New York), Feb. 4, 1920. The article concerned a divorce proceeding that Faun's husband was pursuing against her. Among other things, evidence was presented that implied Faun was receiving money from other men to have affairs with them, Waldo being one of them.

2. "Thorp is Convicted on Several Warrants," *RTD*, Aug. 24, 1915.

3. "Capias is Issued for Arrest of Waldo Thorp," *RTD*, Nov. 10, 1915.

4. "Locals," *BET*, June 12, 1916, and "Newark Man is not Allowed to Enter Canada," *NA*, Jul. 27, 1916.

5. "Locals," *BET*, June 12, 1916.

6. "Real Estate and Courts," *RTD*, May 27, 1916. The date that Thorp sold the Hippodrome to Somma is reported on the property deed, City of Richmond, Assessor of Real Estate, which also named the accoutrements that went with it. The *Richmond Planet* reported the cost of the real estate transaction ("Bragg Brothers and Co. Make Big Realty Transfers," *RP*, May 27, 1916).

7. Richmond City Directory, 1916 (692, digital image s.v. "Hoover Wm H"), Ancestry.com. The 1917 Richmond City Directory does not show Thorp affiliated with any theater.

8. Cox, "Woman," *RTD*, Jan. 10, 1926. It is noted, however, that Thorp may have had financial help from William Morey when she opened Wonderland in Bucyrus.

9. Richmond City Directory, 1918 (839, digital image s.v. "Klein Walter P"), Ancestry.com.

10. "Bluebird Theatre Opens Today," *RTD*, Mar. 2, 1917. A *News Leader* advertisement for the Bluebird on the same day listed "Mrs. A. C. [sic] Thorp and Mr. W. P. Klein," as proprietors.

11. "Bluebird Theatre Opens Today," *RTD*, Mar. 2, 1917.

12. There is scant, conflicting, literature concerning the availability of Richmond movie theaters to Black patrons in the late 1910s and through the 1920s. Unlike the Bluebird, some theaters, especially the big legitimate theaters, had

segregated seating in the gallery (balcony) that were made available at least some of the time to Black patrons, but which theaters did so are not well documented. The Bluebird did not have a balcony, so there could have been no segregated seating available to Black patrons.

13. "Bluebird Theatre Opens Today," *RTD*, Mar. 2, 1917.

14. "New Theatre, the Bluebird Opens," *RV*, Mar. 2, 1917. The website, https://richmondtheatres.tripod.com/, accessed June 9, 2021, states the first Wurlitzer organ in Richmond was placed in the Brookland Theater built in 1924 by Charles Somma and Walter Coulter; whether or not that is true may depend on whether or not the Bluebird Hope-Jones instrument could be considered a Wurlitzer. The most famous Wurlitzer in Richmond, and quite famous in theater histories in general, is the one in the still-functioning Byrd Theatre. The Byrd, built in 1928 by Coulter and Somma, today is a National Historic Landmark on Cary Street. The organ there continues to be played at special events at the theater. The reference to the organ at the Bluebird as a "style Z" is likely a typo as no organ with that designation appears to have been manufactured by Wurlitzer at that time. Not much is known about the architect of the Bluebird theater, Henry T. Barham, though he was also known for designing the iconic Emrick Flats building in Jackson Ward, Richmond. Built as an automobile dealership, it is unique for its triangular shape. For more information about him, see Justin Grenzebach, "Emrick Flats," Architecture Richmond, accessed Jan. 5, 2022, https://architecturerichmond.com.

15. "Bluebird Theater Organ and Organist," *RV*, Mar. 14, 1917. Though further identifying information on Houston could not be located, the *Virginian* also noted that he had played in various cities and towns in England and Scotland and had made an extensive tour in the United States.

16. "Bluebird Theatre Organ and Organist," *RV*, Mar. 14, 1917. The difference in number of reported instruments on the organ may be due to a difference in how the word "instruments" was interpreted. As an aside: Edith Lindeman reported in 1959 that a man named Paul Nevilles or Nelson played the organ at the Bluebird Theater for many years, though there may have been others. She also reported that the Bluebird organ was moved in 1933 to Richmond's Tantilla Gardens, an entertainment venue opened that same year which hosted concerts by big bands and dancing. (Lindeman, "Old-Time Organist Here is Recalled," *RTD*, Mar. 31, 1959.) Located at 3817 West Broad, Tantilla Gardens was started by none other than Walter Coulter. Tantilla Gardens fell into despair in the 1960s and was razed. The organ's fate is unknown.

17. Letter to the editor, *RNL*, Oct. 29, 1925.

18. "Wonderful Music," *El Paso Herald* (El Paso, Texas), Jan. 21, 1916; Theater advertisement, *Spokane Chronicle* (Spokane, Washington), Mar. 4, 1916; and "It Pays to Read the Telegraph: It is Worth While to Go to the Victoria Theatre," *Harrisburg Telegraph* (Harrisburg, Pennsylvania), Jan. 13, 1916.

19. "New Bluebird Theatre in Richmond," *MPW*, Feb. 10, 1917, 884.

20. The Compensarc was an apparatus that helped ensure steady light for showing motion pictures, eliminating the annoying "flickering" of early films which had given rise to the word "flicks" to describe them. Compensarc, advertisement, *MPW*, Jan. 1, 1916, 145.

21. F. H. Richardson, "Richardson has Tussle with Jupiter Pluvius," *MPW*, Mar. 24, 1917, 1909. Richardson visited several Richmond movie theaters and talked to several operators during the visit. He felt Richmond operators were "without exception, bright, wide-awake looking men." Though he praised the Bluebird's operations room, he was less impressed with others, saying that the managers needed to "study the technical end of their business," chiefly in how the projection rooms should be set up. Accompanying the article is a photo of 25 male theater managers that met with the writer one evening at the Murphy Hotel. There is no mention of Thorp in the article, and she does not appear in the photograph.

22. The lights are reported to have been blue in Fuller-Seeley, *Celebrate*, 45. Other details about the sign are from https://richmondtheatres.tripod.com, accessed June 9, 2021. The sign is often remembered in articles reminiscing about the old, but now gone, movie theaters of Richmond.

23. Bluebird Theater, advertisement, *RTD*, Mar. 2, 1917; Joseph De Grasse, director, *Hell Morgan's Girl*, Universal Film Mfg. Co., Mar. 5, 1917. It is noted that the release date noted on the online *American Film Institute Catalog* is after the date it was apparently shown for the first time at the Bluebird; perhaps Thorp had been able to get an advance of the film because of the theater opening.

24. Multiple Bluebird Theater advertisements, *RTD*, 1917.

25. "A Movie Censorship," *RNL*, Apr. 13, 1916. The Richmond population number is an extrapolation of the numbers provided by the census in 1910 and 1920. In the article, the reporter implied that many of the admissions were from patrons who repeated attendance, but there also would have been folks outside of Richmond who came into town to bring in goods, go shopping, or do other errands and who would have taken the opportunity to take in a film.

26. Eric Jay Dewberry, "Jake Wells, Commercial Entertainment Entrepreneur of the South: A Study of His Career in Richmond, Virginia, 1894–1927" (master's thesis, Virginia Commonwealth University, Richmond, 2003), 119–122. Dewberry's work on Wells is unpublished but has much in it for the student of early Richmond and regional theater, not only for the biographical information on Jake but also for its study of local attitudes toward amusements as they evolved in the turn of the twentieth century.

27. "Richmond's Only Exchange," *MPW*, Apr. 5, 1919, 86.

28. "Labor Paralyzed by Fuel Mandate," *RTD*, Jan. 9, 1918, and "Bond Campaign Now Underway," Sept. 28, 1918.

29. "Warning Against Grippe Sounded by Flannagan," *RTD*, Sept. 18, 1918. Though the press, health officials, and others at the time called the flu an "epidemic," it meets the standards today of a world pandemic.

30. "Spanish Influenza makes Gains in Richmond; Cases Total 340; Doctors Busy," *RNL*, Sept. 30, 1918.

31. "Spanish Influenza," *RNL*, Sept. 30, 1918.

32. "Influenza Situation is Considered Grave," *RTD*, Oct. 5, 1918.

33. "Epidemic Forces Drastic Action," *RTD*, Oct. 6, 1918.

34. "Flu Besieges City: 10,000 Cases Here," *RTD*, Oct. 8, 1918.

35. "Theatres Open Monday, Tip Passed Out," *RNL*, Oct. 29, 1918.

36. "Flu Restrictions Lifted by Board," *RTD*, Nov. 5, 1918.

37. Bluebird, advertisement, *RV*, Nov. 5, 1918. Moving picture theaters were on the forefront of ventilation technology. For information about this subject, see Roger Chang, "Historic Theaters and Their Impact on Air Conditioning Today," American Society of Heating, Refrigerating and Air-Conditioning Engineers (ASHRAE), December 2019, 44, https://www.ashrae.org.

38. "A Typhoon Installation," *MPW*, Jul. 31, 1915, 839.

39. "Doctors Meet Tonight to Discuss Influenza," *RTD*, Dec. 13, 1918.

40. The "Spanish flu" continued to bring waves of disease and death to the United States for another two to three years or so, depending on who is doing the reporting, but governmental response largely stopped after fall 1918. Vestiges of the flu are still thought to circulate occasionally. For more information about the experience of Richmond in the 1918–1919 flu epidemic, which parallels the experience in many ways with the COVID-19 pandemic which had its start in 2020, see "The American Influenza Epidemic of 1918–1919: Richmond, Virginia," Influenza Encyclopedia, University of Michigan Center for the History of Medicine and Michigan Publishing, University of Michigan Library, accessed Jan. 22, 2022, https://www.influenzaarchive.org.

41. "Buys Picture Show in Virginia City," *BET*, Sept. 22, 1919, and "Have Two Bluebirds," *BET*, Sept. 23, 1919. The newspaper gave erroneous information about the ownership in the article published on September 22 and partially corrected it on September 23.

42. *BET*, Sept. 22, 1919, and Sept. 23, 1919, and *Petersburg Evening Progress*, Dec. 22, 1919.

43. "Bluebird Theatre Will Open Sunday," *Petersburg Progress & Index-Appeal*, Feb. 19, 1922.

44. Ken Roe, "Hippodrome," Cinema Treasures, accessed June 15, 2021, http://cinematreasures.org. This online article is unsourced, and the information about the organ could not be confirmed.

45. U.S. World War I draft registration, Akron, Ohio, Sept. 15, 1918 (digital image s.v. "Waldo Franklin Thorp"), Ancestry.com; Columbus [Ohio] City Directory, 1922 (1245, digital image s.v. "Thorpe Waldo"), Ancestry.com. At the time of the World War I draft registration, Waldo listed his occupation as a clerk for Firestone Tire and Rubber Co.; he listed his next of kin as Amanda.

46. "Comrades," *Columbus Evening Dispatch* (Columbus, Ohio) (*CED*), May 8, 1909, and "Captain Miller Loses His Place at Statehouse," Sept. 30, 1915. The

article refers to Frank's military rank as "captain"; he actually had been a private in the war. (Captain Miller was another individual who was fired.)

47. "Ohio Deaths and Burials, 1854–1997" (digital image s.v. "Franklin T. Thorp"), FamilySearch.org.

48. "U.S. Civil War Pension Index" (digital image s.v. "Thorp, Franklin T."), Fold3.com.

49. "Bluebird Free to Vets," *RTD*, June 21, 1922.

50. Classified advertisement, *RTD*, Dec. 20, 1914. City directories began to list telephone numbers at around this time; the telephone number in the ad is the one shown as Thorp's in the city directory.

51. Real estate transaction and tax delinquency information was reported over the years in the following periodicals: *RNL*: Jul. 17, 1912, Jul. 24, 1912, and Aug. 21, 1912; *BET*: Nov. 6, 1916; *RTD*: Jan. 25 and Dec. 20, 1914, Feb. 4. and Feb. 7, 1915, and Nov. 6, 1921; *RV*: Jan. 21, 1915, Jan. 13, 1924, June 7, 1925, Mar. 8, 1926, and Apr. 20, 1926; *REJ*: Jul. 25, 1912. Some of these articles were discovered by searches on her name and some by searching on her phone number and 2207 Stuart Avenue home address. Real estate notices are hit and miss in newspapers, and thus there may have been other, perhaps several other, exchanges of property that Thorp was involved in but which were not reported.

52. Richmond city directories 1910–1923 and the 1910 U.S. Census, Madison Ward, Richmond City, Virginia, (digital image s.v. "Amanda Thorp"), Ancestry. com.

53. Edith Lindeman, "Unsung Heroes of Film World Rate Applause," *RTD*, May 23, 1951.

54. Richmond City Directory, 1920 (443, digital image s.v. "Coulter Robt H"), Ancestry.com, and Richmond City Directory, 1921 (407, digital image s.v. "Coulter Robt H"), Ancestry.com.

55. "Capital City Gossip," *MPW*, Aug. 7, 1915, 1039.

56. "Personal Points," *BET*, Apr. 27, 1910.

57. "Virginia Managers in New York," *Billboard*, Mar. 22, 1913, 50.

58. "Among the Exchanges," *MPN*, May 8, 1915, 55.

59. "Mrs. A. E. Thorpe to Open New Theatre," *MPW*, Nov. 18, 1916, 1993.

60. "Virginian Exhibitors Adjourn," *Motography*, Jul. 6, 1918, 38.

61. "Say Uniform Contract is Non-Uniform," *MPN*, Nov. 10, 1923, 2224.

62. "Five Reported Dead in Disaster," *RTD*, May 15, 1923.

63. "No Lives are Lost in Hot Springs Flood; Damage Over Millions," *RTD*, May 16, 1923.

64. Bluebird Theater, advertisement, *RTD*, May 24, 1923. No information could be located about the film, but it probably was a newsreel.

65. Wonderland, advertisement, *BET*, May 11, 1907.

66. "Comprehensive List," *Billboard*, Dec. 15, 1906. In an indication of the rapid growth of these movie theaters, "Combined List," *Billboard*, Sept. 5, 1908, listed several thousand of them across the country.

67. Tom Moore, "Scouting in the Old Dominion," *Film Index*, Oct. 22, 1910, 5.

68. "Virginia," *Tradesman*, Sept. 12, 1912, 54, and "Richmond, Virginia," *MPW*, Sept. 28, 1912.

69. "Mrs. Thorp Doesn't Hesitate," *MPW*, Feb. 21, 1920, 1234.

70. "Say Uniform Contract," *MPN*, Nov. 10, 1923, 2224.

71. "Richmond's Pioneer Movie Exhibitor Quits the Field," *RTD*, Dec. 7, 1923.

72. Richmond City Directory, 1923 (533, e.g., digital image s.v. "Coulter Gertrude Miss"), Ancestry.com.

73. "Washington, D.C., Marriage Records," 1810–1953 (index, s.v. "Walter J. Coulter" and "Clarice MacDonald"), Ancestry.com. The marriage does not seem to have been announced in the Richmond papers.

74. Eric Jay Dewberry discusses these in detail in Dewberry, "Jake Wells in Richmond."

75. "Richmond's Pioneer Movie Exhibitor Quits the Field," *RTD*, Dec. 7, 1923.

76. "Propose New Movie House for South Side," *RTD*, Mar. 31, 1924.

CHAPTER 7

1. "New $15,000 Home Being Built for Mrs. Trorp [*sic*] in Duntreath," *RTD*, Dec. 23, 1923.

2. Though the reporter didn't specifically list the other two, he was probably referring to the Bluebird as one of them, with the other one probably being the Isis, a traditional playhouse formerly known as the Lubin which was converted to movies by Jake Wells at about this time.

3. The location of the Venus is nearly directly across the street from the "New Wonderland" Thorp had briefly opened at 1435 Hull Street in late 1907.

4. The Typhoon ventilating system was a product of the Typhoon Fan Company, New York, New York.

5. "Will Build $75,000 South Side Theatre," *RTD*, Apr. 27, 1924.

6. "Completing New Theatre," *RTD*, Dec. 7, 1924, and "New Management for Victor Theatre," *RTD*, Dec. 6, 1925. It is difficult today to determine where the Victor on Hull Street in Southside was located because street numbers appear to have changed somewhat on Hull Street; the theater may have been demolished and today is an empty lot. All three of Thorp's theaters at this time were within a three-block area in Southside on Hull: in the 1200 (the little Shirley), 1300 (the bigger Victor), and 1400 blocks (the largest, Venus), and all on the same, even-numbered side of the street. Addresses at the time were: the Shirley at 1224 Hull; the Victor, at 1310 Hull, and the Venus at 1412 Hull. The locations today are just outside of Richmond's Blackwell Historic District.

7. Richmond City Directory, 1924 (1351, digital image s.v. "Thorp Waldo F"), Ancestry.com.

8. "Michigan Marriage Records, 1867–1952" (digital image s.v. "Waldo T. Thorp" and digital image "Lulu Irene Cordell), Ancestry.com.

9. 1910 U.S. Census, Columbus, Franklin County, Ohio (digital image s.v. "Lulu Cordell" and s.v. "Clarice McDonald"), Ancestry.com.

10. "South Richmond Turns Out to Attending Opening," *RTD*, Mar. 19, 1925: "Announce Good Program," *RTD*, Mar. 18, 1925; and "Willis Pulliam Speaks," *RNL*, Mar. 19, 1925. "Announce Good Program," *RTD*, Mar. 18, 1925, notes the organist's name as Ernest Loffler; "William Loeffler" was the name based on a correction published the next day. it is not known if Loeffler was from Richmond or was brought in especially for the grand opening. Movie: E. Mason Hopper, director, *Janice Meredith*, Cosmopolitan Pictures, December 8, 1924.

11. "Charlotte Manager Entertains Staff," *MPW*, June 5, 1926, 36.

12. "Venus, Motion Picture Theatre, is Purchased by Goldberg & Rosser," *RTD*, Jul. 2, 1926.

13. "Exchange Opens New Branch in S. Richmond," *RTD*, Mar. 7, 1926.

14. "Virginia, Death Records, 1912–2014" (digital image s.v. "Mrs. Amanda E. Thorp"), Ancestry.com.

CODA

1. All information about Thorp's allegation comes from the Richard Watkins Carrington Papers, 1880–1933, Box 38, folder entitled "1925–1929," Albert and Shirley Small Special Collections, University of Virginia, Charlottesville.

2. There was another reason why Wells was trying to off-load his South Richmond theaters: he was getting out of the theater business entirely and moving into real estate investment. Even as an owner of a large, interstate chain of movie theaters himself, he had found he could not compete against the growing studio-dominated chains. He had already sold many of his theaters across the South, but apparently had kept his Virginia theaters which he felt, for some reason, could be profitable (or perhaps he was emotionally attached to them). He was likely suffering from buyers' remorse after his purchase of the Victor. Thorp, unfortunately, had not reached the same conclusion in regard to competitive status of independent ownership of movie theaters before she opened the Venus. It is noted, however, that Coulter and Somma were having success with their Richmond theaters, but perhaps they were able to come to some kind of accommodation with the studio chains that Thorp couldn't or wouldn't do. Info about Wells' divestments of Richmond theaters: Dewberry, "Jake Wells, Commercial Entertainment Entrepreneur of the South," 19.

3. Thorp's June 1926 visit to the Dardines, who managed the Charlotte, North Carolina, Universal Film Exchanges, may have been a last-minute effort to try to arrange a way to procure better films for the Venus outside the monopoly held by Jake Wells and the Washington, D.C., exchange, Film Exchanges. She may also have been trying to arrange for the sale of the theater to the North Carolina interests which occurred not long afterward.

4. "Virginia, Death Records, 1912–2014" (digital image s.v. "Mrs. Amanda E. Thorp"), Ancestry.com.

5. All information about the resolution of the estate comes from the Richard Watkins Carrington Papers, 1880–1933, Box 93, folder entitled "Estates - Amanda Thorp 1926–1927," Albert and Shirley Small Special Collections, University of Virginia, Charlottesville.

6. "Minstrels Draw Crowd to Victor," *RTD*, Feb. 29, 1928.

7. "Poton to Reopen Victor Theatre," *RTD*, Jul. 11, 1931.

8. Cox, "Woman," *RTD*, Jan. 10, 1926. The quote by Cox has been edited for clarity and to make it more concise. The claim that Thorp was the first woman exhibitor in the United States is unproven as is the claim that she was the first in the South to open a theater exclusively for African Americans, although both are possible.

9. Golden, "Early Movies," *RTD*, Apr. 3, 1939.

10. "Noted Moving Picture Operator of Richmond Here," *Charlotte News* (Charlotte, North Carolina), Dec. 4, 1916.

EPILOGUE

1. Ceased publication in 1991.

2. Much has been written on Jake Wells; see for example, F. T. Rea, "Jake Wells: 'Father of Richmond Movie Houses'," accessed February 5, 2022. https://jamesriverfilm.wordpress.com. In this article, which is often the case, Thorp's contributions to the "movie houses" of Richmond is not mentioned.

3. Cox, "Woman," *RTD*, Jan. 10, 1926.

4. "Movie House Owner to be Buried Today," *RTD*, Jul. 29, 1927. The paper noted in the sub-head and in the text of the obituary that she had "operated [the] first motion picture house in Virginia." It was never her claim that she was the first in Virginia, though she might have been.

5. "Well Known Movie Exhibitor Dies," *Lancaster Eagle-Gazette* (Lancaster, Ohio), Jul. 29, 1927, in an article attributed to the Associated Press.

6. "Thorp" (obituary), *RTD*, Feb. 22, 1928. She suffered an apparent stroke.

7. 1930 U.S. Census, Lee Ward, Richmond City, Virginia (digital image s.v. "Waldo F. Thorp"), Ancestry.com.

8. Iona Park, advertisement, *RTD*, Aug. 1, 1929, and "Notice of Trustees' Selling of Site," Sept. 19, 1932.

9. "Letters from Waldo Thorp to Charles Somma, 1930–1935" (some undated), among papers donated by the Somma family to the Valentine Museum, Richmond, Virginia.

10. "Three-Year Term Given in Tax Case," *RTD*, Dec. 12, 1952.

11. "Virginia, Marriage Records, 1936–2014," Certificate of Marriage, (digital image s.v. "Thelma Pauline Burnette"), Ancestry.com. This was Thelma's second marriage.

12. "Waldo Franklin Thorp," (obituary), *RTD*, June 17, 1956.

13. "New $70,000 Theatre on North Side Planned," *RTD*, May 7, 1924.

14. "Byrd Theatre to Open Doors Monday Night," *RTD*, Dec. 23, 1928.

15. Kate Bredimus, "The Mysteries of the Byrd Revealed," *RTD* online, April 8, 2002, https://richmond.com.

16. Theatre History, Explore the Byrd Theatre's Past," Byrd Theatre, accessed Jul. 7, 2021, https://byrdtheatre.org.

17. Gibson Worsham and Richard Worsham, "Richmond Theater" (part 1 of a 3-part series), *Urban Scale Richmond*, accessed Jul. 7, 2021, UrbanScale RichmondVirginia.blogspot.com.

18. E.g., "Charters Issued," *RTD*, Feb. 5, 1930. This article describes an amendment to a charter of the Bluebird Theater, so the charter existed sometime even before this date.

19. E.g., Tucker, "Main Street," *RTD*, Aug. 19, 1933, but also referenced in several other columns by Tucker.

20. E.g., "Broad St. Methodist Church is Presented $24,000 Organ," *RTD*, Sept. 4, 1936.

21. Tucker, "Main Street," *RTD*, Feb. 15, 1930, and Tucker, "Main Street," Feb. 26, 1930. The alligators were perhaps a friendly competitive nod to the alligators that had been housed in the outdoor fountain of Richmond's venerable Jefferson Hotel since at least 1925 ("Jefferson Hotel," *RTD*, June 7, 1925).

22. E.g., "Clowning Councilmen Clubbed by Addled Aldermen, 19–4," *RTD*, May 31, 1939.

23. "Compromise Ends Tax Case Against Coulter and Blackburn Over Secret Account," *RTD*, June 30, 1938, published the culminating press article for this affair, which had been fully and sometimes salaciously covered in the local press for months.

24. "$362,716.41 Estate Left by Coulter," *RTD*, June 12, 1943.

25. "Miss Coulter, Mr. Somma Will Marry," *RTD*, Mar. 29, 1950; "Virginia, Divorce Records, 1918–2014" (digital image s.v. "Joyce Coulter Somma"), Ancestry.com.

26. Fuller-Seeley, *Celebrate*: 64, 70, and 152. It is important to mention that the Richmond residents and children mentioned here generally are references to Whites. Fuller-Seeley notes that according to a 2002 *Richmond Times-Dispatch* article, the balcony in the Byrd was built with the intention of accommodating Black patrons through a side door during the segregation years, but the theater did not open its front doors to African American patrons until the 1960s which is when the Supreme Court struck down race-based segregation laws (Bredimus, "Mysteries.") It could not be discovered if the Byrd actually ever used the balcony for the purpose of segregating its audience. The original 2002 *RTD* article could not be located.

27. "Washington D.C., Compiled Marriage Index, 1830–1921" (s.v. "Charles A. Somma" and s.v. "Carrie E. Rowe"), Ancestry.com.

28. Fuller-Seeley, *Celebrate*, 82–83. In the 1930s and 1940s, the Abe Lichtman group owned many theaters in the South and East that provided affordable

but segregated entertainment to Black audiences. Lichtman became a nationally known advocate for equal economic opportunities for African Americans. At a time when few White business owners hired African American workers for white-collar jobs, Lichtman was known to have maintained a predominantly African American theater staff at his theaters, but it is not known if that was the case at the Hippodrome specifically.

29. Multiple articles appeared at the time in the *Richmond Times-Dispatch*, including editorials which opposed the deal.

30. "Somma Gives $5,000 Fund to Save Ball Club of City," *RTD*, June 6, 1931.

31. Richmond City Directory, 1930 (1170, digital image s.v. "Chas A Somma"), Ancestry.com, and newspaper articles of the time describing various business deals.

32. "Charles A. Somma, Sr., Dies Here After Short Illness," *RTD*, Dec. 27, 1943.

33. These details on Jake Well's early life and career are taken from Dewberry, "Jake Wells, Commercial Entertainment Entrepreneur of the South," 16–17.

34. Dewberry, "Jake Wells, Commercial Entertainment Entrepreneur of the South," 18.

35. Cara Caddoo, "Colored Theaters in the Jim Crow City," *Envisioning Freedom: Cinema and the Building of Modern Black Life*, (Harvard University Press, 1914), 85–93.

36. North Side Skating Rink, advertisement, *RTD*, Dec. 16, 1906. Roller skating was a popular entertainment in the early 1900s. There were several large White skating rinks in Richmond at the same time that North Side Skating Rink existed.

37. North Side Skating Rink, advertisement, *RP*, June 9, 1906. The information about Bahen comes from numerous *Richmond Times-Dispatch* articles of the era when Bahen was often mentioned due to his position as alderman.

38. "Moseley's European Hotel and Cafe," *IF*, Mar. 23, 1907, and other *IF* articles about Moseley's businesses in Richmond.

39. Newspaper accounts of how many people could be accommodated for a show in the former skating rink ranged from 800–1,800.

40. Globe Theatre, advertisement, *RP*, Sept. 12, 1908.

41. Wm. B. Pizzini Company, advertisement, *RTD*, Sept. 12, 1908.

42. Richmond City Directory, 1909 (1265, digital image s.v. "Orient Theatre"), Ancestry.com.

43. "The New Pekin, Norfolk, Va.," *IF*, Jan. 30, 1909; Richmond City Directory, 1910 (1090, digital image s.v. "Pekin Theatre"); Richmond City Directory, 1911 (1271, digital image s.v. "Pekin Theatre"), Ancestry.com (asterisks indicate it was a theater for Black patrons only); and "The Theatrical Success of C. W. Moseley," *IF*, Dec. 23, 1911, (the latter states Moseley was in business with his brother William and that they owned the Pekin Theater in Richmond and the Idle Hour Theater in Petersburg). Charles Moseley also still owned the Pekin Theater in Norfolk at the time. The Pekin theaters in both Richmond and Norfolk

featured early Black vaudeville acts. Fuller-Seeley says the Pekin in Richmond opened in 1910 and closed in 1915 (*Celebrate*, 169); however, newspaper accounts indicate the Pekin opened probably in 1909. Since city directories often lagged a year between the collection of information and its publication and if the *Celebrate* information is based on city directories as is likely, then the Richmond Pekin would not only have probably opened in 1909 but likely closed in 1914.

44. Regent Theater, advertisement, *Afro-American* (Baltimore, Maryland), Dec. 8, 1917.

45. "To Build New Theatre," *BSun*, Jan. 24, 1920.

46. Richmond City Directory, 1889 (330, digital image s.v. "Klein Walter P"), Ancestry.com.

47. "Building Permits," *RTD*, Oct. 19, 1915, and Richmond city directories, Ancestry.com.

SELECTED BIBLIOGRAPHY

Abbreviations, when used in notes to the text and appendices, are provided.

NEWSPAPERS

Newspapers can be either primary or secondary sources. They are primary sources when they report on events that are current; they are secondary when they are retrospective or reminiscent in nature. Whenever possible, primary sources have been used, but reminiscing pieces are also used to fill gaps or to humanize the story.

Names of some of the newspapers have changed over the years, but they are standardized here as the following:

Afro-American (Baltimore, Maryland)
Baltimore Sun (Baltimore, Maryland) (*BSun*)
Brockway Record (Brockway, Pennsylvania) (*BR*)
Brooklyn Daily Eagle (Brooklyn, New York)
Bucyrus Evening Telegraph (Bucyrus, Ohio) (*BET*)
Bucyrus Journal (Bucyrus, Ohio) (*BJ*)
Bucyrus Telegraph-Forum (Bucyrus, Ohio) (*BTF*)
Buffalo Courier (Buffalo, New York)
Charlotte News (Charlotte, North Carolina)
Cincinnati Enquirer (Cincinnati, Ohio) (*CE*)
Cleveland Plain Dealer (Cleveland, Ohio) (*CPD*)
Columbus Dispatch (Columbus, Ohio) (*CED*)
Columbus Evening Dispatch (Columbus, Ohio)
Daily Ohio Statesman (Columbus, Ohio)
Daily Press (Newport News, Virginia)
Dayton Herald (Dayton, Ohio)
Democrat and Standard (Coschocton, Ohio)
El Paso Herald (El Paso, Texas)
Evening Herald (Norwalk, Ohio)
Harrisburg Telegraph (Harrisburg, Pennsylvania)
Indianapolis Freeman (Indianapolis, Indiana) (*IF*)
Lancaster Eagle-Gazette (Lancaster, Ohio)
Mathews Journal (Mathews, Virginia)

Newark Advocate (Newark, Ohio) (*NA*)

New York Age (New York, New York) (*NYA*)

Petersburg Evening Progress (Petersburg, Virginia)

Petersburg Progress & Index-Appeal (Petersburg, Virginia)

Richmond Evening Journal (Richmond, Virginia) (*REJ*)

Richmond News Leader (Richmond, Virginia) (*RNL*)

Richmond Planet (Richmond, Virginia) (*RP*)

Richmond Times-Dispatch (Richmond, Virginia) (*RTD*)

Richmond Virginian (Richmond, Virginia) (*RV*)

Spokane Chronicle (Spokane, Washington)

St. Luke Herald (Richmond, Virginia) (*SLH*)

Times Recorder (Zanesville, Ohio)

Washington Herald (Washington, D.C.)

Washington Post (Washington, D.C.) (*WP*)

Washington Star (Washington, D.C.)

Washington Times (Washington, D.C.)

Western Sentinel (Winston-Salem, North Carolina)

TRADE MAGAZINES

Billboard Magazine (*Billboard*)

The Film Index

Motion Picture News (*MPN*)

Motography

Moving Picture Weekly

Moving Picture World (*MPW*)

The Tradesman

SCHOLARLY PUBLICATIONS

Alvarez, Max. "The Origins of the Film Exchange." *Film History* 17, no. 4 (2005): 431–465.

Bowser, Eileen. *The Transformation of Cinema, 1907–1915*. Berkeley: University of California Press, 1994.

Butsch, Richard. *The Making of American Audiences: From Stage to Television, 1750–1990*. Cambridge Studies in the History of Mass Communication, ser. Cambridge: Cambridge University Press, 2000.

Caddoo, Cara. "Colored Theaters in the Jim Crow City." In *Envisioning Freedom: Cinema and the Building of Modern Black Life*. Cambridge: Harvard University Press, 1914.

Fronc, Jennifer. "Local Public Opinion: The National Board of Review of Motion Pictures and the Fight against Film Censorship in Virginia, 1916–1922." *Journal of American Studies* 47, no. 3 (2013): 719–742.

Fuller-Seeley, Kathryn. *Celebrate Richmond Theater*. Richmond: Dietz Press, 2002.

Fuller-Seeley, Kathryn and Karen Ward Mahar. "Exhibiting Women: Gender, Showmanship, and the Professionalization of Film Exhibition in the United States, 1900–1930." In *Women Film Pioneers Project*, ser., edited by Jane Gaines. New York: Center for Digital Research and Scholarship, Columbia University Libraries, 2012. Accessed 10 July, 2021, at: https://wfpp.columbia.edu/essay/exhibiting-women-gender-showmanship-and-the-professionalization-of-film-exhibition-in-the-united-states-1900-ndash-1930/

Hillyer, Reiko. "On to Richmond: Richmond and the New Dominion." In *Designing Dixie: Tourism, Memory, and Urban Space in the New South*. Charlottesville: University of Virginia Press, 2015.

Hulfish, David S. *Motion-Picture Work: A General Treatise on Picture Taking, Picture Making, Photo-Plays, and Theater Management and Operation*. Chicago: American School of Correspondence, 1913.

Merritt, Russell. "Nickelodeon Theaters, 1905–1914: Building an Audience for the Movies." In *The American Film Industry*, edited by Tino T. Balio, 83–102. Madison: University of Wisconsin Press, 1985.

Morrison, Craig. "From Nickelodeon to Picture Palace and Back." *Design Quarterly*, no. 93 (1974): 6–17.

Richards, Jason. "Imitation Nation: Blackface Minstrelsy and the Making of African American Selfhood in *Uncle Tom's Cabin*." In *NOVEL: A Forum on Fiction*, vol. 39, no. 2 (Spring 2006): 204–220.

Sampson, Henry T. *Blacks in Blackface: A Sourcebook on Early Black Musical Shows*. 2nd ed. Lanham: Scarecrow Press, Inc., 2014. Two volumes.

Waller, Gregory A. "Another Audience: Black Moviegoing, 1907–16." *Cinema Journal* 31, no. 2 (1992): 3–25.

DISSERTATIONS AND THESIS

Dewberry, Eric Jay. "Jake Wells, Commercial Entertainment Entrepreneur of the South: A Study of His Career in Richmond, Virginia, 1894–1927." Master's thesis, Virginia Commonwealth University, 2003.

Dewberry, Eric. "Jake Wells Enterprises and the Development of Urban Entertainments in the South, 1890–1925." PhD diss., Georgia State University, 2010.

Shockley, Martin Staples, "A History of the Theatre in Richmond, Virginia, 1819–38." PhD diss., University of North Carolina, 1938.

U.S. GOVERNMENT DOCUMENTS

"Broad Street Commercial Historic District," n.d. National Register of Historic Places Inventory Form, no. 127–375. National Park Service, U.S. Department of the Interior, Washington, D.C.

"Jackson Ward." National Register of Historic Places Inventory Form, Jul. 30, 1976. National Park Service. U.S. Department of the Interior, Washington, D.C.

FILMS

Bernhardt, Curtis, director, *Damon and Pythias*, International Motion Picture Enterprises and Metro-Goldwyn Mayer, September 1962.

The Fall of the Mighty, Al Bartlett Film Manufacturing Company, 1913.

Gans-Nelson Fight, Miles Bros., December 1906.

Hopper, E. Mason, director. *Janice Meredith*, Cosmopolitan Pictures, December 8, 1924.

Love vs. Title; or, *An Up-to-Date Elopement*, Vitagraph Co. of America, 1906.

O'Neil, Barry, director. *Uncle Tom's Cabin*, Famous Players-Lasky Corp., July 26, 1910.

Thomson, Frederick A., director. *Uncle Tom's Cabin*, Vitagraph Co. of American, July 26, 1910.

The Unwritten Law, S. Lubin, March 2, 1907.

WEBSITES

American Film Institute (AFI) (catalog). www.afi.com

"The Byrd Theatre" (Richmond). www.byrdtheatre.org

Center for the Study of Social Policy. https://cssp.org/

Encyclopedia Virginia. www.encyclopediavirginia.org

Library of Congress, Washington, D.C. (maps and photographs). https://www.loc.gov/

Organization of American Historians. https://www.oah.org/

Radio Television Digital News Association (guidelines for racial identification). https://www.rtdna.org/

Richmond-Times Dispatch online. www.richmond.com.

Richmond Magazine. www.richmondmagazine.com.

"Richmond Theaters." https://richmondtheatres.tripod.com/

"Urban Scale Richmond." https://urbanscalerichmondvirginia.blogspot.com

GENEALOGICAL RECORDS WEBSITES

Consulted records included U.S. censuses, city directories, vital statistics, military records, etc.

Ancestry.com
FamilySearch.org
Fold3.com

PERIODICAL DATABASES

https://www.newspapers.com/
https://newspaperarchive.com/
https://www.genealogybank.com/
https://www.lva.virginia.gov/
https://archive.org/ (for motion picture trade magazines)

OTHER REFERENCES

Letters from Waldo Thorp to Charles Somma, 1930–1935 (some undated), among papers donated by the Somma family to the Valentine Museum, Richmond, Virginia.

Real Estate Records, City of Richmond, Office of the Assessor of Real Estate.

Richard Watkins Carrington Papers, 1880–1933, Box 38, folder entitled "1925–1929," Albert and Shirley Small Special Collections, University of Virginia, Charlottesville.

Richard Watkins Carrington Papers, 1880–1933, Box 93, folder entitled "Estates—Amanda Thorp 1926–1927," Albert and Shirley Small Special Collections, University of Virginia, Charlottesville.

INDEX

Page numbers in **boldface** refer to illustrations.

Gans, Joe, 54, 194, appx. 2

Gee, Lottie and Effie King, **60**, appx. 3, appx. 5

Gem Theater (Richmond, Va.), 53

Gilliam, Annie, 89–90, appx. 5

Gilpin, Charles, 147, 200

Globe Theater (Richmond, Va.), **64**, 136, 173

gramophones. *See* phonographs

Granville, Ohio, 5–6; Female Seminary, 6, 182

Great Paris Fire Scene (film), 53, appx. 2

Griffin Sisters, The (Mabel and Emma), 60, 87, appx. 3, appx. 5

Hart brothers, 32–35, **32**, **33**, 39, 44–45, 55, 74, **74**, 79, 139, 194, 197, appx. 1, appx. 4

Hell Morgan's Girl (film), 102, 203, appx. 5

Hippodrome Theater (Richmond, Va.), 3–4, 81–94, **82**, **83**, **85**, **86**, 96–97, 107–8, 110, 112, 124, 133–34, 201, 210, appxs. 4–6; Black vaudeville at, 81–94, 97, 124, 133, 159–72; design of, 84–85; original burned down, 157

Holstein, Roy, 106

Hoodlet, Mrs. Emma, 129

Hoover, W. H., 96

Hope-Jones Unit Orchestra (organ), xii, 98–99, 100–103, 202

Hot Springs, Arkansas, fire, 109

Hotel Franklin (Newark, Ohio), 16, **17**, 18–19, **18**, 42, 187

Hotel Seiler (Newark, Ohio), 14

Houston, Henry F., 98

Ideal Theater (Richmond, Va.), 54, 58–59, 194

Idlewood Amusement Park, 46, 55–57, 136, 194–95

illustrated songs, 23, 34–35, 42, 53, 186, 188, appxs. 1–2

Indianapolis Freeman (newspaper), as a source for Black entertainment news, 147

Iona Park Pavilion, 129–30

Isis Theater (Richmond), 102, 206

itinerant exhibitors. *See* exhibitors: itinerant

Jackson Ward (Richmond, Va.), 3, 46, 51–52, 82, **82**, 107, 133, 135, 202. *See also* Hippodrome Theater; Walker, Maggie L.

Jacobson, Jack, 1, 40–42, 45, 55, 181

Jamestown (Virginia) Exposition, 1, 39–40, 46, 190

Janice Meredith (film), 115–16, **115**

Jazz Singer, The (film), 5, 181

Jefferson Hotel (Richmond, Va.), 40, 77, 209

Jim Crow. *See* segregation

Jines, Henry, **60**, appx. 3

Johnson, Jack, 61

Kaiser's Finish, The (film), 110–11, **110**

Keenan, Frank, 102

King and Gee (Effie and Lottie), **60**, appx. 3, appx. 5

Klein, Walter, 97, 100, 105, 107, 111, 137, 157

leisure time, 3, 21, 58, 195

Lewis, Sam, 90

Lichtman, Abe, 134, 209–10

Licking County, Ohio, Jail, 12–13, **12**, 185

Loeffler, William, 116, 207

Love vs. Title (film), 24, 187, appx. 1

Lyric Theater (Petersburg, Va.), 106

MacDonald, Clarice, 112, 115, 128

Madam Calve, 67

Madison, Cleo, 102

Majestic Theater (Richmond, Va.), 54

Manchester, Virginia. *See* Southside/Manchester (Richmond, Va.)

Manvell, Roger, 21

marketing. *See* theaters: marketing of

minstrelsy/blackface, 56–57, 61–62, 87, 200, 208, appx. 5